G000097605

LIVING IN THE KINGDOM

LIVING IN THE KINGDOM

The Ethics of Jesus

David Cook

Hodder & Stoughton
LONDON SYDNEY AUCKLAND

A Catalogue record for this book is available from the British Library

ISBN 0-340-41599-1

Copyright © David Cook 1992

First published in Great Britain 1992

All rights reserved. No part of this publication may be
reproduced or transmitted in any form or by any means,
electronic or mechanical, including photocopying,
recording, or any information storage and retrieval system,
without either prior permission in writing from the
publisher or a licence permitting restricted copying.
In the United Kingdom such licences are issued by the
Copyright Licensing Agency, 90 Tottenham Court Road,
London W1P 9HE. The right of David Cook to be identified
as the author of this work has been asserted by him
in accordance with the Copyright, Designs and
Patents Act 1988.

Published by Hodder and Stoughton,
a division of Hodder and Stoughton Ltd,
Mill Road, Dunton Green, Sevenoaks, Kent TN13 2YA
Editorial Office: 47 Bedford Square, London WC1B 3DP

Typeset by Hewer Text Composition Services, Edinburgh
Printed in Great Britain by Clays Ltd, St. Ives plc

For Kathleen

Contents

Introduction

Christian or Muslim, humanist or Marxist, atheist or agnostic, all of us are fascinated, if not mesmerised, by the figure and teaching of Jesus. Somehow the figure of the gospel narratives still captivates, and the message of the Palestinian Preacher still seems to be considered relevant for today. Most people baulk at any talk of Jesus being God incarnate, at stories of his miraculous powers, and at ideas of his redeeming death on the cross and his resurrection from the dead, but they are still interested in what Jesus had to say. It is not so much his life, his death or his claims about resurrection that hold the attention of even the most cynical today; it is rather the ethical teaching of Jesus which is expressed uniquely and consistently in his life and death. The ethical teaching and the nature of the Jesus who taught it in the way he did continue to draw men and women to study the gospel accounts in order to understand the moral insights of Jesus. Even when people are unable to accept or believe in Christianity, they still feel that Jesus is a man to be emulated and that his teaching would transform the world and people if only it were put into practice. There is an almost audible sigh at the loss because we do not, and, it is thought, we cannot live like that. The question, then, is not just 'What is the ethical teaching of Jesus?' but 'Is it relevant for today?'

Even if we can arrive at a clear understanding of what Jesus actually taught, there remains the problem of the relevance and applicability of that teaching to a technological and scientific world two thousand years on. Much of our work in this book will be to explore the relevance of the ethics of Jesus for women and men today. If they are not relevant, then they may have a great historical interest, but that hardly changes and transforms people or situations. There can be no doubt that people do want to learn about the ethical teaching of Jesus. But to do that properly we shall have to understand the background of that teaching.

The teaching of Jesus does not arrive from heaven without reference to all that has gone before. It is part of the dealings of God with his world and his chosen people. That background is crucial for our understanding of how much of the teaching of Jesus is derived from his Jewish roots and what, if anything, is different and unique about it. Likewise, we cannot easily separate the ethics of Jesus from the setting into which those ethics were expressed. All teaching is teaching into specific situations. Does that mean that the teaching is only relevant to that situation, or can we claim that the ethics of Jesus have a meaning and significance far beyond that specific context?

When teachers teach, they have to use a way of making their teaching clear and understandable. Jesus was no exception, and his moral teaching has different forms and very specific content. One key aspect of the ethical teaching of Jesus is the way that it is closely integrated and bound up with the life and death of Jesus and the significance of those events both then and now. Obviously Christians claim that the life and death of Jesus are fundamental to human being, and that the cross and resurrection have made a crucial change in humanity's relationship with God. This is highly relevant to how we are to understand the ethics of Jesus. But it also leads us to realise that we cannot separate questions of the meaning of the ethics of Jesus from an understanding of the impact and significance of those ethics for people then and now.

It is important, then, that we try to do justice to the different aspects of the ethics of Jesus, ranging from what they are to where they come from, as well as what significance and relevance they have today. We shall follow an order which tries to show what the ethics of Jesus actually are and then moves on to ask what is the relevance of these ethics for then and now. Being clear about the content and significance of the ethics of Jesus, we shall then be able to consider the background and context of those ethics so that we understand the unique contribution Jesus has made to ethics. That will still leave us with a set of hard questions which people quite properly ask about – whether or not the ethics of Jesus are really possible for us to follow today.

But, we may still be asking why we should spend time studying the ethics of Jesus. The short answer is because Jesus matters, and he matters to a whole variety of people. Jesus matters to those who call themselves Christians. What it means to be a Christian is to recognise and confess that Jesus is Lord and to try to live a life which seeks both to be like Jesus and to represent Jesus and his ways to the world. There can be no genuine Christianity which ignores the moral teaching of Jesus and which does not try to put that teaching into practice. If Jesus is Lord, then he must be Lord of the ordinary lives of men and women and his rule must show through in all that they say and do. It is obvious that Christians will and must want to know and reflect on the ethics of Jesus and learn what they are to do with that teaching. They will seek to understand what significance the ethics of Jesus have for twentieth-century people. Jesus and his ethics matter to Christians and to the whole Church of Christ.

Jesus also matters to world faiths. All of us live not only in a multi-faith world, but in multi-faith communities. Ours is a pluralistic society, and we need to face up to and work through what that means for people of different faiths (and none) living together. The presence and reality of people with different religious faiths and traditions create all kinds of questions in our minds. How can we talk to and work with those whose fundamental religious outlook is very different from our own? How can we communicate easily, or even at all, with those whose different faiths create hard questions for us and our beliefs? How far is it possible for us to enter into the shoes of a fundamentally different belief system and understand that system as well as help those believers grasp the heart and message of our own faith? What common ground can there be with those whose starting-point and end result look and feel so alien to our own? It is to Jesus that we may look with confidence as one who is recognised by all faiths and religions; as one who has much to teach us all.

The major religions of the world all offer a surprisingly positive view of Jesus and his teaching. He provides a crucial beginning for reflection and discussion. Of course, there will be disagreement as to who he is and was, and as to whether or not he is the sole revelation and ground of true religion, but that disagreement must not obscure or confuse the general and consistent recognition of the special quality and significance of his ethical teaching and the challenge posed by his life and example.

Jesus is a good starting-point in multi-faith dialogue and discussion. His ethics are universally revered. The critic of religion and its trappings will be quick to remind us that religion in the West is on the decline, and that any interest in Jesus and his ethics must be a purely historical concern – but that is to misunderstand both the nature of Western society and human nature. The Western world is as it is because of the influences of the Greek, Jewish and Christian approaches to life. The Greek and Jewish influences tended to fade as Christianity became the religion and outlook of the Holy Roman Empire and increasingly formed the basis of law, morality, and even the scientific endeavours of the Western world.

Much of who and what we are as a society and as individuals has its roots in the Christian world-view and is derived from the teaching and example of Jesus. Like it or not, we are part of a long tradition which has made us as we are and has shaped the thought-forms, legal practices, and the social and moral attitudes of our modern society, even if religion's role has been diminished. The extent of religion's demise is easy to exaggerate and may lead us to underestimate the continuing role that Christianity in general and Jesus in particular still play, especially at the subconscious level of society's thinking and functioning.

Jesus matters if we want properly to understand who and what we are. However, even if we accept that our modern world is a totally secularised society, there remains a deep fascination with Jesus and his moral teaching. It is that interest which continues to sell new books with the most bizarre and outrageous theories about Jesus. It makes us argue about whether to watch or to ban films and television programmes which continue to explore the gospel accounts and modern people's interpretation and understanding of those accounts.

The film *The Last Temptation of Christ* has again shown that Jesus and his story are still big box-office attractions and are able to create public debate and interest. It is not just the interpretations which are debated, but the reality which lies behind the different interpretations. It would be difficult to find a humanist or a Marxist who would deny the unusual and impressive quality of the teaching and life of Jesus. Many even seek to emulate Jesus in their own lives and to live according to the ethical teaching Jesus is recorded as giving in the gospel records.

Jesus the man and the teacher of moral standards matters to modern people as much as he ever did. The problem is not that no one is interested or concerned to discover the ethics of Jesus, but that it may not be a simple matter to find out what his ethics actually were, or to decide what importance they have for us today. This is not merely a reflection on the difficulties involved in getting back to the Bible and solving any textual problems which may lurk there about the meaning of the text; rather, it is a recognition of the fact that when we approach the Bible or seek to know exactly what Jesus taught concerning ethics, we may wear different pairs of spectacles which radically affect the view of Jesus we adopt. These spectacles may act as a filter through which we take from the ethics of Jesus only what we want, and leave well alone the parts which challenge and make us uncomfortable. This involves something even more serious than the issue of selectivity; it means that we may even misunderstand the true nature of the ethics of Jesus.

Jesus' ethics are not merely a set of ideas which we can take or leave, or which we can choose to try out or ignore. A proper understanding of them requires a living and personal relationship with Jesus Christ. Without knowing Christ, there is no real possibility of understanding the ethics of Jesus, far less of being able to live them out in practice. Without being a Christian, any attempt at the imitation of Christ is inevitably doomed from the start.

Our aim must be to know and understand the ethics of Jesus.

Then we must see how relevant and applicable they are to the world in which we live and work. The hard questions people ask must still be examined and dealt with in a way which does justice both to them *and* to the ethics of Jesus. We must be careful not to push Jesus' ethics into our own comfortable mould, which may be foreign to the spirit and meaning of his teaching. That may mean that if we cannot always see the significance and relevance of his principles, it may say more about ourselves than about the ethics of Jesus.

Karl Barth was probably the leading theologian of the twentieth century. Reflecting on how successful he had been in understanding the nature of God, Barth would say that the angels in heaven always roared with laughter when they saw him pushing his wheelbarrow of books containing his thousands of words about God – as if you can capture God in books and reduce him to words! It is much the same with the ethics of Jesus. No matter how hard we try to encapsulate and describe them, we shall fail to do justice to all that Jesus' teaching means. The danger is that we use divisions which are artificial and build systems which obscure the heart of the ethics themselves. Our systems need to be nothing more than the means of allowing the ethics of Jesus to shine through. The inadequacies of these systems, and the fear of trying to push the teaching of Jesus into a rigid and false framework, should drive us back to the pages of the Gospels. They provide a useful check and corrective to make sure that in our desire for neatness and order we have not missed out what is crucial, nor that we have failed to do justice to the whole message of Jesus Christ.

To make sure that doesn't happen, we need help in finding a way to look at the ethical teaching of Jesus, unless we want merely to repeat what the Gospels say word for word. (Actually, that might not be a bad thing, for at least it would make sure that we paid proper attention to the text.) All of us need a handle on things to understand what we are reading. Some key theological themes lie at the heart of Jesus' teaching and form an over-arching framework to help make sense of the meaning and relevance of what Jesus taught. This will lead us to the heart of the matter: it is the good life. Jesus teaches us what the good

life is and how to live it. The gospel writers often call this living
in the kingdom, and the New Testament describes what kind of
good life kingdom people are meant to live.

No book is written without a great deal of work by many folk,
quite apart from the author. The idea for this book came from
Michael Green, whose work, witness and example have been a
tremendous encouragement to me from the days even before he
led the team at St John's College, Nottingham, of which I had
the privilege of being a member. His international ministry still
leaves time for him to encourage others in making the gospel
real and relevant to this generation. Hodder & Stoughton have
been very patient and constructive, especially in the reworking
of the original manuscript. My grateful thanks go to Michael,
David Wavre, Lindsey who did the typing, and Anna Hall for
the indexing.

This book is dedicated to my long-suffering wife, who continues to put up with me, my schedule and my workaholism,
which is being overcome by inches. Her patience and love are
worthy manifestations of the ethics of Jesus in practice. This
book is dedicated to her with my love.

1

The Good Life – In the Kingdom

In Great Britain there was a popular television comedy series called *The Good Life*: it was about a young couple who were totally disillusioned by the materialistic rat-race of twentieth-century living. They decided to drop out and to turn their suburban home and garden into a self-sufficient unit, growing their own food and keeping the odd animal and a few hens. Part of the fun of the series was the contrast between the folk next door who were very materialistic and unable to imagine life without all the luxuries we call necessities and the young couple struggling to come to terms with the awful reality that it is very hard indeed to be self-supporting and self-sufficient and that bartering is not a readily accepted substitute for paying bills. Yet living in a simple way and doing without the so-called necessities of modern living did bring a quality of life which they saw as 'the good life' and which offered a challenge to friends and neighbours alike.

Our aim in these pages is to discover what exactly the good life pictured in the ethics of Jesus involves, and what this means for us in practice. Are these simply interesting ideas from a bygone age, or are they living standards which are necessary and relevant today for twentieth-century women and men?

All too often at Christmas, relatives (usually my wife's) give me presents that I certainly didn't expect and that I would never have chosen for myself. My problem is always what on earth to do with these presents. They often seem to have no use at all, except as dust-gatherers and constant reminders of what her relatives must think of me and my needs. Is it the same with the teaching of Jesus? Are the ethics of Jesus just an interesting set of ideas, or do they provide a way of living which challenges us all and which transforms men, women and situations?

It is always crucial to begin in the right place. Christian ethics are not about human beings, either in terms of their weakness or their strength. Christian morality is not about sin or about our human need to strive to reach some human ideals. The ethics of Jesus are about God's love to us. At the heart of them lies God's grace, where he shows his kindness to us in Jesus. The God who made heaven and earth, and who is ruler of the universe and humanity, in his sovereignty reveals himself and his ways to us in love through Jesus. Jesus embodies and establishes the fact that God is ultimately in charge. God sets the standards. God gives us the capacity to live up to those standards. God shows how poor our own efforts at keeping his laws are, and it is God who demands and requires that we live all of our life under his rule and authority.

Jesus came preaching salvation and demanding conversion. This implies that there was something to be saved from and something that needed to be changed. Every parent will tell you that you only change a baby's dirty nappy when you have to. You know when it needs to be changed, and you get on and do it for the benefit of the baby and for everyone else's sake. Jesus preached salvation because humanity needed to be saved from itself and from its selfish sinfulness. He preached conversion because men and women had to turn round if they were to know and keep God's moral standards and live as they ought to live.

Jesus called people to repent and to turn to the God who had taken the initiative in coming to them. The grace of God is shown in the fact that God took the initiative in sending Jesus to show men and women how to live properly. The human response is a response to the grace of God. Ethics for the Christian are an ethics of response to the revelation and grace of God. It is because God has done something and taken the lead in Jesus that we are meant and able to respond properly to that initiative. People are to repent from their sin and selfishness and turn to God and follow his will and way. Jesus in his ministry confronted people with the need to be changed. Whether it was the religious leader Nicodemus, a loose-living woman at a well in Samaria, a tax-collector cheating his countrymen, a rich young ruler who was trying to be good, or ordinary fisherfolk working by the sea, Jesus called them to turn round and change in a fundamental way. They were called to respond to the grace of God and to follow the ethics of Jesus. Jesus taught that we are to take our moral cue from God. We are to love because he first loved us.

It is no wonder that children who have been abused by their parents grow up not knowing how to love their own children properly. You would think that having suffered and been abused yourself as a child, the one thing you would make sure never happened is that your own child should suffer in that awful kind of way. Yet all the statistics clearly show that the pattern of abuse is carried on from generation to generation, with the abused themselves becoming abusers and continuing the frightening pattern. Why? Because without the experience of being loved properly it is very hard indeed to know how to love. It was tragic to hear a young woman from Liverpool tell how her older brother abused her sexually when she was not even ten. She wept because she didn't even realise that it was wrong till much later. She became so used to it that she thought this was what always happened to everyone. Her view of 'normality' could all too easily have led to that pattern being repeated in her children's lives. It is because of the experience of being loved that we are able to know what love means and how to love. Because of God's love, we can love God and our neighbours. Our love is the proper response to the loving grace of God.

But to love means that we have to experience the love of God and what that means in experiencing repentance and salvation as Jesus taught. We need to be changed and the problem of our own self-centredness and sin needs to be dealt with and overcome. Jesus came not just to teach men and women about being good and doing God's will, but to free them to live as they ought to live.

This means that the ethics of Jesus are based not on knowing

Jesus primarily as a great teacher, but as the Saviour. For his teaching to have its full meaning and significance we need to know and experience his saving grace and to repent from what we have been, to become what we ought to be. It is in and through that experience that we discover that God's grace enables us to live morally. To live and love properly depends on knowing and experiencing the love of God in our lives. It is the grace of God which enables us to keep the commands of God. All of the ethical teaching and standards of Jesus have their basis and root in God; that is why there is no separation of religion from ethics in Christianity. All true religion leads to good ethical fruit. Knowing the moral truth must lead to doing that truth, or else we do not really know it properly.

Karl Barth (whom we mentioned earlier) was horrified that his theology teachers could sign a letter in support of the Kaiser and going to war against Britain in 1914. Barth had accepted their theological teaching and based his life on that teaching. Suddenly he realised that there was something seriously wrong. If all that he had been taught was true, then it should have led to good results and not evil. But what was being done by the Kaiser and Barth's theology teachers was totally wrong. Barth then realised that it meant that there was something fundamentally wrong with their theology. Good theology should lead to good living; if it does not do that then there must be something wrong with the theology.

Ethics are part and parcel of knowing and loving God. Ethical behaviour for the Christian is based on a living relationship of faith in God. So again we see that God is the source and originator of morality. The ethics of Jesus express the will of God for humankind.

But this is not just a revealing of what God wants us to do. Football writers and fans are more than capable of telling their team what they ought to be doing in order to win every match easily. The problem is that knowing what to do and actually doing it are quite different things. Christians are not simply called to live according to God's will and ways, they are given the power to do so. If Christians live in loving communion with

God and obey him, then they will be able to do what God wants by his power and in his strength.

Jesus' revelation of God is the fulfilment of God's dealing with humanity. Jesus drew on the fact of our creation by God in his image and on the summons by God to live and act like God. We are meant to be like our heavenly Father and to show that we are truly God's children by the nature and quality of our lives. As good children, we are called on to obey our Father's will. The central theme of so much of the life and the praying of Jesus is his prayer to God, 'Thy will be done.' If God has revealed his will and ways for human beings to live, then the desire to obey the will of God ought to be the mark of the Christian's life and prayers. It is from the will of God that we know what goodness is, and it is by the power of God that we are able to achieve the standards he sets. God is the source of the ability to attain goodness. It is in fellowship with God that we are able to reach the ideals that God requires of his people.

In this sense the ethics of Jesus are ethics of duty. It is the duty and responsibility of every Christian to obey the will of God. But such obedience has a further aim and purpose beyond pleasing God and doing what we ought. It is part of what it means to bring in the kingdom of God. How does the kingdom of God arrive in the world? Jesus brings in the kingdom: he announces that the kingdom of God is at hand; he shows the values of the kingdom by the kind of life he leads; he announces what standards are to be followed by members of the kingdom of God, and it is by the living out of these standards that the kingdom of God is revealed to the world and God's reign is ushered in in a real and living way. This is part of why the follower of Christ is to hand himself or herself over to God, be subject to him and obey his will. This is why we are as Christians summoned to deny ourselves, take up the cross and follow Jesus (Matt. 16:24; Mark 8:34; Luke 9:23). It is this pattern which provides a comprehensive account of what it means to live the Christian life. But all of this, both in terms of what is revealed and how we are enabled to respond to that revelation, stems from the grace of God. We are responders to the grace of God. The ethics of Jesus are ethics of grace and ethics of response.

Jesus: God and goodness incarnate

God has revealed his will and his way though creation, law and his prophets. The way the world operates and the way human beings function provide some basic indication of what is good and bad for people. If I smoke forty cigarettes a day and drink three bottles of whisky every day, then it is not good for me. My body was not designed to cope with that kind of abuse. 'What we sow we reap' is not just a theological truth; it is also a clear fact about the way the world and human nature operates. If God is the Creator, it is clear that the world and human beings have a moral dimension which is no accident. Thus it is possible to know something of good and evil, especially in terms of what is good and bad for people, by careful attention to the world and to human being.

In the Old Testament it is clear that God revealed what he wanted from his people, the Jews, in the law. This law expressed God's will and his way of living for human beings. The law covered every aspect of human life from the religious to the civil and social. God was concerned about right behaviour and attitudes in every area of life. It is no surprise to discover that every culture down through the ages and across the world has as part of its legal, moral and religious codes the kinds of rules God requires of every human being. Laws about stealing, truth-telling, the sanctity of life, sexual behaviour and what belongs to us and what does not belong are God's universal, absolute laws for all human life: they form the necessary conditions for the preservation and continued existence of human life and society. Without these basic rules, society and human life would disintegrate.

But even God's people did not remember or obey his laws, and so God in his mercy and grace reminded them of his will and his ways. His word came to the people through his prophets. They spoke out God's word which summoned his people back to obedience and a proper relationship with him.

The lessons of history are that words are not enough, and even the excellent teaching in the word and the lives of the prophets did not restore God's people to living the kind of life he requires from those who follow him. People need more than words; they need a concrete example to see and grasp what it really means in practical terms.

Jesus is God's visual aid; he came to show men and women what God is like. Jesus revealed God's character by incarnating (making flesh) God's perfect life. Jesus is God incarnate. While modern scholars may debate the sense and purpose of the resurrection, the New Testament writers were in no doubt that Jesus was God incarnate. Jesus was God's Word made flesh (John 1:14).

This fact gives authority to what Jesus did and said. When he spoke, it was God speaking directly to humanity. When Jesus acted, it was the action of God in the world in terms which all could see and judge for themselves. Jesus knew a deep sense of God's authority (Matt. 5:17–48; John 13:34). It was this divine authority which enabled Jesus to set himself up as an authority, or rather as one under the direct authority of God. When Jesus said, 'I say to you . . .', he did not invite a debate or seek to argue in support of his claim. Jesus simply commanded obedience. The fact that these were commands is as important as what was being commanded. The direct commands showed that Jesus had the right to make such demands. He brought God's word and will to human beings, and their role was to receive God's commands and to obey them fully.

For the New Testament this theological point is crucial. Jesus is God incarnate. This means that the ethical teaching in the New Testament and in the Gospels in particular is not just the writers' views about morality, or merely an expression of the concerns which were worrying the early Church. The ethical teaching of the New Testament is teaching about Jesus himself. In a sense, the message of Jesus is a message about Jesus. Here the medium is literally the message. Jesus is the ethics of God in flesh-and-blood terms.

In Jesus, character and teaching are in total harmony. There is no gap between who and what he is, what he says and teaches, and what he does and does not do. Jesus was the supreme master of the art of human living; he taught not just by his words, but by his example and his life. Jesus is the religious and ethical centre of Christianity: they become one in him. He illustrated how people were meant to live. We cannot separate the ethics of Jesus from who and what he is. This means that we can only understand Jesus' ethical teaching properly if we realise that he is the Messiah, the Son of God, the incarnate Word, who has come to save and transform the world and humankind. Thus, Jesus is the model for all to imitate. He is the example to be followed *par excellence*.

Thus Jesus did not so much bring moral rules which are to be obeyed without question at all times, as reveal a character and live the human life which all human beings are to emulate and imitate. Christians are called not just to follow an interesting teacher with some fascinating ideas. They are to follow Jesus himself (Matt.10:38; 16:24–7; Mark 8:34–8; Luke 14:26–33). If we want to take the ethics of Jesus seriously and try to live by them, then the only way is by the personal, simple, down-to-earth following of Jesus Christ. It is only by such an obedient following in the footsteps of Jesus that we will succeed in living the good life.

The King and his kingdom

The hope of every Jew was that the Messiah would come. A people invaded and subjugated held on to their hope of deliverance and freedom from the Roman oppressors. It was to the Messiah they looked for such transformation. When he came he would usher in a new era. Everything would be different and everything would be all right then. In trying to describe what it would be like when the Messiah came, the Old Testament writers and the prophets looked back to the golden age of the reign of King David. The Messiah would be God's king, as David was. He would usher in the same kind of military success and prosperity. The only difference would be that the Messiah would rule for ever. So the Jewish nation still looked for a new kingdom. It would be a place where God's will was done and God's reign was known and enjoyed with all its blessings. If Jesus was indeed the Messiah, then he was the new king bringing in God's kingdom. This is exactly what the gospel writers claim and portray.

Matthew records the first message Jesus preached, 'Repent, for the kingdom of heaven is near' (Matt. 4:17). Mark records how after John the Baptist was imprisoned, Jesus went into Galilee and preached the good news of God: 'The time has come . . . The kingdom of God is near. Repent and believe the good news!' (Mark 1:15). Luke uses the words of the prophet Isaiah to give more specific content to the nature of the kingdom, as he records Jesus claiming that Isaiah's prophecy was fulfilled in his own coming:

> 'The Spirit of the Lord is on me,
>   because he has anointed me
>   to preach good news to the poor.
> He has sent me to proclaim freedom for the prisoners
>   and recovery of sight for the blind,
> to release the oppressed,
>   to proclaim the year of the Lord's favour.'
>   (Luke 4:18–19; Isa. 61:1–2)

In John's Gospel it is the reaction to Jesus which reveals that the King has come. John the Baptist said, 'Look, the Lamb of God, who takes away the sin of the world! This is the one I meant when I said, "A man who comes after me has surpassed me because he was before me"' (John 1:29–30). When Andrew had met Jesus, the first thing he did was to find his brother Simon; he said, 'We have found the Messiah' (John 1:41).

Towns and cities in Britain know something of the excitement when the Queen is coming to town. The preparations are endless, but the really important thing is the moment when the Queen actually arrives. Then the crowds come out just to catch a glimpse of royalty. When the Queen talks they listen carefully. The journalists write it down word for word, and everyone repeats what the Queen said to them. It was the same for the gospel writers and those who met the Messiah. Jesus is carefully pictured as the Messiah King who brings God's salvation. He continually uses parables to show what the kingdom of God is like and means. He describes it, how to enter the kingdom, the benefits of being in the kingdom, and the cost of living the life of the kingdom. For Jesus, his ethical teaching is really the ethics of the kingdom. The good life he described was only a possibility for those who entered and lived in the kingdom. It was a good life made possible only under the reign of the King.

The setting of the kingdom

Some scholars help us understand that when the New Testament talks about the kingdom of God it does not mean that the kingdom is a place, rather the word really means kingship. It signifies a living relationship. I do not now live in Scotland, but being Scottish still influences how I live. Our family are great home-made soup eaters. Visitors from some countries find this unusual. For many, soup comes out of a tin; but my wife was brought up believing that home-made soup keeps people healthy and supplies fresh vegetables in a way that even the most unwilling boy will eat. You just have to see a Scottish Pipe Band in the streets of Canada to realise that the Scottish influence is still very strong on people who have long since left Scotland, or maybe have never even been there. Being in a living relationship with the King affects the way we live. What it means to be part of the kingdom of God is to live according to God's will. It means being under his authority. It means recognising that he has absolute control over all that we are, have, and do. The key to membership of the kingdom of God is the quality of our relationship with the King.

The crisis of the kingdom

The kingdom of God created a crisis for people. When Jesus proclaimed the message of the kingdom, it was not a take it or leave it matter. People were forced to respond. They were faced with a crisis. The original meaning of the word 'crisis' is a moment of judgement. People were faced with the need to make a decision for or against Jesus. People were challenged whether they wanted to join the kingdom or not. What this entailed was what could only be described as being reborn. The Jewish leader

Nicodemus came to Jesus to try to discover the secret of this new teacher and what God was revealing. Jesus outlined the necessity of being born again in order to be able to see the kingdom of God. Jesus drew a sharp distinction between light and darkness. The kingdom was for followers of the light and meant a radical rejection of evil:

'Everyone who does evil hates the light, and will not come into the light for fear that his deeds will be exposed. But whoever lives by the truth comes into the light, so that it may be seen plainly that what he has done has been done through God.' (John 3:20–1)

To enter the kingdom means an end to evil living, and a start to living by the truth in the light of God. Through the power of God the changed person can live the good life, but that good life begins with repentance.

But entry into the kingdom had that basic requirement. To be a member of the kingdom it was not enough to try to reform your life. You had to repent of the old way of life and start again. Jesus invited people to enter the kingdom. But the individual had to make a response. The fishermen had to leave their nets. Matthew had to leave his tax-gathering tables. There had to be a response to Jesus' offer. This was not a question of being good enough or trying to change enough to get in. There was a stern demand before anyone could participate in the kingdom of God. We must repent of our self-centred way of living. We must try by God's grace to live according to his will. The proper answer to the call of God is to accept and follow Jesus. It is to be converted and to believe in Jesus. This is the only path to the kingdom of God.

In a way, this reminds me of the children of Israel. They had spent forty years in the wilderness on their journey from slavery in Egypt to the freedom of Canaan. When they eventually arrived at the borders of Canaan, they still had to enter the land and claim their inheritance and all that had been promised to them. That process of gaining their inheritance was marked by war and constant struggle. But there had been an earlier moment, forty years before. Under the leadership of Moses they had reached the borders of the promised land of Canaan at a place called Kadesh Barnea. From there they had sent twelve spies into Canaan to see what it was like. Their report was very divided. Ten of the spies said that it was far too difficult to win the promised land. The size of the people, the strength of the armies there and the solid defences meant that there was no way for the Israelites to win. Caleb and Joshua produced a minority report. They knew all the problems, but reminded the people that God was with them. With God on their side, victory was guaranteed. Sadly, the majority carried the day: the children of Israel withdrew. The price they paid was a serious one. Because they had disobeyed God's call and refused to enter into the 'kingdom' he had promised, then death and separation from God were the inevitable results (Num. 13–14). Entry into the kingdom of God requires a turning away from our own ideas and sinful selfishness, and being willing to obey God and live under his sovereign rule. It means obeying the ethics of Jesus, which begins with repentance.

Repentance and the kingdom

Repentance is the key to entering the kingdom of God. That entry is subject to radical requirements. Jesus in his proclamation of the kingdom made unconditional claims on the believer. This was the pattern from the beginning of his ministry. The calling of the disciples to be his followers is recounted in brief, brisk terms. Jesus confronted them at their nets, or as they were collecting taxes, and called them to follow him (Matt. 4:18–22; 9:9; Mark 1:14–20; Luke 5:1–11; John 1:43). There was no contract, no job description, no discussion of salary or fringe benefits, and no limits set to the time and extent of the following. Jesus must have had a remarkable effect on people that they were willing to leave their normal settings and follow him immediately.

The rich young ruler also discovered that following Jesus was a costly business. He was told that in spite of all his excellence he still lacked one thing: 'Sell everything you have and give to the poor, and you will have treasure in heaven. Then come, follow me' (Luke 18:22). There was a serious cost to following Jesus in the kingdom of God. Even the everyday affairs of this world had to take a back seat when it came to following him (Matt. 8:18–22; Luke 9:57–62). To put this at its starkest Jesus drew a startling contrast:

'If anyone comes to me and does not hate his father and mother, his wife and children, his brothers and sisters – yes, even his own life – he cannot be my disciple. And anyone who does not carry his cross and follow me cannot be my disciple.' (Luke 14:26–7)

Jesus set aside family ties and stressed that in comparison with the importance of following him, they had to be ignored. This may well be part of what he meant in talking of carrying the cross.

Matthew's account provides a very clear picture of what Jesus was doing. The disciples had arrived at Caesarea Philippi, which was the ancient site of shrines celebrating the gods of the river, hills and plain. Jesus asked what appeared to be a harmless question about the local gossip. He wanted to know whom people thought he was. Then he turned the question into a personal one which everyone who reads about or meets Jesus has to face: 'But what about you? . . . Who do you say I am?' (Matt. 16:15). This was the occasion for Simon Peter's great confession of faith. There was now no possibility of misunderstanding for the disciples. They were quite clear that Jesus was indeed the Messiah – the King. Immediately, Jesus tried to make sure they understood what kind of king and kingship he was bringing. He explained that he must go to Jerusalem, suffer, be killed, and on the third day be raised to life (Matt. 16:21). This was not well received by the disciples, and Peter led the complaints, earning him a harsh rebuke from Jesus.

After Peter's outburst, Jesus seems to have given each and every one of his followers a chance to change their minds. They had followed him this far without really grasping what that might mean. Now the cost was made totally explicit. Jesus said to his disciples: 'If anyone would come after me, he must deny himself and take up his cross and follow me' (Matt. 16:24–8; Mark 8:31–8; Luke 9:23–7).

To be a member of the kingdom of God was, and still is, a costly business. For many who are converted from another religion, to become a Christian means that they will be thrown out by their families and cut off from their friends. In some communist countries, embracing the Christian faith has meant an end to education, the hope of a good job and a decent standard of living.

The rule of God

The proclamation of the kingdom of God was the announcement of God's reign. God's reign means that God rules. The ethics of Jesus bring together both aspects of what this is. The reign of God is God's gift to humanity. It is God taking the initiative and setting up his rule. But it is also humanity's response and cooperation with God. God's reign means that human beings are to live under that reign and show by their living what that reign actually means. In that sense the kingdom of God is both a gift and a demand.

God's sovereign rule

God's rule is focused in God's sovereign action. God as the sovereign takes the initiative. He does this not because he has to, but because he wants to act. This is an act of free grace and pure love. God exercises his freedom to love and forgive humanity. He decides to draw them back into a proper relationship with him. In this he is being true to his nature. He loves out of no other necessity than that this is the way he is. He is the Creator, who calls his creatures to be what they were created to be – his living images. He is the Lord of all, who summons everyone and everything into relationship and fellowship under his lordship and rule. In Jesus, God has come to redeem his people from sin and to establish his kingdom. In giving humanity his kingdom he does not simply give rules to follow, but rather the means of bringing in the kingdom for others. This is not just a renewal of the covenant God had made in the past with his own people. This is a new covenant which embraces and enfolds the whole world.

God's holy rule

This rule of God is also a holy rule. Holiness in the Bible means set apart for God. It is purity and being undefiled. That is the way we are meant to live in the kingdom of God. But God is good and gracious and does not require that we attain a certain standard before we are loved and can be welcomed into God's kingdom. There is no question of us having to be good enough to enter into God's kingdom. In fact, to be worthy of entering that kingdom only requires that we recognise and understand it. To enter the kingdom is to see that it is holy. Entry only happens because we understand God's rule properly as the reign of the holy and sovereign one. In that spirit we see that we are absolutely dependent on God for everything. Our role is to accept voluntarily God's rule in our lives as the law by which we are to live.

It is when we are in fellowship with God that we find the strength and inspiration to obey his commands and to follow his rule. We then want to turn everything round to his way and will rather than our own. It's the same when we are in love with someone. All the time we want to please them and to make them happy. Our desire is to do what our love wants to do. Our joy is in doing whatever they want. Our obedient loving response is the proper way to accept the rule of the sovereign, loving God.

This does not mean that the rule of God makes no demands or claims on human beings. Already it is clear that there are costly requirements which are part and parcel of what it means for the kingdom to become integrated into our lives. To meet the cost of becoming part of the kingdom of God is just the beginning. Being a member of God's kingdom means a daily living under God's rule. Christians are called to live the life of faith. It is this life of faith which makes possible the good life for the Christian. Jesus' aim was to arouse and kindle faith in those he met. As he revealed the reign of God, the liberating love of God in action set people free and transformed them. It was not just that they gained a new set of ethical ideals. It was more a case that they came directly in contact with the power of God which enables people to realise these ideals in very practical terms. Christian ethics are not another set of wonderful ideals and ideas. In

Christian ethics there is also the power to fulfil those ideals. But this depends on God. God helps us recognise his moral claims. He also enables us to fulfil them. Both aspects of recognition and fulfilment are the activity of God. He reveals the way to live and gives the means of knowing that way, as well as the ability to walk in it. This means that there is no way we can depend on ourselves and our own efforts. To come under the rule of God in faith is to abandon the rule of ourself for the rule of God. We become his obedient servants. We enter the kingdom.

Entering the kingdom

This is not a matter of some performance of faith on our part or living a life of asceticism or self-denial in order to try to show that we are worthy members of the kingdom of God. The gospel writers are quite clear and definite about this. Of ourselves we cannot do anything to gain entry into the kingdom. Indeed, when we have done all that we are able to do, even that will never be enough. In Luke 17:7–10 Jesus told the story of the unprofitable servant. It is a hard lesson that the kingdom of God is not about counting up all our achievements and the things we've done and expecting God to be grateful to us. The servant is there to do a variety of tasks. That is his job, so he can't expect thanks and some special credit for merely doing what he is supposed to do. Jesus applied the point to his own disciples: 'So you also, when you have done everything you were told to do, should say, "We are unworthy servants; we have only done our duty"' (Luke 17:10). This is not some stick to belittle and beat down the value of our efforts; rather it is a liberation from any notion that we have to strive to please God. This is an end to any idea that we have to do well enough to be part of God's kingdom. As if there was some standard of excellence that had to be achieved. Entry into his kingdom is all of God's doing. God's grace and love accepts us and makes us worthy to be members. This means that we can freely love and serve him to the very best of our abilities, without worrying how we are doing and whether or not we are being successful. To enter the kingdom is, in fact, to receive God's good and generous gift.

Receiving the kingdom

How is the kingdom of God to be received? We have seen that it is by faith in response to God's grace. But Jesus is even more explicit. Mark makes the point:

> People were bringing little children to Jesus to have him touch them, but the disciples rebuked them. When Jesus saw this, he was indignant. He said to them, 'Let the little children come to me, and do not hinder them, for the kingdom of God belongs to such as these. I tell you the truth, anyone who will not receive the kingdom of God like a little child will never enter it.' (Mark 10:13–15; cf. Matt. 18:1–9; 19:13–15; Luke 18:15–17)

The kingdom of God is for the childlike, the poor, and for sinners who have clearly done nothing to deserve or earn it. It is God's gift to the helpless and hopeless. This releases all of us from trying to enter the kingdom in our own strength. Our helplessness is God's opportunity. By childlike faith and trust, we enter into the rule of God. It is with nothing in our hands and without any claim on God that we come for entry into the kingdom. The good news is that God only asks that we come in utter dependence and trust, like little children.

The changes in the kingdom

Entering and receiving the kingdom means radical change for individuals. The degree and extent of change can be seen in what happened when Jesus met Zacchaeus. Zacchaeus was a nasty little man. He had sold out to the Roman invaders and had been appointed as a tax-gatherer for them. That meant that he was able to take as much as he could and keep the extra for himself. Such men were hated both as traitors and as thieves. But Zacchaeus was just like everyone else. When he heard that the new prophet Jesus was in the region he wanted to see and hear the man. But when he got near he discovered that the crowds were far too great for him to get even a glimpse of Jesus. The crowds were hardly going to make room for him, so he shinned up a tree to get a grandstand view. He must have had a shock when Jesus stopped at the tree and told him to get down because he was coming to Zacchaeus' house for a meal. The effect of meeting Jesus and experiencing at first hand the love Christ had for an individual transformed Zacchaeus. The change illustrates what can happen when someone is converted. Zacchaeus is completely changed: 'Look, Lord! Here and now I give half of my possessions to the poor, and if I have cheated anybody out of anything, I will pay back four times the amount' (Luke 19:8). That was quite a turn around, and went far beyond what was usual or required by the law. Love is always generous when it acts. Zacchaeus' love for Jesus expressed itself in love for other people.

Coming into the kingdom of God is not just a matter of personal change for individuals. It is also about societies, communities and crowds. For these the coming of the kingdom means revival and social change. Often it is through the changed nature of individuals that religious and social changes come. One clear example is the Evangelical movement of the nineteenth century. Individuals like William Wilberforce and Lord Shaftesbury were converted and became members of God's kingdom. They were convinced that their new life should make a difference not just for themselves, but for other people. They formed a ginger group which came to be called the Clapham Sect, and they were largely responsible for transforming the industrial conditions of the British people. Their most notable victory was in the abolition of slavery. For them true religion meant fundamental change for every aspect of life, and that meant society itself must be transformed.

In the same way the Church, when it lives the life of the rule of God, must be an agent for change in society. That has usually meant that it exercises a prophetic role by criticising and trying to make perfect the very structures of our human existence and society. Serious commitment to the kingdom of God implies that we are to change radically the social, cultural, political, and economic structures of our existence. These structures must be humanised and transformed to allow human flourishing and fulfilment. This change was evident in the way that Jesus brought relief from poverty, hunger, and suffering when he announced the kingdom of God. Such an overcoming of evil is an essential element in the full proclamation and practice of God's kingdom and rule.

The importance of the kingdom

Jesus is quite clear about how important it is to be a member of the kingdom of God:

> 'The kingdom of heaven is like treasure hidden in a field. When a man found it, he hid it again, and then in his joy went and sold all he had and bought that field.
>
> 'Again, the kingdom of heaven is like a merchant looking for fine pearls. When he had found one of great value, he went away and sold everything he had and bought it.' (Matt. 13:44–6)

To live under the rule of God is worth everything. That is precisely the cost of living the good life in the kingdom of God – everything.

The inner reality of the kingdom

In the teaching of Jesus the kingdom of God is a matter of the inner reality leading to action and attitudes. In looking at the ethics of Jesus we saw that he laid particular stress on the inner life and the need for proper motives in heart and mind. Of course, that was never meant to exclude the behaviour in the world which results from meeting Jesus. Rather, it was a safeguard against allowing ourselves and others to be deceived by appearances. Likewise, as Jesus described the reality of the kingdom of God, he stressed that it has an inner core, which then leads to the appropriate outward expression:

> Once, having being asked by the Pharisees when the kingdom of God would come, Jesus replied, 'The kingdom of God does not come with your careful observation [i.e., visibly], nor will people say, "Here it is," or "There it is," because the kingdom of God is within you.' (Luke 17:20–1)

Life in the kingdom is not following the pages and rules from a handbook. Instead, it is to experience the overwhelming power of God at work in us as his rule takes over our lives. An external law cannot control the inner or personal attitudes of people. This has been found time and again as prisoners of conscience have been shut in jails because of their beliefs and yet have remained unaffected by that restraint. In the past, in so-called psychiatric units in the USSR, Christians have been deprived of liberty and forced to follow an imposed regime because of their beliefs, yet they have not rejected or renounced their faith. The inner reality cannot easily be overcome by external sanctions and controls.

Jesus taught a new law of the mind, will and heart. It was the motive spring of action which was crucial. It was the inner desires of anger and lust which had to be dealt with. Control of those inner motives and drives prevents acts of violence, adultery and sexual misconduct. To live under the rule of God is to experience an inward monitor and guide to direct, lead and control. The Spirit of God is to be at the centre of a person's life. It has to affect our basic personality. If the kingdom of God is anywhere, then it resides in the minds, hearts and wills of the followers of Jesus.

Jesus never separated the inner reality from the outward expression of morality, for he was quite clear that external actions are the results and fruit of particular inner dispositions (Matt. 5:28; 12:34–7; Mark 7:18–19; Luke 6:43–5). What we are inside and what is going on in us inevitably shows itself in what we say and do. Both aspects of our human being are important. They are inextricably linked and interconnected: the one reveals the state of the other. What we think, feel and will matters as much as what we do and refrain from doing.

Jesus knew only too well that outward appearances can be misleading. The Pharisees were very enthusiastic about making sure of good behaviour and correct moral practice, but they were not so careful about making sure that they had the right motives, attitudes and dispositions. Jesus went on:

'What comes out of a man is what makes him "unclean".
For from within, out of men's hearts, come evil thoughts,

sexual immorality, theft, murder, adultery, greed, malice, deceit, lewdness, envy, slander, arrogance and folly. All these evils come from inside and make a man "unclean".' (Mark 7:20–3)

It is worth noting that Jesus' stress on the importance of the inner life as well as the outward expression removed all hope of the self-satisfaction and smugness which comes from appearing to keep the law. Indeed, the seemingly impossible nature of the demands of Jesus acts as a constant check against the danger of Pharisaism. Those who constantly fall short of the perfect inner and outer life are in continuing need of forgiveness and of the saving grace, love, and mercy of God. They know that reaching God's standards is a matter of his grace and power, not human achievement.

Behind this stress on the importance of the inner state as well as the outer is the view that thinking, feeling and willing are at the very core of human being; they are our essence. We sometimes say that it is possible to fool some of the people all of the time and all of the people some of the time. When we say that, we are indicating that there is a fundamental distinction between what is happening inside and the external appearance or performance we manage to portray to the world. But who and what we really are lies with that inner reality, which we think we alone know and experience. It is what happens in our minds, wills and emotions which is of supreme importance when we act and fail to act. The inner experiences are guides to who and what we are.

It is this knowledge of the importance of the inner life which Jesus draws our attention to in Matthew's Gospel. The traditional commandments were expressed in external terms. They dealt with what we did and how we behaved. Jesus reinterprets many of these commandments to show that the internal aspect is crucial. Jesus attacked greed and acquisitiveness rather than just wealth. He attacked lustful thoughts and desires rather than just acts of sexual misbehaviour. He attacked hate rather than simply acts of violence and warfare. Of course, such actions are in no way acceptable: but these actions stem from the hearts and minds of people; they are outward expressions of inner realities. If we are to live as God wants us to live, then our hearts and minds must be changed; they must be renewed. We are to will what God wills, and he is to be the source and sustainer of our moral life and aspirations. To do God's will we must first of all want to do it. It is in choosing to do God's will that we are true to our highest and best nature. We are then what we are meant and created to be. This is a turning away from the selfish sinfulness which comes so easily to us, and a turning towards God himself.

With the ever-increasing level of marriage breakdown and divorce, it seems as if taking wedding vows is not quite what it appears to be. The woman and the man promise to take each other to have and to hold from this day forward, for better, for worse, for richer, for poorer, in sickness and in health, until death parts them. But it is not death that seems to be doing the parting. It sounds as if they are making these promises with their fingers crossed, so that the promise does not really count. They seem to be saying to themselves, 'Well, if it doesn't work out I can always find someone else and try again,' which is exactly what happens. But as we stand watching the vow-taking, we don't hear these mental reservations and qualifications.

With Jesus' stress on the state of our hearts and minds there is an end to the qualifications, reservations, compromises and half-promises which we make mentally when we agree to do something. If the motive and the action both have to be right, then we must be committed to God with all our hearts, minds, strength and self. Jesus shows us that the requirements of God are much deeper, more total, more individual and inescapable than we thought. Our motives must be moral as well as our actions. We've seen how easy it is to appear good by doing certain things, even when our motives are bad. I may do what is regarded as good because I want a great reward in heaven; preferably a front-row seat in the heavenly choir. I may do what seems good because I do not want to spend eternity in the burning flames of hell. Both these motives are not really good motives at all. They are utterly selfish and self-centred. We are to do and be good because this is what God requires, what is right in itself, and the will of God for humanity.

There is another result of stressing the importance of the inner. By making the state of the heart and mind of paramount importance, Jesus shifts the emphasis of morality away from exclusive concentration on what we do to the connection between being and doing. So, when Jesus comes calling for repentance and conversion it is not just a matter of doing different things; actors can do that all too easily: it is rather a matter of being different. Our minds and attitudes must be changed to follow the guidance and will of God.

Another way of expressing the relationship between being and doing is to talk in terms of character and conduct. My conduct expresses my character. Morality is not just about good conduct, but is also about good character. When we are training children we ought not just to be concerned with teaching them to do or not to do certain things. We need to be developing their character. The problem with so much of our teaching and training is that we are far more interested in imparting information than in formation. We give people knowledge and then expect them to be a certain kind of person. We ought instead to be concentrating on making people and forming character and developing moral beings. For Jesus, repentance was to be shown in the whole conduct of a person, and that requires a change of character. Morality for him was never just a matter of what I ought or ought not to do; it was far more about what kind of person I ought to be. Moral behaviour springs from inner dispositions and attitudes. Our conduct reveals our character. That character is to be the focus of our attention.

Jesus is suggesting that if we freely submit to the will of God and enjoy constant communion and fellowship with him, then in a very real sense the conduct can be left to take care of itself. In John 15 Jesus told his disciples that he was the vine and they were the branches. The way to be fruitful was to abide in the vine. Grapes don't grow because the branches trim themselves and try to be fruitful. Trimming and making the branches fulfil their proper function is the job of the vine-dresser; he brings about fruit by making sure that the vine is in good shape and the branches are working properly. Fruiting is the natural result of branches being in a proper relationship with the vine. So the more and better we know God in our lives, the clearer and better will be our understanding of right and wrong, and we will more frequently do what is good. It will follow naturally.

When couples are about to be married, they often buy books about love-making. While this may help, it can also hinder. The spontaneity of expressing loving care for the other person can get lost in an overriding concern to get the technique right, by turning to page sixteen at the vital moments. In the same way, the good life ought to be spontaneous rather than studied. There is always something artificial about having to make an effort to be good and to conform to certain standards. Witness the uncomfortable scene of taking your children to a very proper house where in your anxiety that they should behave well and not make a bad impression, you make the whole visit a nightmare for them, for yourself and for the host and hostess. Goodness should be the relaxed, natural outflowing of action from a transformed character. By such devotion to and concern for God's will, what is evil should be kept at a distance, for there is literally no room for it.

Again, this reminds us of the close relationship between religion and morality. The good life is the inevitable product of a healthy religious life. The inner experience of the reality of God expresses itself in holy living. Jesus taught that the kingdom of God is within us (Luke 11: 33–6; John 7:37–9). So the ethical teaching of Jesus writes God's moral law in the hearts and minds of men and women. It is in this way that the Spirit of Jesus becomes the guiding force in the moral life of the Christian. We are not to follow some external codes of practice or list of rules and regulations, rather we are to follow the guidance of the life-giving Spirit who dwells in our hearts by faith.

Love – the heart of the good life

Jesus used a special word to sum up the heart of the good life: *agape* (love). This was love not just as human beings understand it, it was God's love to us. The good news of the gospel was that God offered his love to men and women. God loves us because that is his nature. He loves us because he is love and love is his natural attitude towards us. We love because of what we get, not because we are genuinely loving at all; our love is often a selfish love. God's love is quite different. Jesus showed this kind of love in the way he loved the poor, who were despised by society. He loved the children whom even his disciples wanted rid of and tried to keep away from bothering Jesus. He loved sinners, and that led to all kinds of complaints from the Pharisees that he spent all his time with sinful people. Jesus had to remind the Pharisees that it was the sick who needed help, not the well. He loved people with problems and diseases. Jesus loved those who were looked down on by society. He took time to treat women properly. He helped those who were outcasts as far as society was concerned because of their diseases or race. Jesus touched, talked, ministered to and healed such people. All that they had in common was that no one thought they were worth anything. Jesus loved them, even though they seemed to be of little or no value. That was his nature as love incarnate. That love is quite independent of the qualities of those who are loved. It is not because of who or what they are that they are loved; they are just loved: that love goes far beyond what any of us could expect. Such love was at the heart of Jesus' ethical teaching. When he was asked what was the greatest commandment, he offered the following comment:

'The most important one,' answered Jesus, 'is this: "Hear, O Israel, the Lord our God, the Lord is one. Love the Lord your God with all your heart and with all your soul and with all your mind and with all your strength." The second is this: "Love your neighbour as yourself." There is no commandment greater than these.' (Mark 12:28–34; see also Matt. 22:34–40; Luke 10:25–37)

Jesus was only concerned with *agape* love. He condemned self-love and self-interest concealed in what passed for love. He taught that the primary concern for the Christian was to love God and the neighbour: the neighbour is anyone and everyone in need. The parable of the Good Samaritan illustrates how widely we are to interpret who our neighbour is (Luke 10:25–37).

There is an indissoluble link between our love for God and our love for our neighbour. As Jesus' love for humankind did not detract from his loving of God, so our love of our neighbour does not detract from loving God; rather, it is the mark of loving God properly. That love is only possible because we have ourselves experienced such love through God's grace. It is because we have been and are loved that we are able to love. Such love presupposes that a change of heart has taken place in us. There has to be an end to self-love, and in its place there must be genuine self-denial and self-sacrifice. This love is shown by humility, a quality that was evident in the model of the servant who was willing to wash other people's dirty feet (John 13:1–17).

This *agape* love is an indiscriminate love. It has to be universal. It is colour blind. It knows no boundaries of race, culture, society, sex or creed. This is a tall order. We are all very good at loving our friends and those who love us in return. Jesus taught that we are to love those who have no claim whatsoever on us except that they are in need (Matt. 25:31–46; Luke 10:29–37). Real love never asks what we will get out of this or any relationship. Love is not interested in setting limits or conditions. We do not say that if someone does this and this, then we will love them; we are to love because that is our nature as children of God.

However, Jesus' new focus on love is not just a repetition of the Old Testament requirement of love. Jesus included love for our enemies. We are not to show malice or seek revenge, even when our enemies return our love for them with hatred and abuse.

'But I tell you who hear me: Love your enemies, do good to those who hate you, bless those who curse you, pray for those who ill-treat you. If someone strikes you on one cheek, turn to him the other also. If someone takes your cloak, do not stop him from taking your tunic. Give to everyone who asks you, and if anyone takes what belongs to you, do not demand it back. Do to others as you would have them do to you.' (Luke 6:27–31)

This command to love our enemies is a distinctive mark of the ethics of Jesus. But he goes further in the nature of the love he demands from his own followers. In the context of the loving act of washing the dirty feet of his disciples, Jesus provided both a visual aid and drove home his message in a new commandment. It takes its place alongside the commands to love God and our neighbour – 'A new command I give you: Love one another. As I have loved you, so you must love one another. By this all men will know that you are my disciples, if you love one another' (John 13:34–5). The true indication of being a disciple of Jesus is to show the same kind of love as Jesus showed. We are to love one another in the same way and to the same extent. The follower of Jesus is recognised by his or her love of and care for others. Such love is both individual and social, and finds its expression in forgiveness, reconciliation, faithfulness and practical service.

The *agape* love of Jesus is a gracious love, which is opposed to self-centredness. It puts others before ourselves. It knows no kinds of limits, boundaries or barriers. It is extended to friends and enemies alike. It is summed up in the new commandment. None of us can escape from the demand to be like Jesus and to incarnate his love. Such love is the bond and cement of the Christian community. Nevertheless, it is a travesty to limit this love only to those within the context of the Christian community. That would be to forget all that Jesus taught about our neighbour and the genuine nature of Christian love which loves and expects and requires nothing in return.

The Christian is to show loving mercy, give to the poor and be concerned to ensure that justice is done (Luke 6:36–8; 11:37–54). Such compassion is to be expressed in our response to those in need. In the parable of the sheep and the goats, it is compassion or the failure in compassion to the hungry, the thirsty, the stranger, the sick and those in prison which is the deciding factor in judgement (Matt. 25:31–46). Whether it was in feeding the multitudes or in meeting the needs of individuals, Jesus showed compassion (Matt. 14:14; 15:32; Mark 1:41; 6:34; 8:2–3; Luke 7:13; 10:33).

Such compassion always leads to action. It meets the needs

of people. The Christian is to have that quality of compassion, which makes a difference to people. Such compassionate love is only possible in the context of obedience. Love keeps the commandments of Jesus. It is the person who is closely in touch with God and his power who is willing and able to obey God's commands. The Christian is to do the will of Jesus' Father (Matt. 7:21–3). If we love Jesus, we will obey him (John 14:15, 21; 15:9–14). The wise person is the one who hears the words of Jesus and then does them (Luke 6:46–9; 10:37). Indeed, part of the mission of the Church is to teach the followers of Jesus to obey everything that Jesus commanded (Matt. 28:19–20). Obedience is not an optional extra. It is a primary quality in living in the kingdom.

Forgiveness – love in action

The Christian life is to be characterised by love. The ultimate test of love is forgiveness. In the Old Testament, the *lex talionis* (the law of an eye for an eye and a tooth for a tooth) had set limits to vindictiveness and revenge. It meant that you could not take two eyes, seven teeth, one hand and a leg, when someone knocked out one of your teeth in a fight: Jesus demanded that his followers were to be totally free from that kind of personal vindictiveness. Instead, they were called to show the same generosity to others as God had shown to them. As the experience of being loved encourages and enables us to love properly, so the experience of being forgiven should naturally lead us to forgive others. This is why Jesus revealed the anger of the master in the parable of the unmerciful servant. The man whose huge debt had been cancelled by his master refused to cancel the much smaller debt of one of his fellow servants (Matt. 18:21–35). Christians are to be forgiving people. So, if they pray that God will forgive them their sins, then the clear expectation is that in the same way they will forgive those who sin against them (Matt. 6:12; Luke 11:4). This is to be the case in all praying, and is not just found in what we call the Lord's Prayer: 'And when you stand praying, if you hold anything against anyone, forgive him, so that your Father in heaven may forgive you your sins' (Mark 11:25).

The mark of the Christian is a willingness to forgive. However, as it takes two to make a marriage, it requires two for a relationship of forgiveness to be restored. If I say to someone that I forgive them, they may complain that this is a piece of cheek on my part, for there is absolutely nothing that they have done which needs forgiving. They do not want or need my forgiveness. While their response ought not to change my willingness to forgive, it does make one thing clear. The acceptance of forgiveness implies an admission of fault and guilt and a repentance and change of attitude on the part of the guilty party. This is important, because when we read how often Jesus told his followers to forgive people, it can read like a recipe for becoming a doormat (see Matt. 18:21–2). Luke's account is helpful and clear on this point: 'If your brother sins, rebuke him, and if he repents, forgive him. If he sins against you seven times in a day, and seven times comes back to you and says, "I repent," forgive him' (Luke 17:3–4). It was no wonder that the disciples saw that they would need great faith to be able to do this (Luke 17:5). Nevertheless, repentance is the key. Without such repentance, the relationship cannot be restored. This does not mean that the attitude of forgiveness is lacking; it is and must be there. It does mean that, in order to have the experience of being forgiven, being able to accept that forgiveness and for it to be real, there must be repentance. There are one or two people who have done me serious harm in their dealings with me. Their actions were designed to do me down. It is not easy to forgive that kind of thing. But just saying the words is not enough. The aim in forgiveness is restoration of the *status quo* and going back to the relationship as it was before and ought to be. The problem is not just my willingness to forgive them, but whether they think that being forgiven is really what it is all about. They may not think that they need to be forgiven or that they have done anything wrong at all. There needs to be a recognition of wrongdoing and a genuine change of mind and acceptance of guilt before people can be forgiven.

As God is always ready to forgive and receive even the prodigal who wanders off and wastes all that he was given, so we must always be ready to receive the prodigal back and restore him. In the story of the prodigal son, it is clear that he came to the point where he knew he had made a terrible mistake and decided to go home and tell his father that he was sorry. His father was always on the lookout for his wayward son, and as soon as he saw him he ran to meet him. The son did not even get a chance to say that he was sorry. His coming home showed that. Immediately, he was welcomed, forgiven and restored (Luke 15:11–24). Until and unless the other person comes recognising their genuine fault, the two-way relationship of forgiveness cannot be complete. That is not the fault of the forgiver; it is the fault of the one who refuses to accept the need for forgiveness and take the pardon offered.

One danger here is that we adopt a totally sentimental view of forgiveness. Such a view suggests that sin, evil, faults and crimes are not really important. However, forgiveness is not an easy acceptance of anything and everything. We must not tolerate what is wrong under the banner of forgiveness. Genuine forgiveness treats sin, faults and crimes with the utmost serious-ness and honesty. It tells it like it is, and describes reality as it has happened. It admits that sin is awful, harmful and destructive. But we are not to let sin and evil have the last word. In spite of what has been done, we are to forgive for God's sake. The Christian is not called to cover up evil, nor to pretend that it doesn't really matter. It does matter, and it must be seen and recognised as the destructive force it is. But the Christian is not to gloat over or wallow in sin and its consequences. In love, he or she is required to forgive the repentant person and to re-establish a good relationship with him or her. Jesus knew how hard this was, yet even in the midst of his agony on the cross he was able to forgive his enemies (Luke 23:34). Christians are to offer forgiveness to all who wrong them, and to mean that offer. If the wrongdoer accepts that forgiveness, then there is a reconciled relationship. If there is only refusal, the Christian is still called to be ever open to forgiving and restoring the bond.

No one can call living the good life in the kingdom an easy option. It cost Jesus his life. But he gave his life so that we might be able to live the good life.

2

The Good Life –
Relationships in the Kingdom

We have seen that to be a member of the kingdom of God is at the very heart of living the good life. The qualities of the good life are to be the marks of kingdom men and women. We have also seen that there are some key features of the kingdom which are crucial for those who wish to live the kingdom life. But to appreciate fully the manifesto of the kingdom in the simple starkness that Jesus taught it, we need to see how in the totality of his teaching about the kingdom, relationships were a central focus.

The whole of the Bible is ultimately concerned to describe the relationship between God and human beings. From creation to consummation and from Genesis to Revelation, how human beings are related to God is crucial. At the turning-point of the Bible – the coming of Jesus Christ – that theme of our relationship with God takes the form of God's gracious love reaching out to us and of the need for our response to that grace. To become a member of the kingdom of God is to enter into a living relationship with God. In practical terms, what that meant then and means now is that we become disciples of Jesus. To be a member of the kingdom of God is to be a disciple or learner of Jesus.

In the gospel stories, it is clear that to be a disciple means that we are to deny ourselves, take up the cross, and then follow in the steps of Jesus. The call to discipleship is the call to follow the incarnate Jesus. It is to become an imitator of Jesus. It also means that we must be willing to share in his destiny (Matt. 10:24–5;

Luke 22:24–30). That destiny may mean suffering, persecution and even death (Matt. 10:24–39; Luke 9:57–62; 14:25–35). But the realisation that this was what following Jesus meant dawned slowly on the disciples. At the start, it seemed straightforward enough. Jesus 'appointed twelve – designating them apostles – that they might be with him and that he might send them out to preach and to have authority to drive out demons' (Mark 3:14–15). Some have interpreted this as meaning that the goal for the disciple is that of everlasting communion with Christ and to be God's ambassador in carrying on the ministry of Jesus. Certainly at the very end of Jesus' appearances after his resurrection, Jesus himself gave his followers a specific task and ministry: 'Go and make disciples of all nations, baptising them in the name of the Father and of the Son and of the Holy Spirit, and teaching them to obey everything I have commanded you' (Matt. 28:19–20). He then gave them the wonderful promise, 'And surely I am with you always, to the very end of the age' (Matt. 28:20).

It is important to notice that this task and promise is set firmly in the context of the authority of Jesus. It is an authority which has been given to him by God, and that authority is over all of heaven and of earth (Matt. 28:18). The task of the follower and disciple of Jesus is thus to make more disciples, to enrol them in the Church and to manifest the reality of this discipleship in the obedient observance of Christ's commands. This command came after three years had been spent with Jesus. In that time Jesus not only taught but also showed in practice how his followers were meant to live.

In terms of relationships, Jesus' pattern for his followers reverses the normal order of things. Jesus was the Master yet he became the servant of his disciples. He lived out in practice what he taught. The greatest in the kingdom is the one who serves: 'If anyone wants to be first, he must be the very last, and the servant of all' (Mark 9:35). The life of service was a direct following in the footsteps of Jesus (Mark 8:34–8). What this meant in reality was shown by Jesus when he washed the disciples' feet. We have to remember that this was during what we call the Last Supper. Jesus knew that his hour had come,

John tells us in his thirteenth chapter. He had set his face to go to Jerusalem, and now he had come. He had known that he must suffer and die, and that time had arrived. But before the agony of the cross was this last opportunity to explain to his disciples what was going to happen and to try to prepare them for life without him.

The last thing that someone says to us before they die is often fixed indelibly on our minds. I knew a lady whose husband had died very suddenly. They had had a tiff that morning before he had left for work, and relations were a bit strained. During the morning, he had phoned her. Someone else had answered the phone and told her it was her husband. She told the person to tell him that she was too busy to speak to him. He died later that day. She never knew what he wanted to say to her. She knew only too well that the last thing she had said to him was that she was too busy to talk to him.

It is no accident that John the disciple, whom Jesus loved and who enjoyed the confidence and trust of Jesus in a special way, records in great detail the last meeting Jesus had with his disciples. It was a private party and no servants were there to fulfil the normal courtesies. Usually a servant would wash the feet of an honoured guest before he took his place on the long sofa usually used for meals. The disciples must have realised that there were no servants, but it seems that no one was willing to do the dirty work necessary before everyone could enjoy their meal. No one, that is, except Jesus. He stripped off and wrapped a towel round his waist. Then he took a basin and washed their feet. There is the beautiful detail recorded that he dried them with the towel he was wearing. I always imagine Jesus drying carefully between each toe, doing the excellent job you would expect from the Son of God. After he had taken his place again, he asked them if they understood what he had done. It is not always enough to act out a visual aid. Jesus wanted to be sure that they had got the point. 'Now that I, your Lord and Teacher, have washed your feet, you also should wash one another's feet. I have set you an example that you should do as I have done for you. I tell you the truth, no servant is greater than his master, nor is a messenger greater than the one who sent him' (John 13:14–16).

This is what it means in practice for Jesus to command his disciples that they are to love one another as he has loved them (John 15:12–17). They are to love in the same way and to the same extent as he has done. Thus, the essence of the relationship between Jesus and his followers is that of obedient, Christlike service. But, in telling them to love one another as he loved them, and so to have the same attitude and relationship with each other as he had with them, Jesus went a stage further: 'You are my friends if you do what I command. I no longer call you servants, because a servant does not know his master's business. Instead, I have called you friends, for everything that I learned from my Father I have made known to you' (John 15:14–15). The disciple is not so much a servant of Christ, but Jesus' friend. We have the living and risen Christ with us at all times and in all situations, whether we like it or not. That fact is both a comfort, for it means we are never alone, and it is also a frightening challenge, for it means wherever we go and whatever we do, Jesus is with us.

The relationship between Jesus and his followers is the core, but that inevitably leads to a clear relationship between the disciples themselves. They are to exercise love towards each other. Jesus loved them and gave his life for them. His followers are to be ready to do the same.

In the teaching of Jesus, true brothers and sisters are those who do the will of God, the Father (Matt. 12:50). They are also those who hear God's word and put it into practice (Luke 8:19–21). Christians are to have such a quality of relationship with each other that they are open to mutual correction out of love for each other. If we know that someone is on our side and genuinely wants the best for us, we are ready to accept their criticism, knowing that it is for our good and that it seeks the best for us. Christians are also always to be ready to forgive. Even when a brother or sister regularly sins against another, if the person repents of what they have done, he or she is to be forgiven (Matt. 18:15–20).

The loving quality of relationships between the followers of Jesus is a witness to the world that these people are genuinely the disciples of Jesus (John 13:35). The converse must also be true. If there is no such love shown between so-called disciples, it must raise the question whether they are really disciples at all.

Relationships and the golden rule

Before the coming of Jesus there was a widely-known form of what is called the golden rule. It stated that we should not do to others what we did not want them to do to us. Later we shall explore the way that Jesus' teaching on this theme builds on that but takes it a stage further. The important way he did that was by turning it from a negative into a positive. Instead of the fearful way of avoiding harm embodied in 'Do not do to others what you would not want them to do to you', Jesus made the positive demand on his followers to do to others what we would want them to do to us. This is no defensive tool to look after our own interests, but a call to action and a taking of initiatives to express loving concern for others in a real and genuine way. Jesus was essentially summing up the heart of the law and the teaching of the prophets. 'In everything, do to others what you would have them do to you . . .' (Matt. 7:12). There is a world of difference between refraining from doing harm and actively seeking to do good. It is the difference between the self-centred safety of refusing to get involved unless I am forced into it, and the risky business of serving other people in the world.

Service of others is the basic relationship Christians are to have with all men and women. They are to put the golden rule into practice. They are to take positive steps for the benefit of others. They are to look after other people's interests in the same way as they look after their own. But, even here the danger is that we have too narrow a view of what this means. It is not only that Jesus was concerned to make sure that Christians act in a positive way in serving others; he was equally concerned that Christians avoid the sins of omission.

It is fascinating to see how strongly Jesus condemned sins of omission. We read of Dives, the rich man, suffering in hell because he failed to meet the needs of Lazarus, the poor man, who had been a sick beggar at Dives' door (Luke 16:19–31). In the story of the Good Samaritan, the priest and the Levite pass by the traveller who has been assaulted and robbed. They fail to act in any way to help the person in need. Their religious interests are far more important than helping alleviate the suffering and distress of someone. They are condemned by implication, not for what they did, but for what they failed to do (Luke 10:25–37). It was the same kind of condemnation that was received by the servant who was punished because he failed to use the talent entrusted to him. He had been given the talent to use, but had done nothing with it, even though he knew quite clearly that he was expected to put the talent to work (Matt. 25:14–30). But perhaps the most frightening picture is that of the last judgement. It is an account of the judgement of the sheep and the goats and their separation. The goats are severely punished, not for all the terrible things that they have done, but for all the things they failed to do. They failed to respond to the sick. They failed to feed the hungry. They failed to visit the prisoner. They failed to help the stranger. They failed even to notice the needs of others. They never took up the opportunities for service. They are judged and condemned for their failures and omissions (Matt. 25:31–46).

Social relationships in the kingdom

So often when we talk or think about relationships we do so almost exclusively in terms of personal relationships. In a sense, all relationships are personal in that they inevitably involve us as persons. But our relationships are far more complicated than just family and friends. We have relationships with governments and with every level of society. Part of what it means to be a member of a society and a citizen is that we are inextricably involved in a web of social relationships ranging from the formal and legal to the informal and casual.

Many people imagine that Jesus had little or nothing to say on the social issues of his day. They would argue that Jesus concentrated on the vertical relationship with God. In that way, they see his task as prophetic and spiritual, rather than attempting to make a blueprint for a perfect Christian society. There is some justice in this claim, for he did not offer any detailed plan for the organisation of society along Christian or any other lines. However, Jesus not only exercised a prophetic ministry which pointed people to God and the necessity of a proper relationship with him; he also tried to spell out the implications of that relationship in practical and social terms. If a man or woman became a member of the kingdom of God, then Jesus was adamant that this would lead to certain kinds of relationships and behaviour in society. Those who are in a loving relationship with God are to have different relationships with others. People are to be treated differently. Jesus made it clear that this was the case and gave direct guidance on particular issues of the day. But what is also clear is that he was much more concerned to give the basic ethical principles and ideals of the kingdom than to set out specific formulae for solving social problems.

Jesus went behind the issue to the nub of the problem and gave the framework for thinking and responding to the issue. This is why we can find genuine help from the teaching of Jesus for issues today. While the problems themselves may have a very different form, the basic questions underlying the problems are the same. So often the questions really come down to the kind and quality of relationships we should have with others. We need to be clear what these principles are. We may not actually attain them fully. That we fall short of these ideals is no reason to hold up our hands in horror at the impossibility of the task; nor is it any reason to throw the principles away simply because of our weakness. Rather, this is a constant reminder of our need for renewal and for a deeper and greater reliance on the grace of God. It reminds us that Christian ethics are not about what we are able to do, but about what God is able to do in and through us. If we fall short, it is more a failure in relying on him than any weakness in the truth of the principles.

Relationships with civil authority

All of life seems to require some kind of social organisation. For communities to survive and flourish there need to be some kind of social rules, organisation, customs and norms. Becoming a Christian does not change that need and does not remove the Christian from the social world and its structures. But the Christian is caught in a tension between two different levels of reality and two different structures. The Christian is living life in the kingdom of God. He or she is under the rule of God. At the same time he or she is living under the authority of the civil powers in whatever place and time he or she happens to be. In the case of the gospel writers, they were living under the power of the Emperor and Roman rule. Jesus was certainly not a revolutionary in the obvious sense of a guerrilla fighter with a sword in his hand, battling to liberate his people and his land from an oppressive regime. Yet he was quite clearly involved in a serious struggle against injustice and oppression. At times he was bitterly critical of some expressions of authority, particularly of abuses of authority. The revolution that Jesus came to bring was much more fundamental than the mere use of physical force. Jesus was concerned to change the hearts and minds of men and women, and through them to change the world as a whole. Jesus came as the Prince of peace, riding into Jerusalem on a beast symbolising peace. He did not join the guerrilla bands which were around at the time, and gave no support for any notion that the kingdom of God was to come by the violent overthrowing of the *status quo*. Jesus recognised that the secular state had proper claims. These claims had to be measured against the proper claims of the kingdom of God. This meant that there might well be – we might say there would inevitably be – conflict between the two sets of demands and claims. If there was any conflict, Jesus was in no doubt that God's claims were and are to be absolute, and that his will must be done. We need to remember that in a sense all authority stems from God, and that in creation and providence he has set some people in authority for the good of humanity.

In the Old Testament it is quite clear that all authority is ultimately answerable to God and that the proper function and purpose of authority is for the benefit of humanity. Given that we all live in a fallen and distorted world, the exercise of authority will not always be as it ought. We all live with the hard fact that although there are times when secular authority functions in good and constructive ways, there are other times when it takes on evil and destructive forms. It looks as if Luke's Gospel is trying to make sure that those in authority (presumably the Roman authorities in particular) recognise that Christians are not in the business of trying to overthrow the state by violent means, like the Zealots. John's Gospel appears to be much more concerned to show how secular power can be exercised as if it were only a matter of this world in the here and now, with nothing beyond and no reference to God. John is certain that this is a totally inadequate understanding of the nature of power and authority.

The story of the trap set by the Pharisees illustrates some of this tension and the way that Jesus resolved it (Matt. 22:15–22; Mark 12:13–17; Luke 20:20–6). It is vital to note that the question asked by the Pharisees was not a genuine one. Out to trap Jesus with his own words, they asked the question in a way that, no matter what he said, he would be in trouble. They began their questioning with the flattery which was aimed at deceiving. Then the question came: 'Is it right to pay taxes to Caesar or not?' Jesus spotted the trap and then turned the question and the issue at stake back on the ones who were trying to trap him. He asked for a coin and enquired whose portrait and inscription it bore. He was told they were Caesar's. Jesus then made his famous remark, which was not just a clever response to a tricky question, but also embodied a crucial principle for Christians: 'Give to Caesar what is Caesar's, and to God what is God's' (Matt. 22:21; Mark 12:17; Luke 20:25). From this it is clear that as far as Jesus was concerned, secular authority has a proper place of its own. There is no indication that Jesus was seeking to overthrow all authority and its structures. Nevertheless, in teaching explicitly that God has his own requirements, Jesus makes it clear that the demands of living in the kingdom of God always have precedence over those of the civil authorities. If the two sets of demands come into conflict, there is to be no doubt where one's loyalty is to lie.

Matthew relates another occasion when Jesus was explicit in drawing a distinction between the sons of God who live in the kingdom of God and those who are not members of that kingdom (Matt. 17:24–7). Peter had questioned Jesus about payment of the temple tax which was required of every Jew. Jesus asked Peter, 'From whom do the kings of the earth collect duty and taxes – from their own sons or from others?' Peter responded that it was from others. Jesus then said to him, 'Then the sons are exempt . . . But so that we may not offend them, go to the lake and throw out your line . . .' Jesus then told Peter that he would find a coin for the tax in the mouth of a fish. Jesus and Peter did pay the tax, so as not to offend. This was another aspect of Jesus' recognition of the proper authority of those set over us. It seems that we are not to offend them over issues which in no way conflict with God's authority and the life of his kingdom.

When Jesus is hauled before the authorities, he is always polite: whether before Herod or Pilate, there is no attempt to subvert their role. There is, however, a distinct recognition that the authority they exercise is not their own. They are not free to do whatever they want with the power they have. Jesus reminds Pilate that he is answerable for his use of his power and authority. 'Pilate said, "Don't you realise I have power either to free you or to crucify you?" Jesus answered, "You would have no power over me if it were not given to you from above . . ."' (John 19:10–11; see also Matt. 27:11–26; Mark 15:1–15; Luke 23:13–25).

In the final analysis, all power rests with God. There is no power exercised which is totally out of relation with God. That means there will be a full and final accounting for the use and abuse of power. This is the essence of what is meant by the sovereignty of God. It implies responsibility and answerability to the all-powerful God for how the power human beings exercise is used. But Jesus was also willing to respond forcefully to the abuse of power when he discovered it. We can see this in his response to the cant and hypocrisy of the Pharisees, who abused their religious power and authority. It is also evident in Jesus' response to the way that the temple officials had used their power and abused their responsibility. They were responsible for keeping the temple as a place of prayer. They were meant to create the right kind of atmosphere and to prevent any kind of trouble. But they had allowed businessmen in to sell animals and birds to the worshippers and to change ordinary money into the special coinage used in the temple. Of course, it might seem like the most natural thing in the world, where people needed animals and birds for sacrifice, that convenience shopping was the name of the game. It only takes a visit to a holy site or pilgrimage centre to see the awful effects of this policy.

One summer my family and I visited Lourdes and were deeply impressed by the atmosphere of devotion and moved by the patient suffering and sense of hope in the thousands of chronically sick who had gathered in hope of cure. The authorities there had learned from the Jewish lesson, for the grotto itself was completely free from commercialisation. But the moment you emerge from the gates into the streets of Lourdes you are bombarded by shops and shopkeepers of every kind in a cacophony of languages pleading and cajoling you to buy mementoes and religious favours of every kind from bottled water to neon flashing statues. It is crass and intrusive and so far from the genuineness of devotion and religious piety within the grotto itself.

It must have been exactly like inside the temple of Jerusalem – the most sacred site for the Jewish people. When we read of Jesus driving out the money-changers and salesmen in the temple we might imagine that he was carried away in the heat of the moment and lost his cool. It was nothing like that. Mark records that 'Jesus entered Jerusalem and went to the temple. He looked around at everything, but since it was already late, he went out to Bethany with the Twelve' (Mark 11:11). On the next day there follows the scene of Jesus driving out those who were buying and selling in the temple area. The tables and benches were overturned. Jesus castigated them verbally and used a whip made of cords to drive them out: 'Is it not written: "My house will be called a house of prayer for all nations"? But you have made it a "den of robbers"' (Mark 11:12–19; cf. Matt. 21:12–17; Luke 19:45–6; John 2:13–17). This was a deliberate self-conscious act on the part of Jesus. The results too were just what was intended. 'The blind and the lame came to him at the temple, and he healed them' (Matt. 21:14). To this it must be added that when the temple area was restored to its proper use, the children broke out in praise of God and of the One who came in the name of the Lord (Matt. 21:15).

Jesus was not afraid to use justifiable force when he was confronted with the oppression of people by those in authority. However, we need to remember that this was not a violent spur-of-the-moment reaction to the situation of abuse, but a careful, reflective act designed to restore the temple to its proper use. The immediate success of Jesus' action brought about exactly his intention. The danger for Christians surrounded by the power and authority of civil authorities is that they begin to model their behaviour on those authorities. Christians need to be aware that all authorities, whether they are national, international, local or business leaders, will be required to stand before God and give account for their use of power. But it is also vital that Christians realise that when authority is exercised in the body of Christ, the distinguishing mark of kingdom authority is that of service. Those for whom the authority is exercised are far more important than those who exercise the authority (Mark 10:42–5; Luke 22:27; John 13:12–15).

Nationalism and relationships in the kingdom

It is in the application of the gospel in the letters of Paul that we find an end to the spirit of nationalism. Yet the seeds of that destruction of nationalism are to be found in the life and teaching of Jesus, though often in an indirect way. Jesus came as the Messiah. He came to the Jewish people. But he came to them as part of the fulfilment of God's promise that in and through Israel all the nations of the earth would be blessed.

Jesus' ministry in fact reached out beyond the boundaries of the Jewish nation. One of his most notable encounters was with a woman at Jacob's well in Samaria (John 4:4–42). She was a Samaritan, and the Jews and the Samaritans not only had nothing to do with each other, they hated each other with a deep religious hatred and distrust of the kind which sadly marks the troubles between so-called Protestants and so-called Catholics in Northern Ireland. There can be no doubt that Jesus took the initiative in asking the woman at the well for a drink.

It is obvious that she was a loose-living woman whose lifestyle made it impossible for her to come to draw water at the normal times. So she was forced to go in the heat of the day, which was when she met Jesus. She was shocked at his greeting her and asking her for a favour. Jesus challenged her about her life and offered her insight into a different kind of life, all based on their discussion of water. She recognised that this was indeed the anointed one — the Christ. She was changed, and brought many of the villagers to meet Jesus. In spite of her reputation they came to hear the man who had told her all she had ever done. I am not sure that I would have been rushing to meet a man who was able to tell me and everyone else all I had ever done. But the Samaritans came, and many believed and accepted that Jesus was the Saviour of the world.

Jesus' behaviour must have scandalised the disciples and the Jews, but that did not prevent him from making sure that they realised that God was not interested in nationalism and national-istic prejudices. The kingdom of God is about relationships and how men and women treat each other. It is no accident, then, that when faced with a trick question about the law by a legal expert Jesus used a shocking example (Luke 10:25–37). The lawyer had been bested by Jesus and was trying to save face by pushing him to define who was a neighbour. Jesus then told the story we call the parable of the Good Samaritan, where a man who has been robbed and assaulted is left to die by the priest and the Levite, but helped by a Samaritan. (Luke's Gospel paints a vivid picture of the lengths to which the Samaritan went to make sure that the man was cared for.) Jesus then asked the legal eagle which of the three men who passed that way was the injured man's neighbour. We can almost feel how the answer stuck in his gullet and he carefully avoided saying the dreaded words. It was 'the one who had mercy.' Unable to bring himself to say that it was the Samaritan, he still could not escape from the reality of mercy and love in action. Jesus was making it plain that nationality was not the issue. What matters as far as the kingdom of God is concerned is how we respond to our neighbours in need. On that basis the Samaritan passed the test with flying colours.

Later in Luke's Gospel the same point is made not so much by

Jesus himself, but in terms of the response to what he had done (Luke 17:11–19). Jesus had been travelling along the border between Samaria and Galilee and was met by ten lepers. They pleaded with him to have mercy on them. He told them to go and show themselves to the priest, which was what the law required of anyone who was healed from leprosy. The priest acted as the community health officer and had to pronounce people clean before they could be accepted back into society. As they went, the lepers were healed. We then read that only one of them came back when he realised he was healed. He threw himself at Jesus' feet and thanked him. At that point in the story, almost as if it were an afterthought, Luke adds the sting in the tail: '. . . and he was a Samaritan'. Jesus expressed surprise that only one returned and that he was a foreigner. It made no difference to his healing or his faith, for Jesus told him, 'Rise and go; your faith has made you well.'

Mark and Matthew record another insight which calls in question national exclusivism and superiority (Mark 7:24–30; Matt. 15:21–8). A Greek woman born in Syrian Phoenicia came and begged Jesus to drive the demon out of her daughter. It seemed that Jesus was responding as a single-minded Jew interested only in the Jews and their salvation and healing: 'First let the children eat all they want, for it is not right to take the children's bread and toss it to their dogs' (Mark 7:27). Her reply was pointed and successful: 'Yes, Lord, but even the dogs under the table eat the children's crumbs' (Mark 7:28). Jesus rewarded the woman and her faith. Her daughter was healed. Salvation and transformation were not only for the Jews, but for all those in need who came in faith.

Luke and Matthew give one further example of how a non-Jew impressed Jesus and gave him the opportunity to tell the Jews that the kingdom of God was far wider and greater than their narrow national understanding and hopes (Luke 7:1–10; Matt. 8:5–13). A centurion had a sick servant and asked Jesus to heal him. The centurion seemed to recognise the authority of Jesus and told Jesus that he need not bother to come to his house. It would be enough for Jesus simply to say the word and the healing would happen. This astonished Jesus: 'I tell you the truth, I have not found anyone in Israel with such great faith. I say to you that many will come from the east and the west, and will take their places at the feast with Abraham, Isaac and Jacob in the kingdom of heaven' (Matt. 8:10–11). The boundaries of the kingdom of God were clearly meant to stretch far beyond anything most Jews could conceive. This was an implicit challenge to the spirit of nationalism which excluded others and believed in native Jewish superiority. Relationships in the kingdom must be totally different from typical nationalistic exclusiveness.

Relationships with the poor and with money

The primary aim of the ethical teaching of Jesus was to bring the message of the kingdom of God. This expressed the righteousness of God in terms of how we are to live in the kingdom. Jesus did not offer some pattern for economic life in terms of a blueprint for society. It would be unreasonable to expect such a thing, given the nature of Christ's life, death and ministry. He came to save people and to move them from darkness into light and from death to life. Yet there is quite a lot of teaching directed to the subject of wealth and poverty.

Jesus was deeply concerned with people's attitudes towards wealth and towards the poor. He did not separate our relationship with our money from our relationship with the poor. How we use and spend our money shows what kind of concern we have for poor people and how selfish we are. Broadly speaking, Jesus attacked wrong attitudes towards riches and made it clear that his ministry was focused on the poor and needy. However, it is not wealth itself which is condemned, nor poverty in itself which is commended (Matt. 5:3; Luke 6:20; 12:15–21; 16:14, 19–31).

Even before the ministry of Jesus began, it was clear how he would respond to the rich and the poor. In the Magnificat, Mary proclaimed, 'He has filled the hungry with good things but has sent the rich away empty' (Luke 1:53). Luke also records the very first public sermon and teaching Jesus gave. It expressed his special role in relation to the poor by using Isaiah's words, 'The Spirit of the Lord is on me, because he has anointed me to preach good news to the poor' (Luke 4:18; Isa. 61:1–2). In the Sermon on the Mount, which we shall look at more closely in the next chapter, Jesus taught that the poor were blessed and the rich were woeful (Matt. 5:3; Luke 6:20, 24).

Jesus was faithful to this outlook when he was in situations where the rich and the poor might gather. When he was at a meal in the home of a prominent Pharisee, he saw how the guests picked out the places of honour at the table. His reaction was to tell the parable of the wedding feast (Luke 14:1–14). At this feast the order was reversed and the humble were given the places of honour and those who thought they should sit at the top table had a rude shock. Jesus then applied the parable to his host: 'When you give a luncheon or dinner, do not invite your friends, your brothers or relatives, or your rich neighbours; if you do, they may invite you back and so you will be repaid. But when you give a banquet, invite the poor, the crippled, the lame, the blind, and you will be blessed' (Luke 14:12–14).

The poor have a very special place in the kingdom of God. Some theologians even go so far as to call this God's 'bias towards the poor'. Certainly Jesus was quick to notice the loving giving of the poor. He watched a poor widow giving an offering far beyond her means and what she could afford. This generosity stood in sharp contrast to the selfish, calculated token giving of the wealthy (Mark 12:41–4; Luke 21:1–4).

Jesus also noted how some people loved money too much. He was quick to point out that some Pharisees, the rich young ruler, and the rich fool who planned to pull down his barns to build more all illustrated the dangers of the love of money (Matt. 19:16–30; Mark 10:17–31; Luke 12:13–21; 18:18–29). The heart of the lesson was summed up by Jesus in Matthew's version of the story of the rich young ruler: 'I tell you the truth, it is hard for a rich man to enter the kingdom of heaven. Again I tell you, it is easier for a camel to go through the eye of a needle than for a rich man to enter the kingdom of God' (Matt. 19:23–4).

In another parable, where he appeared to commend the shrewdness of the worldly manager (Luke 16:1–13), Jesus was quite explicit about the dangers of money: 'No servant can serve two masters. Either he will hate the one and love the other, or he will be devoted to the one and despise the other. You cannot serve both God and Money' (Luke 16:13). The rich young ruler illustrates Jesus' point exactly. He was a good man, who kept the law and was desperate to know the path to eternal life. Jesus confronted him with the fact that his riches were the real stumbling-block to following him. He told him that all he had to do was to sell all that he had, give it to the poor, and then follow Jesus. Unfortunately, the young man was so attached to his wealth that he refused to follow Jesus (Matt. 19:16–30; Mark 10:17–31; Luke 18:18–29).

Three incidents in the life of Christ illustrate the dangers of riches and God's concern for the poor. These show what kind of relationships Christians ought to have with both. In the parable of Dives and Lazarus – the rich man and the poor man – the failure of Dives to respond to the need of the poor man at his gate reaped a terrible reward (Luke 16:19–31). Yet this does not mean that rich people cannot enter the kingdom of God. The story of Zacchaeus and his remarkable conversion shows that. He used his wealth generously – to put right the wrong that he had done, and, even more importantly, to give away half of his wealth to the poor (Luke 19:1–10). Such sacrificial giving, expressed in sharing what we have with those who have little or nothing, is the mark of Christian living in the kingdom. Yet it was not everything that was given away, and it was not a case of meeting the needs of the poor at all costs.

The story of the woman with the alabaster jar is a painful corrective to any simplistic equation of the gospel with concern for the poor. Though that concern is fundamental to the Christian gospel, it is not the only thing that matters. It is all too easy for us to become hypocritical about our attitudes to the poor. Some fellow guests responded very indignantly when the woman broke the alabaster jar and poured expensive perfume over Jesus' head. 'Why this waste of perfume? It could have been sold for more than a year's wages and the money given to the poor' (Mark 14:4–5).

Jesus responded to their criticism, 'Leave her alone. Why are you bothering her? She has done a beautiful thing to me. The poor you will always have with you, and *you can help them any time you want.* But you will not always have me' (Mark 14:6–7; see also John 12:1–8). In accepting the woman's gift of love, Jesus recognised that there may be other priorities than giving to the poor, though he was absolutely clear that his and her critics were simply using the poor as a stick to beat the woman. They had no real or continuing concern for the poor. It seems that while they could have helped the poor at any time, they did not do so.

There is no doubt that Jesus taught that the wrong relationship with our money is dangerous. If we are over-attached to it and love it, then that is a serious hindrance to entering the kingdom of God. Living in the kingdom means a genuine commitment to supporting and caring for the poor and to meeting the basic physical needs of people. That we always have the poor emphasises the constant need to re-evaluate our priorities and to use the wealth we have been given to relieve the distress and suffering of others.

Sexual relationships in the kingdom of God

Despite our twentieth-century preoccupation with sexuality, Jesus had remarkably little to say about it. Perhaps this shows that it is not nearly as important as we like or are made to think. What he did say, however, calls in question many of the attitudes and responses that we tend to take for granted today.

At the heart of all Jesus' teaching on sexuality is the centrality of the marriage relationship. But that teaching is mostly set in the context of the Pharisees trying to trap him. Their interest was not in ascertaining what should be the right attitude towards divorce, but in trying to make Jesus criticise the law of Moses and so alienate the Jewish community – but they were destined to be disappointed. Jesus explained why Moses had allowed divorce in the first place, and then he went behind the question of divorce to the fundamental ground and nature of marriage. Divorce was only allowed because of the hardness of people's hearts. It was never part of God's original creation-pattern or intention. Divorce arises because men and women are sinful beings and we all live in a sinful world where we have to come to terms with situations which are less than ideal. But that does not invalidate the ideal, nor does it make that ideal less important or something we ought not to bother to aim for.

Jesus explained that from the beginning God's intention was the lifelong exclusive relationship which we call marriage. In the beginning male and female were created. It is not the case, as some of my feminist friends tell me, that God made Adam first and then thought that he could do better. According to the Genesis account, woman was created because man on his own was inadequate. It was not good for man to be alone. Thus human beings were created to complement each other (Gen. 1:27–8; 2:18–25).

There is a simple biblical pattern for male and female relationships. It is leaving, cleaving and becoming one flesh. Jesus reaffirmed and restored the importance of that basic God-given pattern and foundation. It begins with a leaving of the old relationships of family loyalties. We all know that when couples are forced by circumstances to continue to live with their in-laws it creates tremendous strains on a marriage. If parents refuse to leave their children alone to develop proper relationships in their new marriages, then this is a recipe for disaster. But cleaving is to follow the leaving. Usually cleaving is understood in terms of being so stuck together that any separation produces harm and hurt. If two things are glued together, taking them apart is a painful process and often leads to two pieces which are less than complete. There then follows the becoming one flesh. This is not just a sexual unity, but is a union between a man and a woman such that the two become one by the grace and power of God. They ought not to be separated (Matt. 19:1–11; 5:27–32; Mark 10:1–12; Luke 16:14–18). Yet it is quite clear, now as it was then, that separation does happen. So how are we to respond?

Jesus' teaching is expressed by Matthew with total clarity: 'But I tell you that anyone who divorces his wife, except for marital unfaithfulness, causes her to become an adulteress, and anyone who marries the divorced woman commits adultery' (Matt. 5:32). God's pattern is that of total commitment to faithfulness in marriage. God's ideal is that marriages are for ever. But, confronted with the reality of divorce and marriage breakdown, people are faced with the question of remarriage. Given that divorce is obviously permitted under certain specifiable circumstances, is remarriage possible? The honest answer is that there is no absolutely clear answer given in Scripture. So people have argued from silence, from the context and customs of the day, from other biblical passages, and from the history of the Church.

Mark and Luke seem to indicate that to remarry is in fact to commit adultery (Mark 10:2–12; Luke 16:18). That also seems to be the thrust of Matthew 5. The issue is not totally clear-cut, however, because of a key passage in Matthew 19 which is paralleled by Paul's teaching in 1 Corinthians 7. Both passages stress that divorce is not the norm, but allow exceptions to that general rule. Matthew allowed divorce if adultery (literally *porneia* or sexual misconduct) was the cause of the breakdown, and Paul allowed divorce where a believer and an unbeliever decided that they wanted to end their relationship. The problem is that neither passage explicitly mentions whether or not this exception also applies to remarriage after such situations. This has led to the use of arguments from silence and to close examination of the customs of the day. One side argues that in Jesus' time remarriage among divorced Jews was the norm and order of the day. It was so obvious that remarriage was acceptable that Jesus did not need to say it. The other side is equally certain that in the light of what Mark and Luke have to say, remarriage is always wrong. Even if divorce may be permitted under exceptional circumstances, the nature of the marriage bond implies that it cannot be dissolved or undone, so any idea of remarriage is a logical impossibility. Christians will and do come to different conclusions, and none of us can be categorical about remarriage in such circumstances. But we can be categorical that divorce is less than ideal and that we should all strive to avoid such situations.

Some commentators suggest that Jesus never gave any permission for divorce, and that what we have in Matthew is an addition from the early Church to try to harmonise the teaching of Jesus with that of Moses. This is speculative and in no way escapes from the plain fact that this teaching which was given to the Church allowed divorce only in a very narrow range of instances. This was far more stringent a standard than obtained in the culture of Jesus' day. What Jesus was doing, it is argued, was raising the status of women by safeguarding them and their interests and tightening up on an open abuse of the law of Moses. This view is supported by the realisation that the manifesto of the kingdom set far more rigorous and stringent standards than even the Pharisees held. For Jesus the lustful look is as wrong as the act of adultery. Jesus knew that the look of lust is the first step towards the committing of the act. It reveals sin in the heart and mind. The motive is as wrong as the action (Matt. 5:27–8). None of us can feel easy before such a standard. All of us will fall short, and so we must be driven back to the grace and love of God and realise that there is no way we can achieve the standards of the kingdom without the help of God. Yet we are left with the fact that people will and do fall short of the kingdom's standards, and not only have lustful desires, but also commit adultery.

The Pharisees again tried to trap Jesus (John 8:1–11). They brought before him a woman who had been caught in the very act of adultery. The fact that it was only the woman showed their low view of women and their lack of any real concern for the law of Moses. They were trying to trick Jesus into some open breach with the law of Moses which would have destroyed his credibility. His reply is a famous challenge to all of us who are quick to accuse others and ignore our own faults and weaknesses: 'If any one of you is without sin, let him be the first to throw a stone at her' (John 8:7). It is interesting that as the members of the crowd slink away the oldest leave first. The older and wiser knew that when matched up against such a standard, every one of us is condemned. In the end, no one was left to condemn the woman. Jesus did not condemn her either, but that in no way implied he condoned her sin. He sent her away with the clear call to leave her life of sin. Adultery is a serious matter, but it is no more and no less serious than any other sin which breaks and destroys our relationships with other people. The proper way of dealing with such sin in our lives is repentance and rejection of the sin and old way of life. Then we shall know the forgiveness of God.

The only other recorded discussion of marriage and divorce happened in the context of yet another trap. This time it was set by the Sadducees (Mark 12:18–27; Luke 20: 27–40). It sounded like an excellent example of a theological conundrum, like 'How many angels can you get on the head of a pin?' A woman married seven brothers in succession after each of her husbands died. The question was, after the resurrection, whose wife would she be in heaven? Jesus turned the question by suggesting that marriage will be the last thing on our minds when the resurrection comes. He then cleverly opened up the debate between the Pharisees and the Sadducees. Obviously when the kingdom comes in all its fullness, marriage will not be important. The quality of our relationship with God will be far above and beyond the best we experience here and now. Our human life will be transformed so that even the union of marriage will be surpassed.

This does not detract from the importance and significance of marriage. But it is a useful reminder that marriage is not and ought not to be the first or only priority in our lives. Jesus said, 'For some are eunuchs because they were born that way; others were made that way by men; and others have renounced marriage because of the kingdom of heaven. The one who can accept this should accept it' (Matt. 19:12). Jesus himself never married, and many have followed in his footsteps, being willing to set aside marriage and that kind of family life for the sake of the gospel. By their selfless commitment to God and to other people they have shared in ministering the good news of the kingdom of God. Sexuality and its genital expression are not the most important things about us or our lives. The proper place for sexual expression is within the context of a lifelong commitment in marriage. For those in the kingdom of God, its place is recognised, but that is never to be worshipped or followed slavishly.

Kingdom values and relationships

When someone enters the kingdom of God all their relationships are affected. To be in the kingdom is to have a new relationship with God through Christ. In following his example servant-love is the core value and the guiding principle for all behaviour and relationships. The golden rule expressed positively the good that the Christian is to do to others. That good is to be seen in every relationship, ranging from those with civil authorities to those with the poor and needy. Nationalism and the wrong attitude to money are called in question by our new relationship with God. Every aspect of our human being is affected by that relationship, including our sexuality and the settings in which it is to be expressed. In Christ there is not only new life, but also a new lifestyle. The one is the mark of the other. This new lifestyle is based on a manifesto that Jesus taught his disciples; it is usually called the Sermon on the Mount, and is the subject of the next chapter.

3

The Manifesto of the Kingdom

'Blessed are the poor in spirit,
   for theirs is the kingdom of heaven.
Blessed are those who mourn,
   for they will be comforted.
Blessed are the meek,
   for they will inherit the earth.
Blessed are those who hunger and thirst for
                           righteousness,
   for they will be filled.
Blessed are the merciful,
   for they will be shown mercy.
Blessed are the pure in heart,
   for they will see God.
Blessed are the peacemakers,
   for they will be called sons of God.
Blessed are those who are persecuted because of
                           righteousness,
   for theirs is the kingdom of heaven.

Blessed are you when people insult you, persecute you and falsely say all kinds of evil against you because of me. Rejoice and be glad, because great is your reward in heaven, for in the same way they persecuted the prophets who were before you.'

(Matt. 5:1–12; cf. Luke 6:17–23)

The upside-down values of the manifesto

Familiarity breeds contempt and robs us of the initial power and amazement which must have greeted this manifesto. It is a grave loss. Because we know the words and ideas so well we are no longer challenged by them. We have translated them from a strident attack on the values of the world around us to a saccharine set of pious phrases. In fact these sayings call in question the very basic assumptions of life and should cause us to reflect on the nature of our ethical ideals and values.

The manifesto appears in two slightly different forms. In Matthew we have the sermon on the mount (Matt. 5–7) and in Luke we have the sermon on the plain (Luke 6:17–49). In Matthew's account we are given the most sustained presentation of direct teaching from Jesus. The detail and the form of expression show the impact these words must have had not only on the crowds, but especially on the disciples. The way the manifesto is set out encourages easy remembering, but the impact must also have come from the unusual content of the ideas. Here Jesus set out the pattern of life required of everyone who enters the kingdom of God. It is no surprise that John Stott calls this 'the Christian counter-culture'. Its form owes much to the parallel with Moses as the law-giver, but these laws embody a set of values and issue a call to live in a way which thoroughly contradicts the qualities that the world admires. If this is indeed the way to be a successful Christian, then these are certainly upside-down values.

The teaching of Jesus here is completely out of step with our usual way of looking at things. It declares that the truly fortunate or blessed ones are those who seem desperately unfortunate from an ordinary worldly point of view. Both Luke and Matthew make a point of stressing that Jesus was speaking to his disciples, though a much larger crowd of people was present (Matt. 5:1–2; Luke 6:17–20). The crowd seems to have been like a set of spectators sitting on the sidelines watching a noteworthy event. Here was the master teaching his team of disciples what it meant to belong to the kingdom of God. These men had left everything immediately when Jesus had called them to be his disciples. As far as the things of this world went, they had very little. They lived in a way which must have brought them face to face with hunger, poverty, hardship and deprivation. But those who had responded to the call of Jesus were now hearing again the call and the cost of discipleship in the context of the benefits, blessings and promises of Jesus.

Jesus was presenting a picture of a new redeemed humanity. His manifesto indicated and illustrated what it meant to obey God and belong to his kingdom. He outlined the basic essentials of Christian living in the kingdom of God. If anyone wanted to be a real disciple, then this was what you had to do. Jesus presented the ideals which ought to motivate his followers. Inevitably he drew from many themes and ideas which were well known in Judaism, but what makes this manifesto original and different is the twist Jesus gave them.

The good Jew was concerned to live according to the law of God. To help people to do this the Jewish religious leaders had created sets of commentaries on the laws. These offered interpretations of what the law meant and what actually constituted keeping the law. With the growth of such commentaries, there also arose the idea that you had to keep all the rules about keeping the laws. This in itself encouraged a spirit of legalism. Legalism grows when people become more concerned with keeping the letter of the law than with fulfilling the purposes intended by the laws. Keeping the letter of the law for the law's sake rather than for God's sake is an ever-present danger. Part of the purpose in Jesus' ushering in of the kingdom was to remind people that the will of God is not focused on the letter of the law, but rather on getting our motives and inner attitudes right so that we can know and do God's will properly. The only genuine motive for godliness must be a desire to please God.

God's rules are there to help us. But we can become obsessed with keeping the rules for their own sake. The sad history of many Victorian parents seems to be that they were desperately keen to be good and to keep the moral rules, especially in the eyes of other people. But often they were so utterly selfish in their keeping of the rules that they became tyrants at home and at work. They lost their humanity and damaged their children and their workers as they pursued their moral ideals at the cost of other people. Love was missing both from their vocabulary and their lives. If we are left to our own devices in morality we shall either fail miserably or else we will care too much for ourselves and too little for our neighbours. We can so easily become totally obsessed and absorbed with ourselves and keeping the moral rules for ourselves. The picture we have of the scribes and Pharisees is of just such people.

When Jesus healed people in need on the Sabbath day the scribes and Pharisees complained that he was breaking the Sabbath law. You were not allowed to do any work on the Sabbath, and healing people was work, so Jesus was breaking the Sabbath. Jesus took them to task and complained that they were more interested in the rules than the point behind the rules and what they were meant to achieve. Surely it was better to do something good on the Sabbath day than something evil. The Sabbath was meant to be a time for human recreation, and healing was part of that recreation. So, in healing people on the Sabbath day, Jesus was fulfilling the original purpose of the Sabbath. The Pharisees had lost sight of that meaning in their obsession with the rules themselves. They were more interested in keeping themselves guiltless than in helping people. The manifesto of the kingdom challenges our legalism and the self-centredness behind it.

The manifesto is also a challenge in that it describes the kinds of attitudes and aspirations which ought to characterise the life of the disciple in the kingdom of God. But Christians need to ask whether or not this is the case. Each beatitude and all the teaching of Matthew 5–7 is a direct challenge not only to the conventional contemporary ideas of the day, but to every follower of Jesus. The manifesto provides a test for the reality of our discipleship. Jesus suggested that we are in fact blessed and fortunate in conditions which most of us regard as less than ideal and a curse.

Jesus turned values upside down. The manifesto is full of contradictions to normal expectations. It works by a series of contrasts between what most people believe and what God provides. These contrasts are set in the context of a series of promises. The apparent successes and failures in the here and now will be totally reversed in the future when the kingdom comes in all its glory. This is not so much a reward for having a hard time now, so inviting people to grin and bear it; rather it is the very opposite and antithesis of the present understanding of reality. Our problem is that the beatitudes seem like a set of mildly stirring precepts for a group of other-worldly people. If we are honest, they seem of little use or relevance to the difficult situations of everyday life. Such a response fails to accept the genuine challenge to discipleship and the test of obedience implicit in the teaching. It also misses any reference to the power of God to bring about this quality of life by the Spirit in God's kingdom.

As it is set out in Matthew, the teaching is in the form of a catechism or teaching plan. The manifesto gives the required marks of the one who follows Jesus. It describes the kind of character, outlook and qualities which stem from having the kingdom of God within us. The ideals of humility, a hunger for a goodness like God's, mercifulness, singleness of direction, and being a peacemaker lead to genuine satisfaction and wholeness. If and when we live like this, we shall be what we ought to be and were created to be. This blessedness comes from obedience to the call of Jesus. At the very heart of this call lie the themes of justice and righteousness. We cannot escape the necessity of being right with God and living in just and true relationships with each other.

Luke's woes

In Luke's account of the manifesto, there is a parallel passage which also provides a sharp contrast to traditional ideas (Luke 6:20–49). Happiness is the fruit of poverty, hunger, weeping and persecution. Pain and displeasure are the fruit for those who have lived their lives in luxury, have satisfied their own hunger, have had no experience of sorrow, and have never experienced opposition. The contrast is too exact to be accidental. Luke is expressing negatively a reinforcement of the positive form of the manifesto in Matthew. The kingdom turns upside down the values we all take for granted. An easy life in the present can lead to spiritual blindness and a closed mind as far as the kingdom of God is concerned.

The overall picture from the 'woes' is of self-centred, self-satisfied people who, by implication, have been careless of the needs of others, as Dives seemed to be unaware of Lazarus starving at his gate. A life which is lived only for the present fails to realise the spiritual dimensions of existence, which stretch far beyond the present. It is not riches, being well fed, laughter, or having a good reputation which are in themselves the problem. There need be nothing wrong with any or all of these in their proper place. However, the state of mind on which these things can breed and the selfishness which all too often is the hallmark of people who live in relative luxury are very real dangers. Luke records Jesus' challenge to contemplate how we live. He does this by the very starkness and the unexpectedness of the contrasts Jesus presented. The true meaning of the 'woes' is to be found in the positive statement of the manifesto.

The beatitudes

'Blessed are the poor in spirit, for theirs is the kingdom of heaven.' (Matt. 5:3; cf. Luke 6:20)

I remember a discussion on the Governing Body of my Oxford college. We were debating the relative merits of two candidates for a fellowship – a senior position in the college. The candidates were pretty well matched academically, so how were we to choose between them? One fellow was quite clear that he had a definite preference. One of the candidates was, as far as he was concerned, a good mess mate! There was no higher compliment from an ex-military officer who was willing to share his dining mess with such a companion. Others agreed that he was indeed 'clubbable'. It sounded like he would make a good member of the club and fit in with the life of the college. In fact, when they elected him it was on the basis that he was our kind of person.

It may be easy for us to recognise what our kind of person is, but the manifesto begins by making it clear what sort of person God's kind of person is. Luke's Gospel expresses it simply and boldly: 'Blessed are you who are poor' (Luke 6:20). Jesus' concern seemed to be the poor hard-working ordinary people. This is not just a matter of those who are at the bottom of the heap in an economic sense. It also covers those who are disadvantaged at every level of life. All too often, they are the victims of oppression. By necessity and not because of choice their lifestyle is a simple one. They have little choice about most things. They are trapped by their economic position. They are poor too in the sense that they are excluded from the privileges that wealth brings. To be a fellow of most Oxford colleges brings with it the amazing privilege of being able to walk on the grass within the college boundaries. If you are not a fellow, then it is the path around the grass for you. The poor are excluded from far more weighty privileges and necessities. Even the realm of education (and by this Jesus was probably thinking of religious and moral instruction as well) was closed off from the poor. It is often the case in a society that it is the relatively well off and upwardly mobile who have access to education. The way up is often through that education, so the poor may be doubly discriminated against. In Jesus' day the poor were poorly educated, and that meant that they knew little about the law and will of God. Such knowledge and its control was in the hands of a few: it had become the privileged domain of the wealthy elite.

In the Old Testament there is developed a clear understanding of the poor. The poor are those who have little or no influence. Because they have no clout and are unable to affect what happens, they become victims in so many situations. They become oppressed and have nowhere to turn except to God. It is this turning to God on the part of the poor which gives us the meaning of the saying, 'Blessed are you who are poor.' In terms of the Old Testament, the poor had become identified with the saintly. They were the ones who were faithful to their religion and tried to keep the law as far as they understood it. In contrast, it was the better off who tended to be easily affected by the worldly standards and values of the cultures surrounding Israel. The religious life of the rich became mere public show and the heart of the matter was lost. The rich all too easily degenerated into oppressive exploiters. It was different for the poor. They were seen as simple devoted people who were self-sacrificing, caring, and genuinely humble. They are God's kind of people. They belong to God's kingdom. They accept God's will for their lives.

Jesus' disciples had abandoned everything to follow him. They were genuinely poor as this world counts things. But in the kingdom of God their situation would be reversed. True wealth is not in material things or financial security; it lies in dependence on God. If we allow anything to become a substitute for God, and think that we can find security in anything other than God, we are in for a serious shock.

Some argue that Jesus is not just referring to the despised, the oppressed and the destitute, but that the gloss in Matthew of 'the poor in spirit' (Matt. 5:3) clearly identifies the people who recognise their spiritual need. They realise that they have no 'riches' of their own, but that they are utterly dependent on the grace and love of God. It is people like that who are open to receiving the kingdom of God like a little child. Theirs indeed is the kingdom of heaven. They are the sort of people that God can use and do something with. The problem with the rest of us is that we are tempted to try to do everything in our own strength. We fail to recognise that when it comes to divine matters we are poor. God has no place in our reckoning. We can do it ourselves and do it our way. The kingdom of heaven is not entered or lived out in that way.

'Blessed are those who mourn, for they will be comforted.' (Matt. 5:4; cf. Luke 6:21)

It was those in exile in Babylon who wept when they remembered Zion (Ps. 137). Anybody who has been a stranger in a far-away place, with no prospect of getting back home soon, knows only too well the terrible waves of homesickness that sweep over you and bring tears to your eyes. Weeping and mourning were not something new to the people of Israel. But it seems as if Jesus was trying to encourage those who do weep and mourn that there will be a reversal of their situation. Their tears and grief will be transformed into comfort and laughter. But it is far more than just a clever play on words which suggests that the unhappy will be happy one day. All of us realise that sorrow can just as easily destroy people as be used as a means of growing and showing tremendous human courage in the face of tragedy and adversity. Sorrow can just as easily break people as make them saints.

When Jesus talks of mourning here, it is not so much at the awfulness of our own situation as because of our sin and the sin of others. It was said of Robert Murray McCheyne that when he walked down the street in Dundee people were so struck by his holiness that they wept for their sinfulness and resolved to change. It is also told that he would mount the pulpit steps on a Sunday and look out over the congregation and be so conscious of sin – his own and that of the people present – that all he was able to do was weep in the pulpit and say nothing. Yet that weeping led to many being changed and converted as they too became conscious of their own sin, and that led to despair. The despair then led to a search for freedom from sin, and so they experienced the grace of God and his loving forgiveness.

Jesus challenged his followers to mourn for their sinfulness. This only really happens when we see the holiness and purity of God and the total inadequacy of our efforts to be like him. One of the reasons that the Church of today has so little sense of sin is that we have lost any real understanding of the holiness of God. We have forgotten that God hates sin and cannot bear to look on it. God takes sin seriously. The cross is God's remedy for sin. It cost Christ everything. It cost his life. We need to recover an awareness of sin, and I am sure that that will only happen when we see again the holiness and purity of God.

True mourning is as concerned about other people and their situation as about our own sinfulness. After the lethal rioting of football fans in Brussels some years ago, many people remarked that they were ashamed to be British. Such a sense of shame because of what others have done ought equally to mark the followers of Jesus. When we reflect on the state of our societies, the condition of the world, and the gross inhumanity of people against each other, then we ought to mourn.

Genuine compassion shares the grief and sorrow of others. In fact, Martin Luther even translates this section in a literal way as, 'Blessed are the sorrow-bearers.' Inevitably this reminds us that the disciple is to be like his or her master – 'a man of sorrows, and familiar with suffering' (Isa. 53:3). As Jesus suffered for others, wept over their sinfulness and bore their sorrows on the cross, so the members of the kingdom of God are to carry the sorrows of a broken and twisted world. This is surely part of the tremendous ministry of prayer which lifts the sorrow of the world up to the throne of God and begs for his mercy and intervention in our world.

But the promise of Jesus is that there will be a contrast between the present and the future which will be as sharp as the difference between tears and laughter and grief and joy. God himself will be the comforter and bring laughter into the lives of those who have mourned and wept for their own sins and those of the world. God is the one who is called in to help and who supplies the necessary strength to bear the pain and sorrow. He gives hope to the hopeless. This is not just some future aspect. It is at the core of what it means to live in the kingdom of God now. We are able to be comforted by God here and now.

What this means is revealed in one of the most touching verses in the New Testament. It tries to describe the final outworking of the kingdom of God and what that will be like: 'God will wipe away every tear from their eyes' (Rev. 7:17; cf. 21:4). That picture of the loving heavenly Father taking out his handkerchief and using it to wipe away the dropping tears is a remarkable account of the reality of the comfort that can be known by those who dwell in the kingdom of God.

'Blessed are the meek, for they will inherit the earth.' (Matt. 5:5)

The apostle Peter, writing of Jesus, summed up the heart of this beatitude: 'When they hurled their insults at him, he did not retaliate; when he suffered, he made no threats. Instead, he entrusted himself to him who judges justly' (1 Pet. 2:23). The psalmist echoed a very similar thought about the fruitlessness of retaliation and the fruitfulness of meekness:

> Refrain from anger and turn from wrath;
>   do not fret – it leads only to evil.
> For evil men will be cut off,
>   but those who hope in the Lord will inherit the land.
> A little while, and the wicked will be no more;
>   though you look for them, they will not be found.
> But the meek will inherit the land
>   and enjoy great peace. (Ps. 37:8–11)

Our problem is that we see the word 'meek' and the picture that springs to mind is of weakness and ineffectiveness. The modern world teaches us that the assertive grab the earth, both in terms of what is theirs and what is somebody else's. 'What's yours is mine and what's mine is my own' is the philosophy of the day. If you don't stand up for yourself, no one else will stand up for you. As my boys would say, 'Don't be a wimp!' But there is nothing weak, ineffectual or wimpish about Jesus. Surrounded by the brutality of others towards him, he was silent – not as in a huge fit of the sulks, but a patient enduring which challenged the most bloody-minded and even transformed a hardened Roman centurion (Matt. 27:54).

According to Jesus, members of the kingdom of God are to stand in sharp contrast to the values of the world around them. But this is not always the case. We live in a society where everyone is very insistent indeed on having his or her rights. We seem so caught up in a constant set of demands for this right or some other one. We appear to have many rights today which our parents and grandparents didn't even realise were rights at all: the right to work, the right to have a baby by any means, the right to have an abortion, the right to do as we please, the right to . . . and so it goes on and on. The community of God's people is not to seek its own rights. The term for meekness here really means never being angry at the wrong time, but also implies that there is room for being angry at the right time. That anger ought never to be concerned about things which are simply affecting us, but must always be concerned about things that affect other people.

Thus the community of the kingdom is to be in the forefront of ensuring and safeguarding the rights of others, especially of the poor and oppressed.

Any attempt to protect one's own rights smacks of greed and selfishness. Instead, there is to be a gentle willingness to be put upon as far as other folks are concerned. Meekness is a lack of self-concern. It stems from the realisation that we all have much to learn and a great deal to be forgiven. The meek person does not claim his or her own rights, for they know that they are not really in any position to do so. They recognise their own weakness, ignorance and need. Because of this they leave their own defence to God. Their aim is to control themselves and to reject any idea of looking after number one.

Thus, rights are not to be claimed for oneself. They are to be renounced in order to live for the sake of Christ and for others. In the face of reproaches, the Christian is not to leap to his or her own defence. When treated with violence, the Christian is to endure it patiently. The Christian is not to make a scene when treated unjustly. God himself will restore and give due recompense. This means that the mark of the Christian is to be the gentleness which forbears and considers others before oneself. There is to be no hint of domination or any desire for power over others. Instead there is to be only a gentle service of the needs of others.

The second half of the beatitude is equally surprising. We might think that the natural reward for such gentle people is that they will have a front-row seat in heaven. Surely they are too good for this world! In the kingdom of God, the meek will inherit the earth. The very sphere of violence and aggressive power is won in the end, not by the violent and powerful, but by the gentle and meek. They are to rule the earth, for they are the genuine heirs who own and deserve the earth. This will be the renewed earth, which becomes theirs in all its fullness when the kingdom comes in all its glory.

'Blessed are those who hunger and thirst for righteousness, for they will be filled.' (Matt. 5:6; cf. Luke 6:21)

For the members of the kingdom of God, the renunciation of

one's rights is to be paralleled by the renunciation of any idea of one's own righteousness. The aim of the good Jew was to stand right before God. It was to be good enough to be able to stand in front of God, look him in the face, and not be ashamed. You had to earn that yourself by the way you lived and were righteous and good. The religion of Jesus' day was marked by the earnest struggle to achieve as high a standard of goodness and righteousness as possible. The disciple of Jesus had to recognise that the righteousness he or she can achieve is never going to be good enough. The only goodness that counts is the goodness that comes from God and his grace. The best and indeed the only thing that we can do is to hunger and thirst after this kind of righteousness. God created us to be good and to do what is good, so we can find no real rest until we find that goodness. It comes from God alone. It is not a 'do it yourself' job.

Thus, the attitude portrayed in the beatitude is that of people who know that they have not been able to attain the righteousness they ought to have. At the same time, they are desperate to have it. There is nothing complacent or self-satisfied about them. Their sense of need is so great that it is like a starving man looking for food or a thirsty person gasping for a drink of water. The desire for goodness is to be like a physical craving for food and drink. If we don't get what we need we shall die. These appetites are crude physical necessities. Unless these basic appetites are satisfied we will shrivel up and die as people. The desire for goodness and righteousness is meant to be as basic as that. It is to be the bread and butter of our existence.

What Jesus is demanding is that his followers should never be satisfied until they have reached the totality of God's righteousness. It is not simply living up to God's standards, but rather a complete conforming to the goodness and character of God himself. This is why Jesus is so important. He is God's incarnated goodness. He unveils God's righteousness for us to copy. To hunger and thirst after righteousness is to long to be like Jesus.

It is also to long for all righteousness. Being right and good means being right in all our relationships. We are to be right in our relationship with God. We are to be right in our moral relationships with each other. Our character and conduct are to be good and right. Our homes and family life, our work and business dealings, our social and political activities are all to be marked by goodness and righteousness.

All too often we may feel that we are not very far down the road towards Christlikeness. So often we are neither righteous nor good. The promise is that we shall be filled and satisfied. The only failure at issue here is not of attainment, but of wanting, of not hungering or thirsting. This beatitude is not about getting something, but about wanting it. As the branches are to abide in the vine and leave the fruiting to the vine and the vine-dresser, so we are to concentrate on wanting to be like Christ, and the Christlikeness will follow as promised. We don't have to worry about doing anything except really desiring goodness.

In a sense, the beatitude shows us that what it means to follow Jesus is to want more of Jesus and to be more and more like him. The more we get, the more we want and ought to want. The contrast between the present and future reality is the difference between a famine and a feast. The good news is that in the kingdom of God we can feast on the bread of life here and now and participate in the messianic feast. But the final and total satisfaction of our desire to be like Jesus will only happen when we shall see him face to face (1 John 3:2).

'Blessed are the merciful, for they will be shown mercy.' (Matt. 5:7)

The essence of being human is the capacity for relationships. The nature and success of these is the test of our humanity. At the heart of this New Testament teaching for those in the kingdom of God are the ideas of *reciprocity* and *mutuality*. As husbands have duties and responsibilities, so too do wives. As parents have responsibilities, so too do children. As masters have duties and responsibilities, so too do slaves. This New Testament teaching derives quite clearly from Jesus. He described the essence of good relationships as beginning and ending with reciprocity. We are, in the words of the golden rule, to treat others as we would want them to treat us. But in the kingdom of God the right perspective for this is that of mutual forgiveness. In the prayer given to the disciples, we read, 'Forgive us our sins, for we also forgive everyone who sins against us' (Luke 11:4). This is echoed in the Gospel of Mark, 'And when you stand praying, if you hold anything against anyone, forgive him, so that your Father in heaven may forgive you your sins' (Mark 11:25). This is the heart of the command to be merciful. The kingdom-follower is to be forgiving and merciful.

The failure to live like this reaps a terrible reward, as we can see from the parable of the unmerciful servant. He had been forgiven a great deal by his master and released from his debts; yet he was unwilling to do the same to others who owed much less. In spite of his own experience of mercy, he refused to be merciful and forgive (Matt. 18:21–35). This was no case of 'I'll scratch your back, if you scratch mine.' It lies at the core of the gospel. God has acted to forgive humanity in the coming of Jesus. Jesus died to bring forgiveness of sins for us all. The members of the kingdom of God are those who have accepted and experienced that forgiveness from Christ. They are, then, to be like Jesus in forgiving others. It is the mark of the truly forgiven person that they show mercy and forgiveness. It is only those who are truly merciful who will be shown mercy. This was in sharp contrast with the example of the Pharisees. Their lives seem to have been geared to making sure that God would be merciful to them. They searched for mercy, yet they were pitiless towards others. There was no hope that such people would experience mercy. They might not even have recognised it if they had got it.

But mercy is not a vague feeling, nor is it sentimental. Mercy seeks justice for all. It tries to make a difference. It begins by getting inside another person's situation and understanding what he or she is experiencing. It then acts and reacts appropriately to the person's needs. The merciful do not stand on their own dignity. They are quite prepared to get down in the mud with people, not to wallow in it with them, but to lift them out of the mud of their situation. As the Lord Jesus came down from the glory of heaven, refusing to stand on his dignity, and transformed the lot of men and women, so we are to do the same in terms of the transformation of people and situations. This merciful compassion is not an emotion, but an activity. Genuine pity ought to move us to vigorous action.

The call of Jesus is very clear: 'I tell you the truth, whatever you did for one of the least of these brothers of mine, you did it for me' (Matt. 25:40). As the Good Samaritan showed mercy, Jesus told the lawyer to go and do the same (Luke 10:37). Because we have experienced the mercy and forgiveness of God, we are to show mercy to others. Only those who deal mercifully with human need and distress will be shown mercy in the kingdom of God.

'Blessed are the pure in heart, for they will see God.' (Matt. 5:8)

The psalmist cried, 'Create in me a pure heart, O God, and renew a steadfast spirit within me' (Ps. 51:10). Purity in heart involves the whole of a person's personality. It is much more a matter of the will than a question of what we feel. Both Jesus and the psalmist stressed the inner nature of this purity. They knew only too well how easily outward show can cover an evil heart and mind. We can all be incredibly good actors and our public performance can be very different from what is actually going on inside.

Jesus stressed that purity was to affect our minds, intentions, motives, will, and heart. This demand is offered as a contrast and challenge to any purely ceremonial religion. Appearance should never be confused with reality. Thus the kingdom life is to be a life of singleness of purpose. That purpose is to be pure like God. Human standards will not do as substitutes for that kind of purity. Our human attempts to achieve purity usually concentrate on trying to be pure in one aspect of our lives. We interpret purity in a narrow way, rather than realising that it is a matter of the whole of a person's life. Purity is a matter of holiness. Such holiness is to cover every aspect and facet of our lives. As holiness is essential to the very nature of God and who he is, so holiness is to become second nature to the followers of Jesus.

For Jesus' listeners, talk of purity must have reminded them of the steps you had to go through to come to worship in the temple. Before you could come into the presence of God, there had to be ritual purification to make you pure and worthy to stand before God. In the Essene community there were sets of baptismal baths for ritual washing and cleansing. This was a necessary part of a proper approach to God. Jesus was saying that there is no bar to coming before God for those who have purity in their motives and lives. The pure in heart will see God.

The history of Christianity has been punctuated by mystics who have sought the perfect vision of God. Jesus was saying that the vision of God comes not so much by or through mystical experiences, as through plain, ordinary holiness. There can be no substitute for right living before God. But the harsh truth is that for most of us holiness means very little and it is certainly neither plain nor ordinary in our experience; it is non-existent. We have little sense of our sinfulness, and that is often the key to holiness. Holiness is the opposite of sin. Rejection and avoidance of sin is the path to holiness. Holiness means an end to sin in our lives. If we want to be holy we must make sure that our hearts and minds are pure. That purity of heart leads to the vision of God. While Job was not perfect, he had done nothing wrong and yet he suffered. In the midst of his suffering he tried to make sense of why bad things happen to good people. He pleaded with God to reveal himself face to face to him, for then Job knew things would get sorted out. Eventually, after all his disasters and complaints, Job was at last to see God. That vision of God transformed his attitude and his life. Seeing God provided him with a perspective which enabled him to cope with whatever happened in life.

In Christ we see God, but in the fullness of the kingdom we shall see God properly and fully. Before we get to that stage we need to know and experience the purity of heart which loves good and hates evil. The vision of God transforms our lives, for it shows us what we can be and what we will be. That vision will transform us more and more into the very likeness of Jesus himself as we are changed from one degree of glory to another.

'Blessed are the peacemakers, for they will be called sons of God.' (Matt. 5:9)

Jesus came as the Prince of Peace. Nowhere in the Bible is his work as the perfect peacemaker expressed more clearly than in the second chapter of Ephesians:

> For he himself is our peace, who has made the two one and has destroyed the barrier, the dividing wall of hostility ... His purpose was to create in himself one new man out of the two, thus making peace, and in this one body to reconcile both of them to God through the cross ... (Eph. 2:14–16)

The followers of Jesus are to be like him in making peace, breaking down barriers between people, putting an end to hostility, and being instruments of reconciliation. The New Testament writers taught that Jesus was their peace, and that peace was Jesus' gift to his disciples (Eph. 2:14; John 14:27). But the disciples are not only to know and experience this peace for themselves. They are also to be peacemakers, bringing and sharing that peace with others. Obviously, this is not just the negative virtue of non-resistance to evil, but it is an overcoming of evil by good as a positive step. It is not merely an absence of conflict, but a making up where there have been quarrels, and a reconciliation in the place of discord and strife. The followers of Jesus are to establish the peace of God in the midst of a world of warfare and hatred. It is as they work for peace that they will be blessed.

I recently saw my first example of a sign which said, 'Jones and Daughter'. It was a timely reminder to me as the father of two boys of the great delight a parent must feel when his or her business sign can be altered by adding the name of the son or daughter who is following in the parent's footsteps and carrying on the family business. Most parents in business would be more than happy for their children to work with them and to take over from them. Jesus said that those who are peacemakers will be called the sons and daughters of God. This recognition as sons and daughters comes from the God who himself adopts and acknowledges those who make peace in his name and act as their heavenly Father would act and want them to act. These people are truly the new Israel. They are the children of God and partners with Christ in his work of reconciliation. Their job is to keep the family peacemaking business going.

> 'Blessed are those who are persecuted because of
>   righteousness,
>   for theirs is the kingdom of heaven.
>   'Blessed are you when people insult you, persecute you and falsely say all kinds of evil against you because of me. Rejoice and be glad, because great is your reward in heaven, for in the same way they persecuted the prophets who were before you.'
> (Matt. 5:10–12; cf. Luke 6:22–3)

In teaching students philosophy and theology in Oxford, one question I encourage them to ask after each tutorial and lecture is, 'So what?' They need to be asking what difference all this information and learning makes. What is the practical effect of what they have been taught and learned? In a sense, the last of the formal beatitudes was set out in both Matthew and Luke's Gospels as a response to exactly the question, 'So what?' If the followers of Jesus are to put into practice the manifesto of the kingdom of God, what kind of reaction should they expect? What will the world do with people who try to live the kingdom life? It is quite clear that Jesus promised that it would be rejection rather than recognition. Such a quality of holy living will sting people into an unpleasant yet predictable response – persecution.

Those of us who live in the West have no real grasp of what it means to suffer for our Christian faith. I recall a conversation with a Yugoslavian Christian who said that he pitied the Western Church. I was surprised, and asked him why. He said that the Church in the West was not worthy to suffer for its faith. It was a fascinating perspective on suffering and the way in which our Christianity should be a challenge to others. Perhaps the Western forms of Christianity are so insipid that there is no need to persecute us. We don't make that much difference.

In many other parts of the world, however, Christians have

suffered and continue to suffer because of their faith. Their Christianity still has that bite which evokes a response. Our tepid Western expression of the kingdom life is treated only with apathy and indifference. It does not challenge in any way, and causes no offence whatsoever. The danger in such a situation is to settle for that poor caricature of Christianity. This beatitude should make us stop and ask why there is no persecution, insults or slander for Western Christians. Perhaps it is an honest reflection on the quality and worth of our Christian living. Nevertheless, there are dangers too for those who do suffer persecution.

Jesus is quite clear that he is not talking about the ordinary troubles and ups and downs of life, nor about suffering for conscience or conviction's sake. Jesus states that it is suffering for the sake of righteousness, because of him, or, as Luke expresses it in his exact way, because of the Son of Man (Luke 6:22). The suffering mentioned here is a suffering for a just cause and for Christ's sake. If we are truly men and women of Christ, then we can expect to be hated, reproached, excluded, driven away, slandered and have evil things said against us. The hostility, opposition and persecution will be for the kingdom's sake. It ought not to be because of our personalities, approaches or styles. Some of us are all too ready to excuse ourselves and our unpleasant behaviour by trying to explain away quite natural reactions to us and what we do. This is not suffering for Christ's sake; but no one is fooled by such manoeuvres.

Jesus is stating a bald fact of life about the way that the world will respond to people who live by the manifesto of the kingdom. But at the same time he is giving encouragement. The experiences of suffering and persecution are neither to surprise nor to discourage Christian people. Rather, their reaction is to rejoice. They are to be glad that this suffering is evidence that they are really following in the footsteps of their master and of God's prophets. They are to rejoice that it is only a temporary state of affairs and that it is certainly not the last word. The reward of the kingdom of God is theirs. This will more than compensate. As we saw before, it is only spiritual reward which makes any sense in the kingdom of God. There is no question of suffering in order to get a front-row seat in the 144,000, as some sects believe. (They think only a given number of exceptional people will be in heaven, a view they base on Rev. 14:1, 3.) Instead, the reward is simply the natural and inevitable consequence of living the kind of life that Christ lived and that he now desires for his disciples. The actual content of the reward is the latter part of all the other beatitudes – the kingdom, comfort, inheritance, being satisfied, being shown mercy, seeing God and being children of God. Of course, to the world with its values this list seems pretty insignificant. But to the children of light it is worth everything. There is no sense in seeking some other reward when the kingdom comes in all its fullness, for that reward will be exactly the fulfilment of what Christians experience here and now. The only difference will be that it will be far more so then than now. We can see beyond and through the present experience of hardship and suffering. We can even understand why it is happening. We can look forward to the end of that experience and the complete presence of God with us in all his fullness.

Salt and light (Matt. 5:13–16; Mark 9:50; Luke 14:34–5; and Matt. 5:14–16; Mark 4:21–2; Luke 11:33–6)

The final beatitude concerns the point of living according to the manifesto of the kingdom; what follows is a description of how we are to put the kingdom life into practice. We are to be salt and light. Matthew continues his way of presenting ideas by a set of contrasts: salt and loss of saltiness; light and darkness. These are the kinds of contrasts we should find if we were to compare the life Christians live as members of the kingdom of God with the way that the rest of the world behaves and lives.

Christians have a very particular job to do – they are to be salt. If they are loving, meek, merciful, forgiving, peacemakers, and pursuers of the righteousness of God, then they will be salt. This stands in sharp contrast to the picture the world has of the Church and the way it expects Christians to behave. Perhaps even Christians have bought that package and try to live as 'sweet' people. Saccharine Christianity is what seems to be expected. The little bit of 'sweetness' is to help the medicine of belief go down. Jesus is quite clear that Christians are to be salt, not sugar.

The role of salt was crucial in the times of Jesus. Salt was a purifier. It was white and stood for being pure and unsullied. Christians are to be purifiers and to bring purity into situations where there is none. Salt was also a preservative. It stopped things going bad; it prevented decay and corruption. Christians are to be salt and to prevent decay; they are to safeguard against corruption; they are to prevent things, people, society and the world going bad.

Salt was also used as an antiseptic; it stopped wounds going bad. I remember when my wife came home from hospital after the birth of each of my sons. She had stitches, and the doctors and midwives had given her advice on how to help the healing process. Hot baths with lots of salt added. The salt would help mend the wounds. Salt is part of the healing process; it guards against infection and helps restore. But salt is also a necessity for life. Our bodies need salt. Salt sustains life and both literally and metaphorically adds flavour to what we eat. There is nothing worse than a hot plate of soup without enough salt in it – it's as bad as soup with too much salt. A proper amount of salt is needed to bring out the appropriate flavours. Christians are to be like salt in bringing out the flavour of what it means to be a human being and also in showing the full flavour of life as it is supposed to be lived. God meant humankind to enjoy all the good things of life and to taste them to the full. Christians are to help others and show them how to enjoy the full flavour of human being.

Christians are called to be the salt of the earth; so it is very much the here and now and the down-to-earth which is to be affected by Christian influence and action. Salt as a preservative and purifier will exercise a restraining influence in society and on individuals. This fits well with the way the apostle Paul argued that God has given us those in authority to reward the good and to restrain evil (Rom. 13:1–7). But in that restraint and in bringing healing to the wounded, Christians, as salt, will have a bite and a cutting edge. When my wife soaked in the salty bath, it was a painful experience. The salt nipped. This was itself part of the healing process. Christians will and must have that kind of cutting edge and not be afraid to be direct and to act in ways which may even be painful; but the aim and result must clearly be healing.

Christians are to be the salt of the earth, whether or not they like it. They are to be what they are. This is not a living for another world. It is very much living in the here and now, and that is to be the salt of the earth as well as the light of the world. The earth and the world are very much part of our ordinary life. But perhaps we also need to remember that too much salt really spoils things and destroys both the flavour as well as the capacity to taste. Christians perhaps need to spread themselves around and not form great salt heaps which do no good to anyone else. It makes no difference whether we are talking about lots of Christians or just a few. A pinch of salt is all that is needed for it to do its work. One Christian can make the difference that is needed, at work in the office or factory, in a home, or anywhere else.

Jesus goes further with his picture of salt, for he says: 'But if the salt loses its saltiness, how can it be made salty again?' (Matt. 5:13). It can't. It is then good for nothing. It is literally dumped in the street as rubbish was thrown out of doors. It is worthless. This verse has led some interpreters to suggest that salt was used as a fertiliser on certain types of soil in the East. So when Jesus condemned unsalty salt to be thrown out in the street, he was in fact contrasting it with salt which might be thrown on to the fields as a fertiliser. In this sense, salt is meant to help things grow. So Christians are meant to help men and women grow up into the full manhood and womanhood which God created them for and intends for them. But if Christians fail to be what they are meant to be – salt – then they will be thrown away.

One main danger facing the Christian community is that it fails to live according to the manifesto of God. Its profession of religion may be nothing more than a hollow show. If the Christian community fails to live as it should and fails to be the kind of influence it ought to be, then it will be cast away. It is worthless. Once salt has lost its flavour and capacity to bring flavour, then there is no hope of recovery. Salt only salts other things. It exists for the sake of others. If the Christian fails to be salt, then she or he will be cast away (Matt. 8:12; Luke 13:28).

There is a second picture Jesus uses to indicate the impact that Christians are meant to have on the world around them. Christians are to be the light of the world (Matt. 5:14–16; cf. Mark 4:21–2; Luke 11:33–6). It is a theme John uses and develops in his Gospel. As this was heard and read by generations of the followers of Jesus, it must have immediately brought to mind Jesus' self-designation as the light of the world (John 8:12). As Jesus is the light of the world, so his followers are to be light in the darkness of the world.

Again, this is not just a matter of what is said and done; it is the disciples themselves who are the light. This is genuine incarnation. They are to embody light and to burn clearly in the darkness. Light is not and cannot be hidden. How often has a spy been spotted by a watching sentry when a cigarette was lighted by a match or lighter? It is hard to conceal light. It is highly visible. Christians are to be distinctive; they are meant to be seen. They are to have a high profile and to be visibly different. People ought to be able to see that we are Christians by the way we are, the way we live, and the way we behave.

But light also shows up the reality of evil. A student friend and his wife kindly invited us to spend a holiday in their family villa in Malta. We had a splendid time. The days were spent lounging on the beaches by the then still blue unsewaged waters of the Mediterranean. We'd linger till dusk, and as the darkness descended we would drive back to the villa. After we stumbled up the pathway to the door, we would switch on the light and then watch the cockroaches scuttling for cover. The light showed us the evil hidden in the darkness. It's the same with my study. I have a system of filing which involves extensive use of the floor. When the lady who cleans comes in she always offers to tidy and dust my papers on the floor. I insist that they are all carefully filed and in constant use, and encourage her to leave them alone. But every now and then the sun shines in Oxford, and as the light streams in through the window it shows up the dust caked on the undisturbed papers. When the light comes, evil is shown up. Light reveals the true nature of things. Christians are meant to show things and people in their true light.

Light also shows people where and how to go. My sons are keen scouts, and sometimes they go on night exercises. Apart from lots of warm clothing and an inordinate amount of food, especially chocolate, the one thing they must have is a good torch. They need to be able to see where they are going and to be able to help others find them. Light helps people see where they are going. Light helps us see things as they really are and enables us to move freely and safely through all that puts us at risk. Christians are meant to be guides to people in the darkness of this world. They are to help people see where they are going and to show them the safe places to go and be.

Light is unaffected by the darkness around it. Indeed, it seems to shine all the brighter when there is only darkness around. For the Jew, the phrase 'the light of the world' was used to refer to God, to Israel, the law, Adam, the temple, and to Jerusalem. For the Jew, to be the light of the world was to reveal God. Our poor English language may blind us to the stress here on the group and the community. It is not so much that each individual is to be the light of the world, as that the community of the kingdom is to be. The very existence of the Christian community is in itself intended to be the reality of the light of the world.

Scientists tell us that light is crucial in creation and that without light there cannot be life. The world depends on light and on life, for light is the source of life. Christians are to bring life by bringing light to the world. As Christians fulfil this command and description of being light they will challenge men and women:

> This is the verdict: Light has come into the world, but men loved darkness instead of light because their deeds were evil. Everyone who does evil hates the light, and will not come into the light for fear that his deeds will be exposed. But, whoever lives by the truth comes into the light, so that it may be seen plainly that what he has done has been done through God. (John 3:19–21)

The theme of visibility is continued in the picture of the disciples as a city set on a hill (Matt. 5:14–16). Such a city can be seen for miles around. All eyes will be on the disciples. It is no good trying to hide or extinguish the light. Those who live according to the manifesto of the kingdom are to show by their lifestyle that they belong to God. Christian people are meant to be conspicuous, not anonymous. There should be no room for mistakes about them. Their Christianity is to be obvious to everyone they meet and to all who observe them – something that can be a bit daunting.

Because I occasionally take part in radio programmes and have a Scottish accent, people tend to remember my voice and recognise it. There is nothing more disturbing than to be talking to someone on a train and have someone interrupt and ask whether I am the person on *Thought for the Day* on Radio Four. When I tell them I am, I have a worrying moment during which I try to recall what on earth I was saying over the last few minutes. Will there have been a gap between what I say on the air and what I say on a train journey? There ought to be no such gap.

The result of such holy living – being salt and light – is not some massive ego trip or praise and applause for the quality of our efforts. It is that other people will see not so much the disciples, as their good works, and then will praise, not them, but God, their Father himself. Good works are really the works of God. He produces them in the members of his kingdom. The lives of the disciples of Jesus are to be loving examples of God's power and grace transforming people. Those who live out the qualities of the kingdom are to be salt and light, and like a city set on a hill. There is to be no confusion as to their presence or their role. They are to be totally visible and transforming in their impact. Then people will turn to give praise to the God who is able to change people.

The fulfilment of the law (Matt. 5:17–20; 23:1–39)

This passage is central to the ethics of Jesus and the Sermon on the Mount. The beatitudes seemed to be such a great reversal of all that the disciples had previously accepted. Their values were almost literally turned upside down. It is not surprising, therefore, that Jesus now took great care to ensure that they understood what this reversal implied.

As good Jews, they must have been asking, 'Has the old law been destroyed?' Jesus wanted to show both the continuity with the old law and the genuine discontinuity with the way the law had been practised. He wanted to prevent any misunderstanding of what he had said thus far, and what he was going on to say. In a real sense, he was describing the content which follows in Matthew's account. Elsewhere he stressed the discontinuity of his teaching from the old understandings of the law (Matt. 11:12–13; 15:11; Mark 3:1–6; 7:15; Luke 13:10–17; 16:16), but here his purpose was different. He began by stressing the fulfilment of the law and of the prophetic teaching. Jesus himself is the meaning and fulfilment of the Old Testament prophecies.

In stressing that there is no abolition of the law or the prophets, Jesus emphasised the continuity between the law of the old covenant and his teaching. For Jesus, the continuity rested in the covenant and the covenant relationship itself. The God who made the old covenant is a God who keeps his word and fulfils it. Jesus is the fulfilment of God's word. In a sense, Jesus Christ added nothing to the commandments of God. He was instead driving people back to the original meaning of God's law and the purpose and will of God expressed in the commandments. The key difference is that now at last, for the first time, the commandments were fulfilled. Jesus kept them perfectly. In keeping the commandments, he fulfilled the purpose of those commandments and turned people's attention to the moral heart of the law rather than to the ritual. Jesus led people back to the motive and spirit of the law rather than to its letter.

It is clear that even as he began this section ('Do not think . . .'; Matt. 5:17), Jesus realised that there might be misunderstanding. The abuse of the law by the scribes and Pharisees might have led the disciples to the conclusion that the only cure for such abuse was a total rejection of the law. Jesus did not reject the law just because it had led to the abuse of the law. The law itself was not responsible for the way the hypocrites had abused it. By fulfilling the law and showing what was possible if a person lived as God intended (and so was enabled to keep the law), Jesus showed the real point of the law. It was a way of living properly in relation to God. In that sense, Jesus redeemed the law and bought it back for its original purpose. He fulfilled it in order to show how men and women might be right before God.

For the people of his day, the law was about keeping up standards and appearances. But all too often, there was a gap between the public external behaviour and what was actually going on inside a person. Jesus fulfilled the law and kept all the external rules and standards, but he went much further than that, for he recast the stress on the external appearances into an emphasis on the inner reality for will, attitude, motivation, and heart.

The law and keeping the law meant that there was to be no gap between our external behaviour and our inner attitudes. But in stressing the importance of both, Jesus did not belittle the law in any way. It is clear that no disciple was to disparage the law itself – it was to be fulfilled. Even the smallest detail of the law was and is to be obeyed. Jesus was concerned in case his disciples misunderstood what he was doing to the law and teaching about it. His teaching about the law was no excuse for licence or doing whatever people wanted. The law was to be kept. It was to be fulfilled and more. Both the external and the inner demands made by the law of God on all who came to worship and serve God were to be kept. The disciples were not to relax or loosen the law in its true reality. It was to be lived and taught without any false easing of the real standards and way of life to which it pointed. The followers of Jesus were not to commit themselves to any less than the law required; they were not to allow what it forbade; they were not to exempt themselves or others from the law's positive requirements. The law was still binding on the followers of Jesus. They had to sustain the law. There is a proper conservatism here, which preserved what was good and right and maintained the genuine point and purpose of the law.

To make matters worse, Jesus then set what looked like an unattainable standard: 'For I tell you that unless your right-eousness surpasses that of the Pharisees and the teachers of the law, you will certainly not enter the kingdom of heaven' (Matt. 5:20). What this righteousness actually means is defined in the rest of the Sermon on the Mount. Jesus was getting to the heart of the matter. True righteousness will show itself, not in an outer show of piety, but in a real and vital way. This was how the disciples of Jesus were to be distinguished from the Pharisees. It was by their better righteousness. This seemed like an impossible requirement. The Pharisees held a great place of honour because of their achievements and their goodness. If anyone counted as holy and good in the society of Jesus' day, it was surely the Pharisees. Yet their goodness was not good enough. Jesus required even more than just doing the right things. He also required people to have the right motives and intentions, to do what is right as well as have the right attitude and motivation. This cannot be done on our own in our own strength, or even with the help and support of others. It is only possible through the grace of God.

This high standard set out by Jesus is the death of all human achievement and the foundation of the grace of God. It means that I will always fail if I think that I can achieve or even try to do it in my own power. We will all need God's help to keep such standards. To reach that standard of righteousness is always a gift and never an achievement.

Once Jesus had established the *how* of fulfilling such stand-ards, the rest of his teaching – the *what* – was outlined. He went on to show the nature of Christian morality in the rest of the manifesto of the kingdom. In the whole section, Jesus' assumption was that this morality and his teaching pointed back to the original intention of God expressed in God's law. The only way that the law and its intended purpose could be fulfilled was in and through obedience to Jesus. This is what it meant to be a follower of Jesus.

Murder (Matt. 5:21–4; Luke 12:57–9; cf. Exod. 20:13; 21:12; Lev. 24:17; Deut. 5:17; 17:8–13)

In drawing attention to the difference between the mere keeping of the law and having the right attitude as well as keeping the law, Jesus used contrast. He is recorded as saying, 'You have heard that it was said ... But I tell you ...' (Matt. 5:21–2, 27–8, 31–2, 33–4, 38–9, 43–4). Jesus contrasted old accepted understandings and interpretations of the law with his own. This is not the mere prophet speaking on behalf of a greater authority. With the typical prophetic opening of 'Thus says the Lord ...', Jesus spoke with his own authority, setting this over and against all other authorities. It was the authority of God himself which was being claimed implicitly. Jesus was offering God's direct challenge and interpretation. But this rested on the principles on which the law was based. In all his comments on the commandments, Jesus was always concerned to deal with the principles behind and enshrined in the law. Actions were to be related to proper intentions. The intention to sin is itself sinful, and that sin needs to be nailed and seen for what it is. There is to be no gap between what we think and what we do.

But Jesus also goes a step further, for he moves away from the simply negative form of law to a positive expression. Christianity is not a series of 'Don'ts'. It is to be stated and lived positively. Jesus constantly expanded the aim and application of the commandment away from the merely particular to make it apply universally. Some have tried to argue that the commandments in the Sermon on the Mount only apply to the Christian community. But what this does is to set unacceptable limits to the

notion of who my neighbour is. There is no limit to my neighbour, nor to the responsibility we have for others. The whole
context and general thrust of Jesus' teaching is to include people
and increase responsibility rather than to limit it. There are no
limits to who my neighbours are, nor on those who require
proper responses from me. Everyone falls into that category.
There are to be no exceptions here. The exceptions which were
the stock in trade of the Pharisees were dismissed and the true
scope of the law was reinforced in an inescapable way.

In the synagogues of Jesus' time, where the law was read aloud,
everyone must have heard the sixth commandment with great
regularity. But perhaps that regularity had dulled the senses of
the listeners and they thought that it couldn't possibly apply to
them, for they were certainly not murderers. It is not hard for
all of us to condemn the taking of life by a murderer. Murder
should be and inevitably is subject to judgement. But Jesus went
a stage further. He stressed the sanctity of life. Murder is to be
forbidden. The old law is reinforced, but Jesus now extends
the commandment to anger and the reactions that accompany
anger. It is to the root cause of murder that Jesus turns his
attention. It is the spirit of anger which leads to murder, so
that anger must be dealt with as well as the acts which result
from wrong attitudes. Jesus is widening not just the scope of
the command but also its very content: malice and anger are
included.

Sins of thought and feeling are just as serious as the actions
which result from those feelings. Anger and malice are, in effect,
attacks on my brother and sister's life and well-being. These
emotions make me want to hurt, hit out and destroy. These
feelings are wrong and need to be dealt with. The first step
in dealing with such feelings must be to recognise what they
are. They are sinful and wrong. They are forbidden. We are
as responsible for what we feel and our attitudes to others as
we are for our treatment of them.

Jesus' teaching is not simplistic, for he recognised a set of
distinctions which are hard to translate accurately. Feelings are
harmful, but there is even more harm done when the feelings
give vent to words. Anger brings judgement, but insult – anger

put into words – is even more serious. Jesus saw that we do
each other harm at many different levels. We do it when we
harbour grudges and ill-will against each other. We do it when
we insult, belittle, and do each other down. We do it when our
anger boils over into violence and murder. The pattern and
progression is clear: feelings lead to harsh words, which in turn
lead to violent actions. There is a graduation from the feeling
of being angry to the casual angry word, then the deliberate,
studied insult, to the act itself. The punishments are also scaled
in relation to the ascending order of anger and its expression.
But what is crucial is that we realise that every level is totally
unacceptable for those who are members of the kingdom of
God. Every level of sin is serious and has to be rooted out
and dealt with. It is obvious that these levels of anger are not
all the same, but they are all equally serious and equally to be
avoided.

Jesus did not leave the question of right attitudes to relationships there. He urged those who were making an offering,
whether in the form of a regular sacrifice or one with a special
significance, to be reconciled with their brother or sister before
they went ahead with the offering. Jesus taught that it is impossible to come properly into the presence of God if there is some
blockage between your sister or brother in Christ and yourself.
You can no longer have access to God if there is a barrier
between you and your brother. The sacrifice and worship are not
acceptable. This is not just a clear message that Christian people
are meant to live in harmony with one another. It also makes
it clear that true worship involves and requires the whole of a
person and touches every aspect of their life and relationships.
Part of a right standing before God is a right relationship with
each other. Later John was to write that he did not see how we
could claim to love the God we do not see if we are unable to
love the brothers and sisters we do see (1 John 2:9–11; 3:14–18).
Jesus knew that worship was important, but so was a proper
attitude to worship. To come into the presence of God means
that everything else in our life ought to be right as well. While
there is still an opportunity to be reconciled with our sisters and
brothers we are to make the most of it. The seriousness of Jesus'

point is made clear by his reference to the court. If things are not sorted out before you get to court, then you will be liable for whatever sentence the court decides to inflict. It is no wonder that people are encouraged to settle disputes out of court (only lawyers are guaranteed to make money in court cases): we might find that we lose the case and face a heavy fine and punishment. Good sense as well as Christian morality argues for restoring relationships.

Adultery (Matt. 5:27–30; 19:8–9; Mark 9:43–8; Luke 16:18)

In the ten commandments, adultery is forbidden (Exod. 20:14). Adultery breaks the law of God and destroys the fundamental human relationship of marriage. Jesus offered new insight into the nature of lust and adultery. In this section of the Sermon on the Mount Jesus clearly condemns the deliberate intention to sin for what it is – sin. It is not only the act itself which is wrong – the intention to commit the act is equally forbidden. As with anger and murder, lust leads to adultery, and both are wrong. We are not dealing here with the natural response by a member of one sex to an attractive member of the opposite sex. Here Jesus is dealing with the question of raw lust. Lust is the desire which longs to act out what we feel and to make use of the object of the desire. It has no concern for the other person. It is entirely a matter of self-gratification. Lust is about pleasing oneself and fulfilling one's selfish sexual greed and desire. But lust is also a calculating activity. It plans how to act and enacts the working out in the mind. This is not the momentary flash of temptation which affects us all and is part and parcel of what it means to be a fallen human being living in a fallen world. My sin makes me selfish and leads me to treat the opposite sex in ways which are less than ideal. It transforms the good feeling of love and sexual desire into a twisted parody of the real thing which we call lust. That lust plays with sexual desire in a deliberate way. It is like fantasising. In our minds we can commit adultery as in our imagination we run over the details of the act and savour each aspect, moment and thrill.

We may pretend that we do not understand what Jesus meant, but that is only trying to avoid the force of the commandment. We know quite clearly the difference between a twinge of desire and a raw lusting after the opposite sex. This applies to both sexes. For in spite of men trying to kid themselves, lust is not the sole prerogative of the male. We are not to play around with our sexual drives, which are such a vulnerable part of our human condition. Of course, this does not mean that sexual desires and drives are wrong and evil. Sexuality and the physical desire to express it are natural and God-given. Sexual desire finds its proper expression in the context of marriage. But these desires are so strong that they can play havoc with us if we allow them to control us. Jesus recommended sexual purity in our attitudes as well as in our actions. We all need this kind of self-discipline.

Some of this emphasis was foreshadowed in the commandment that we are not to covet our neighbour's wife (Exod. 20:17; Deut. 5:21). Sexual desire in the form of lust and covetousness is just as culpable as adultery. Jesus emphasised the gravity of sexual impurity by stressing the kind of discipline which is necessary and appropriate. To Western ears it sounds so brutal. But it reveals that it is better to live a maimed life than to be damned. The safe life is better than the complete life which is twisted and where we are the mere victims of our desires. The loss of an eye or hand is of little significance compared with the loss of Christ. That is the stark choice to which unfettered sexual desire can lead us.

We are not to give free rein to our sexual impulses. We are not to stimulate our desires in deliberate ways. Such feelings and intentions are actually a barrier to following Jesus. Our natural desires and human passions are to be tamed and controlled at all costs.

The apostle Paul made a similar point: 'I beat my body and make it my slave so that after I have preached to others, I myself will not be disqualified for the prize' (1 Cor. 9:27). There is a splendid picture in one version of the beginning of the twelfth chapter of the book of Romans: 'Do not give the flesh a chance to have its fling.' Those who have seen the Scots dancing a Highland Fling will know exactly what that means. The wild abandon of the dance sums up so well the way that the flesh can come to control us and take us over, rather than be controlled.

Divorce (Matt. 5:31–2; 19:3–9; Mark 10:2–12; Luke 16:18; cf. Deut. 24:1–4)

The issue of divorce was as divisive in Jesus' day as the question of divorce and remarriage is today. As the rabbinic schools divided over their interpretations of the old covenantal law, so modern church people are divided over the possibility and propriety of divorce and remarriage. What is clear is that Jesus was concerned to put a stop to a serious abuse of women. Simply by handing a woman a bill or note of divorce on any ground whatsoever, a man could dismiss his wife. Burning the dinner or not being what he expected were in themselves taken as sufficient grounds for divorce and dismissal. Jesus cut through the debate and set it in its proper perspective. He went back to the original pattern quite literally. He went back to creation.

From the beginning God had created marriage. It was meant to be a lifelong union which only death would break. Marriages were made to last. However, as we find elsewhere in Matthew (19:3–9), the hardness of men and women's hearts led Moses to allow divorce. He was faced with the harsh reality of broken relationships and broken marriages. There were situations which were a kind of living hell for women and men. So divorce was permitted. But human nature being what it is – when you give people an inch they take a mile. Allowing divorce as a means to deal with extreme breakdown was the gap through which all kinds of excuses had become considered adequate grounds for divorce.

Jesus tightened the grounds for divorce into one narrow category, using a criterion which fitted with what he had already taught about the seriousness of sexual misconduct. It was only on the grounds of sexual impropriety that divorce was to be permitted. Matthew is quite insistent that this is Jesus' exception to the ideal of lifelong marriage. There have been attempts to set this aside by arguing that it is a later addition by Matthew himself to help cope with the Jewish situation in the Church. But this is in danger of missing the point that from the very earliest times Christians recognised and accepted the importance of the exception. Such a setting aside of the teaching also raises very serious questions about how we are to interpret the Scriptures and what authority we recognise or accept about God's word. Even in marriage, the follower of the kingdom life is told how to behave. The exception is meant to be just that – exceptional. Exceptions do not destroy general rules as long as they are genuinely exceptional and rarities. It is only when they become the regular norm that we need to have a real concern that the rule and the general law is being totally abused. Marriage is God's creation pattern for life. It is intended to be lifelong and ended only by death. Only in exceptional circumstances which have destroyed the heart and nature of the marriage relationship is divorce to be contemplated or permitted.

Oaths and truthfulness (Matt. 5:33–7; 23:16–22; Jas. 5:12; cf. Lev. 19:12; Deut. 6:13; Amos 8:14)

Jesus began with a reference to the third commandment (Exod. 20:7; cf. Num. 30:1ff.; Deut. 5:11; 23:22). It seems that oaths and swearing were as much a part of everyday life in Jesus' day as they are now. All too often people say, 'Oh, my God' or 'Jesus Christ'. My reply is, 'No. Just one of his humble servants!' It is all too common for people today to profane the name of God and that of his son, Jesus.

An oath is meant to be a call made in a public setting to God as a witness to some statement or claim that it is truly the case and a true representation of the facts. The very existence and need for oaths shows that there is a problem with lies. It is because people tell lies that we have had to resort to swearing an oath to tell the truth, the whole truth and nothing but the truth. Jesus was concerned to wipe out all lies and to deal with the problem of the lack of truth. In the kingdom of God there is to be no room for lies or half-truths. Jesus intended to achieve this aim by abolishing oaths themselves. This does not mean that we can say anything we like, but rather that everything we do say is to be completely true. Every word spoken by the disciple of Jesus is to be uttered as if it were spoken in the very presence of God. It *is* spoken in the presence of God, for he is the unseen listener to every conversation. That means that the followers of Jesus are to be completely truthful. Sincerity is to be shown in our speech as well as in all the other aspects of our lives. There is to be no gap between the appearance and the reality. Our word is genuinely to be our bond. It is to fall below the standards of what it means to be a disciple if we imagine that we are only bound by an oath, but not bound by what we say in ordinary speech and our usual conversation. Even worse would be to imagine we are more bound by an oath and less bound by what we usually say. All the language and conversation of the follower is elevated to the same level as that of an oath. Whatever we say is to be said as seriously as when we take an oath. We are always to mean what we say; so our 'Yes' means 'Yes' and our 'No' means 'No'.

Jesus was doing something more than stressing that truth is one of the key foundations of any and every society. Unless we can rely on what other people say, we cannot function together. If we cannot believe what people say, then society will collapse and all relationships will be thrown into confusion. Jesus was sweeping away the mechanism of swearing oaths and was destroying lies by making truthfulness the regular and only characteristic of what Christians say. We are to speak the truth and not just part of the truth. It is all too easy to make the truth into a lie by only telling a part of the story or by careful equivocation. It is all too easy to be economical with the truth. As a member of the kingdom the Christian is to be totally committed to truth. Truth must always go along with all the other kingdom virtues.

Some have argued that this command forbids the followers of Jesus from the public taking of oaths in courts and the like. However, it does seem that both Jesus and Paul did take oaths (e.g. Matt. 26:63). What is clear is that the Christian has the most serious responsibility to speak truly at all times.

An eye for an eye (Matt. 5:38–42; Luke 6:29–30; cf. Exod. 21:22–5; Lev. 24:19–20; Deut. 19:21)

One key element in the whole idea of punishment is that of retribution. It is the giving back of what is owed. The aim of Gilbert and Sullivan's Lord High Executioner was always to make the punishment fit the crime; in other words, to ensure a proper and appropriate retribution. The picture which lies behind the idea is that of the scales of justice. When a crime is committed the scales are thrown out of balance. It is as if the crime was in one dish of the scales. Something is needed in the other dish to restore the balance of the scales. When a punishment is put in the other scale then a balance is achieved. But we must realise that the punishment must not be too heavy, or it will outweigh the crime and not maintain a balance. The criminal is to get what he or she deserves. The danger is that if punishment is left just to those who have been wronged then they can easily go too far in taking vengeance. Instead of a proper response we end up with a crude revenge which is out of all proportion to the crime actually committed.

It was to put an end to such extremes that the *lex talionis* – an eye for an eye and a tooth for a tooth law – was introduced. When someone harmed you and made you lose your eye, you were entitled to have compensation: you were entitled to punish them. But that punishment meant that the criminal should lose an eye, not an ear, nose, leg and two arms as well. The *lex talionis* was a form of restraint on a very basic human instinct.

Jesus was going a stage further in his teaching. He was commanding not so much moderation in revenge, but rather the complete end to any notion of taking revenge. Paul expressed the same kind of point in the book of Romans:

> Do not repay anyone evil for evil . . . Do not take revenge, my friends, but leave room for God's wrath, for it is written: 'It is mine to avenge; I will repay,' says the Lord. On the contrary: 'If your enemy is hungry, feed him; if he is thirsty, give him something to drink. In doing this, you will heap burning coals on his head.' (Rom. 12:17–20)

If we are honest, we are horrified at this kind of teaching; we regard the refusal to hit back as showing cowardice and weakness. However, Jesus is not interested in human reactions, but in what reaction comes from God. This command can only be achieved by the power and in the strength of God. He can help us to accomplish it. There is, though, no suggestion that evil is to be tolerated or accepted. Jesus was concerned with the evil person who treats us badly in our personal relationships. If we are to deal properly with that evil person and try to regain them, then the way to requite them is not to resist. Here Jesus was not talking about the business of politics or the way a legal system operates. In those settings the role of law and of leaders is to restrain and punish evil. Jesus was offering his teaching to individual members of the kingdom who were asking how they should respond when evil is done to them. They are to refuse to pay back in the same coin. Jesus knew only too well that violence breeds violence. He condemned violence and showed that it is a pointless exercise when the only thing it does is evoke counter-violence. We have seen in this century the effects of attempts to take this teaching of Jesus seriously. Gandhi and Martin Luther King both brought about remarkable societal transformations by their strategies of non-violence. Christians are to be non-violent in response to personal violence and abuse not simply as a strategy; they are to be like that because their Lord commands it and that is now the way they are.

Always the danger is that in leaping to defend ourselves we will become vindictive. The injured person tends to be vindictive, seeking far more than their pound of flesh. Revenge is poisonous, not sweet. Revenge leads to escalation and breeds yet more violence. We are not to resist the evil person, nor to get in the first blow. Jesus opened up the possibility of a radical review of how we are to regard personal harm done to us by others. He then applied this teaching to the legal system. If we find ourselves the victim, we are to refuse to resist legal injustice. This runs contrary to all our notions of standing up for our rights. In fact it is the duty and responsibility of others to stand up for us and our rights. But Jesus is concerned here with motives and attitudes. He taught that our motive ought to be one where self-interest has no part. As with personal violence, extortion is to be coped with and defeated by love, not by violent resistance.

Likewise, exploitation is not to be resisted by violent means. The picture Jesus used was that of public officials making demands on citizens. They were legally entitled to do this, but it was a form of legalised exploitation. We are not simply to fulfil the letter of the law, but to go further: Christians are to walk the second mile. In some communist countries Christians have shown us what this means in practice. They have shown no resistance to unfair demands and unjust treatment in labour camps and in psychiatric hospitals. Instead, generosity of spirit and action are to be the markers of the members of the kingdom of God. However, we must not misunderstand: we are not asked to tolerate evil or to tolerate the evil done to others: evil is still evil. We are called on elsewhere to resist the evil and injustice done to others. But, when it comes to the personal harm done to us by groups or individuals, we are to show that suffering willingly is stronger than evil, and, in the end, destroys the point of evil. As a person living the life of the kingdom of God, we can have victory over evil by having the love and strength of Christ within us.

The new law of love – love for enemies (Matt. 5:43–8; Luke 6:27–36; cf. Exod. 23:4; Lev. 19:18)

We have already seen how Jesus extended the notion of neighbour to include those like the Samaritans who seemed more like enemies than neighbours. Here in Matthew's account Jesus' command is quite explicit. The Jewish law had commanded love towards one's neighbours. Jesus was now stating that our enemies are neighbours too. There was a deeply moving scene in Tiananmen Square before the tragedy of repression and massacre. A student demonstrator gently placed a flower in the barrel of the gun raised against him. He was treating that soldier as a neighbour and as a person. Those who curse, hate and insult the members of the kingdom of God are to be loved. Those who are unresponsive to the love of the disciples are still to be loved. Indeed, the greater the enemy's hatred, the greater is his or her need of being loved. Jesus based his command to love on God's way and will. God as our loving heavenly Father provides for everyone through the creation order in nature. God's love is totally indiscriminate. So too is to be the love of the follower of Jesus.

This is not some kind of social rule or merely a description of ordinary human relationships. There is no virtue in loving those who love us. We all do that, and it will not distinguish the members of God's kingdom in any way. It is loving the unloved, the unlovely and the unloving which is to be the mark of the kingdom. We are to welcome, entertain and be concerned for our enemies. This is God's way of dealing with enemies and persecutors: it is to love them. Enemies are to be destroyed and overcome by love. We are to pray for those who persecute us. Jesus himself prayed that his Father would forgive those who nailed him to the cross. Jesus loved his enemies. It is hard to hate someone if we are praying for their good. Love shows its concern by praying.

This section in Matthew is rounded off by a statement which is frightening in its simplicity: 'Be perfect, therefore, as your heavenly Father is perfect' (Matt. 5:48). At first sight this seems impossible. If we are supposed to be that good, we might as well give up now. This is not a recipe for despair, but is instead an invitation and encouragement to be fully grown and mature. The ultimate aim of the disciple, and the point of the manifesto of the kingdom, is to be like God. If salvation depends on God, so too does perfection. By God's grace we shall be perfect, mature and whole, so we are encouraged to press on into God's life, light and fullness. The standards of the kingdom are only daunting if they require our own efforts and achievement. They are only impossible if it all depends on us. If it is down to me, then I'm lost. The secret of the kingdom is that God's power is given to us in order to help us keep God's perfect standards. With the right ideal and the right power to fulfil the ideal, we can be perfect, as the Father is perfect.

These commandments are not simply some new social rules for life in the kingdom, though they are at least that. They are a challenge to live as God intended humanity to live. They are descriptions of the new righteousness which belongs to and is required from those who live in God's kingdom. At this point Matthew goes on to record the very specific teaching of Jesus and to describe the qualities and the character required of the members of the kingdom of God.

Giving to the needy (Matt. 6:1–4)

Again the theme here lies in the realm of motivation and attitude. Jesus knew that there are many different reasons why people give help to others. We can give a beggar a few pence to get rid of him. We can stop and give money in order to make a bit of a show and to draw attention to our generosity. If you have ever collected money for a charity with a collecting tin, you usually get one or two individuals who make a great show of opening their purse or wallet and unfolding a note and then, ever so carefully, folding it through the slot in the tin.

Almsgiving was part of the Jewish faith. Giving to the needy was a sign of your righteousness. Of course, if people happened to see you giving, then your good works brought you credit in the eyes of others. Jesus made it clear that if we only give to others in order to make ourselves great and appear good, then we have our reward in the here and now, but that is the end of it. It is not so much the reward itself which is offensive, but rather the motive of seeking the reward. In a way we are using other people and their need for our own selfish purposes – to make a good impression. Genuine love of our fellow human beings is concerned to meet their needs because they are needy.

Jesus forbade all ostentation in doing good. The righteousness of the kingdom is a hidden righteousness which is not at all concerned with how we appear. The virtue of the kingdom is not to be displayed in this way. The motives as well as the actions are to be pure and good. Genuine love is not concerned with ourselves or what we get out of a relationship: genuine love is only concerned for the needs of the other person. People who blow their own trumpets may well get some praise and attention from others, but there will be nothing more to come for them; that is their lot – their receipt has been paid in full. But for those who practise a genuine love and concern for others and give to those in need for God's sake, there will be a proper reward from the God who commands such loving action.

The charity which gratifies the vanity of the giver is not genuine charity. It simply humiliates the recipient by making the giver the important person rather than the one in need. The secret act of charity is known by God, who can tell the purity or otherwise of our motives. Discreet helping of the poor and needy removes any possible wrong motive in terms of public display. That reward is not worth having. A genuine reward follows the genuine loving giving of help to the needy as surely as the night follows day.

Prayer (Matt. 6:5–15; 18:23–35; Mark 11:25–6; Luke 11:2–4)

Almsgiving, prayer and fasting were (and still are) three key aspects of Jewish piety. They were and are still to be part of the life of the member of God's kingdom. In the same way that a public show over helping other people is to be avoided, so too is a public display when the followers of the kingdom pray. Jesus is quite adamant that what we sow we reap. Conduct gets its reward. Public performances may well receive public acclaim and applause, but worldly motives only get worldly rewards. The genuinely spiritual life avoids public display of itself. Real holiness avoids self-display, especially in prayer.

In our Western culture, we are not so familiar with the sight of people standing, kneeling or even prostrate in prayer, as may still be seen in many Middle Eastern countries today. But those who attend prayer meetings in the West know only too well the temptation to pray for the benefit of the audience rather than praying to God. True prayer is more concerned with God than with ourselves, and it is in keeping with that emphasis that Jesus used the framework of the Lord's Prayer to teach his disciples to pray.

Jesus knew that prayer can lead to all kinds of subtle temptations to be proud. Prayer can also become a meaningless repetition of gibberish, which, while it may take the form of pious, well-worn phrases, is quite hollow in its meaning and intention. It is significant that Jesus had to teach the members of the kingdom how they were to pray. What they knew already about prayer was not good enough. Our praying is to avoid all play-acting and hypocrisy. If we are enjoying a direct personal relationship with God, then honesty and sincerity are the necessary prerequisites. To pretend in the presence of God that we are different from what we really are is utter foolishness.

In Jewish thought, to know someone's name was to know exactly who and what that person was. Jesus called God 'Father' and encouraged the members of the kingdom to do the same. We are to come to God not in some formal or mechanical way; we are to come to him as to our father who knows all about us and our needs, before we even open our mouths. For the followers of Jesus' way, God is the Father. He is the Father of all the disciples. They stand together in solidarity before God. He is not simply 'my Father'. He is to be addressed as 'Our Father'. The Lord's Prayer is the clearest example of the shape, form and content of prayer for the disciples of Jesus. Elsewhere, it is presented in response to the direct request from the disciples to be taught how to pray (Luke 11:1–4).

It begins, like the story of salvation, with God. It sets first things first. God, our Father in heaven, has his name to be hallowed. His kingdom and his will are to come and to be done. God's nature, his kingdom and his will are the setting and the actual content of the prayer. God's name is to be sanctified. His revelation of himself and his nature is to be accepted. He is to be given his proper place. That can only happen when his will is being done. The kingdom of God will be fully realised when his will is done on earth as it is in heaven. The disciples have to crucify their own wills, and in their place they are to put God's will and way. God's will is to be at the very centre of their lives. Everything is to be seen in the light of God and his will for the world and for humanity.

Having set God first and stressed the intimacy of that personal relationship with God, then there is a proper place for human need. As we ask our parents quite naturally for all the things we need, so we are to come to God with our requests. We can be confident that he already knows what we want and need and is ready and willing to respond.

We are to pray for our daily bread. The exact phrasing is difficult to capture, but the sense seems to be that we are only to ask for enough bread for one day at a time. This is immediately reminiscent of the story of the children of Israel travelling through the wilderness who were provided with manna. That bread came every day and there was just enough for a day at a time. They were to be utterly dependent on God every day for what they needed to survive. Bread is a necessity of life and every culture has some kind of basic bread or bread substitute to eat. God is the giver and sustainer of life, so it is the most natural thing in the world to ask him for our bread. In this age of hunger in the world, to pray for our daily bread is to recognise that we all share in our hungry brothers' and sisters' plight across the world. I cannot be satisfied to eat my bread in comfort, careless of those who have nothing or not enough to eat. If I have more than enough bread, then that must be shared with those who are hungry. God gives us our daily bread in order to feed the world.

The prayer then focuses on the issue of forgiveness. The content of the prayer is that our debts, trespasses and sins may be forgiven. What we owe, what we have done wrong, and what we have failed to do all need to be forgiven and wiped away. But Jesus added a qualifying clause which reminds us of the pattern of forgiveness in the manifesto of the kingdom. It is not enough merely to acknowledge our guilt and confess our sins both in terms of falling short of God's standards and in terms of failing to do our duty as members of the kingdom; we must also be in right relationships with others. We cannot be right with God unless we are right with each other. There is a kind of circle here where God takes the initiative in forgiving men and women. They in turn are to forgive others and thus experience again the forgiveness of God. But to fail to forgive others is a failure in the proper response to the experience of being forgiven. 'Be kind and compassionate to one another, forgiving each other, just as in Christ God forgave you' (Eph. 4:32).

Jesus then taught his followers to pray that they might not be put to the test of temptation. Such a prayer reveals the extent we are to distrust ourselves, knowing that if we are left to our own devices, we shall fall into sin on every occasion. Jesus added a prayer for deliverance from the reality of evil and the reality of Satan. The followers of Jesus can only be protected and delivered from Satan by the power of God. He alone can deliver us. The hard reality of the gift of forgiveness is restated, and this brings to an end Matthew's version of the Lord's (or is it the Disciples'?) Prayer. God and his nature, kingdom and will come first, our needs, forgiveness, defence, and deliverance follow in the light of who God is and our relationship with him. The originality of the prayer lies in its totality. It is no wonder that in worship, in every kind of church and denomination, this prayer has formed the basis of public, communal prayer. Jesus gave it so that his followers would use it.

Fasting (Matt. 6:16–18; Mark 2:18–22; Luke 5:33–9)

All too often the disciples of Jesus were taken to task for their behaviour. The scribes and the Pharisees could not understand why the disciples of Jesus did not appear to fast, but seemed to enjoy their food – and with it every kind of company. The tradition of many of the great religions of the world has been to fast and pray. Jews and Muslims alike observe certain fasts, and the Christian Church, particularly in the season of Lent, has itself a long history of fasting. There is no contradiction between the public behaviour of the disciples and Jesus' advice about the secret discipline of fasting. The danger, as so often, is of the wrong kind of public display and hypocrisy. People can want to appear holy, and that appearance might earn other people's respect. But that is neither true holiness nor respect honestly won. It is just show, and will be revealed as such. Jesus took it for granted that people would fast.

Discipline ought to be at the heart of the life of the disciple. The very words have the same root. To be a learner is to be under the discipline and regime of learning. This fasting is not fighting the flab, but rather a controlling of the body. Both Jesus and Paul were concerned to control their bodies (Luke 4:1–2; 1 Cor. 9:27). The object of fasting is not to show that the body is evil, for it isn't; the object is to bring the body under control. We are far too self-indulgent. Abstemiousness ought to be the discipline of the disciple. But we are never to force our piety on others, nor display it. We are not to cause offence.

A well-known Oxford philosopher of religion tells the delightful tale of a student who always had his tutorial lesson just before dinner. He was always offered a glass of sherry and he always took one. At the end of the year both student and tutor were at a party, and the tutor overheard the same student refusing a glass of wine on the grounds that he was a teetotaller. The tutor quizzed the student, who replied that he did not wish to give his tutor offence, so he always accepted the sherry. While the motive may have been sound, the practice seems more than a little odd. It is all too easy to cheat in this area of our bodily desires. We need to discipline and control our bodies, but we are not supposed to advertise the fact. It is a secret and private discipline, and it will receive its appropriate reward.

Treasure in heaven (Matt. 6:19–24; Luke 16:13)

People delight in telling stories about heaven. There is the story of the wealthy woman who arrived in heaven and was taken on the grand tour to see the heavenly sights. She was shown a sumptuous mansion where her former maid now lived. She thought that if this was what maids lived in, then she would do very well indeed. Finally her curiosity got the better of her and she asked to see her heavenly home. She was taken to a ramshackle, broken down hovel – she was horrified. The response from her heavenly guide was, 'This was the best we could do with the material being sent up.'

In a sense, the story captures something of the spirit of Jesus as he drew the distinction between true and false treasure and wealth. For Jesus the contrast was between the accumulation of riches in the earthly scene and heavenly treasure. As we have seen already, the seeking of wealth for its own sake inevitably takes the focus away from following the path of the kingdom. Worldly possessions are fraught with danger for the disciple, for they can take away the single-minded seeking of God. Wealth in the here and now is fraught with risks and worries, and in the end it can lead to total loss. It is not just that moths and rust can get at what has been accumulated; it is also the fact that we can't take it with us when we go. In contrast, true treasure is to be found in trusting God: he is the ground of genuine security and consolation.

The crucial thing is the attitude of heart and mind. One flaw can have fatal effects, and hoarding is a kind of niggardly idolatry. Wealth becomes an idol in the name of which everything else can be sacrificed. In the last analysis there can only be one master and one aim in life, otherwise conflict is inevitable. So Jesus raised with his followers the question of their desire for security and the place where they thought they would find it. He was quite clear that possessions simply add to one's insecurity. A divine deposit of faith in God pays dividends, never deteriorates, and provides real tranquillity. In the end, we have to choose between God and money; we can't serve both. 'Keep your lives free from the love of money and be content with what you have, because God has said, "Never will I leave you; never will I forsake you"' (Heb. 13:5; cf. Deut. 31:6).

Do not worry (Matt. 6:25–34)

Jesus went straight on into dealing with the very natural response we might have when money and possessions seem to have been set aside so easily. How then shall we live? Do not worry. Do not be afraid or anxious. That is the advice of Jesus. One of the many ways we misuse what we have is as a kind of insurance against the problems of all our tomorrows. There is a wrong kind of concern about the future which can actually destroy the capacity to live and enjoy life here and now. The present can be destroyed by worry about the future. Anxiety all too easily distracts us, especially if we try to rely on our own strength. There is a selfish egocentricity at the very root of the matter here. The problem is that we are thinking about ourselves, rather than seeing ourselves in light of being God's and belonging to his kingdom. We need to come to terms with our creaturely existence and our utter dependence on God. The way to do that is to concentrate on God and on his will for us. The God who gives us the gift of life will provide for all our temporal needs.

Of course, this is not a recipe for doing nothing. Rather it is the proper response to destructive worry. We all know how worrying can paralyse us and thinking about what might happen can make us totally incapable of doing anything. We are not to be victims like this. The victory is won when we do not worry. How we avoid worry is by having a correct view of God and by seeing our lives in the light of his sovereignty. Jesus expressed the priority of the kingdom in crystal-clear terms: 'But seek first his kingdom and his righteousness, and all these things will be given to you as well' (Matt. 6:33).

One is inevitably reminded of the story of Solomon and how God came to him in a dream and offered him one wish. He chose not the obvious things like fame, wealth and power; instead he chose wisdom. God gave him his desire for wisdom and all the other things were given to him as well (1 Kings 3:4–15). They are important and necessary, but they are never to be the most important things in the lives of the followers of Jesus. God is to come first, and the life of the kingdom guarantees that we need not worry about our future. That is secure in the hands of God. Tomorrow will worry about itself. We are to concentrate on living the kingdom life here and now, and developing the character and qualities required of those who live in God's kingdom.

Judging others (Matt. 7:1–6; Luke 6:37–42)

Jesus was an expert at using pictures, parables and the proverbs and sayings of his time to help illustrate the nature of life in the kingdom of God. Here again in Matthew 7 Jesus raises the question of right attitudes towards other people. Jesus has already taught that it is the merciful who obtain mercy. Now he is dealing with the specific problem of the critic who is censorious.

We all love to criticise others. Usually our criticism is not constructive. We are much more at home when we are being destructively critical. We all know that it is far easier to knock things and people down than to build them up. What we often forget as we criticise others is that we ourselves are equally open to criticism. Jesus was only too well aware that the disciples might be taking in all that he had said and then might turn round and compare themselves with the hypocritical Pharisees rather than with God. This is the 'Oh what a good boy am I' syndrome with which we are all familiar, and Jesus did not want to create a new type of Pharisee. In judging others in this critical kind of way, the danger is twofold. We overestimate ourselves and we underestimate other people. We are very good at adopting a superior attitude towards the rest of the world and doing nothing but condemn others. All too often we are clearly identified with the caricature of a Christian, who looks down his or her nose at everyone else: smug self-satisfaction is a widely pervasive disease. Jesus made it clear that such judging of others has its direct retribution. God will judge us all.

Jesus was not saying that we are to stop exercising our judgement or our critical faculties. The advice not to give to dogs what is sacred and not to throw away pearls to pigs showed that we need to judge what is sacred, valuable, and has worth, as well as which settings are appropriate and which are inappropriate for sharing those special things.

We must all pass judgements in order to live and function as human beings, but Jesus was teaching that we may simply be looking for the evil in others in order to justify ourselves. We need to remember that we are evil and fall short of God's standards, and that everyone has a claim on us to be treated and judged fairly and justly. Too quick a condemnation and too censorious an approach to people reveals more about us than about those judged. With the measure we judge others by, we ourselves are to be judged. We ought to listen to the advice given to those who brought before Jesus the woman caught in the act of adultery: 'If any one of you is without sin, let him be the first to throw a stone at her' (John 8:7). Paul said, 'You, therefore, have no excuse, you, who pass judgment on someone else, for at whatever point you judge the other, you are condemning yourself, because you who pass judgment do the same things' (Rom. 2:1). Jesus' command is clear. Do not pass critical judgements on others in a negative way. Do not throw away what is holy and sacred, but safeguard it and use it with discretion as you share the kingdom with other people.

Ask, seek, knock (Matt. 7:7–12; Luke 11:9–13)

This passage has usually been seen as teaching on prayer and the discerning of God's will. Jesus taught that his followers are to have confidence in their praying. They are to pray in faith and to pray expectantly. There seems to be a kind of movement suggested like trying to find the right house on a first visit. We ask someone the way, try to follow the instructions and find the place, then knock and check that we have arrived safely and correctly. Jesus pictured a good God, who loves the followers of the kingdom like a good earthly father, and who is ready and willing to give what is needed by his children. It is the good things that they ask for that they will be given. That seems to suggest that silly requests and asking for harmful things will not be very productive. The confidence for the kingdom believer is in how much more our Father will give.

At this point in his account of the Sermon on the Mount, Matthew includes the golden rule. We have already mentioned how it is a positive statement and encourages the active seeking of and doing of good for others, rather than the mere avoidance of doing harm. The key seems to be such an identification with and sympathy for the other person that we treat them and care for them as well and as much as we look after ourselves. This is what it means to fulfil the teaching of the law and the prophets.

The narrow and wide gates (Matt. 7:13–14; Luke 13:22–4)

To round off the Sermon on the Mount, Matthew records a series of final warnings from the lips of Jesus. Having heard all that Jesus had to say in the manifesto of the kingdom, it is no surprise that the disciples might have felt totally inadequate for the task. It hardly sounds like a popular manifesto guaranteed to win universal support and a huge following. Jesus was well aware of that and described two gated roads. The one road was narrow and the other broad. The worthwhile and noble way is often extremely difficult. The path of discipleship is a narrow one and hard to follow. The realistic recognition is that few will actually take that way. Nevertheless, the warning must be given clearly. Any alternative route, even though it may appear an easy attractive option, will end up in a destruction and annihilation worse than mere physical death.

A tree and its fruits (Matt. 7:15–23)

Jesus taught the kingdom followers how to play 'Spot the False Prophet'. Jesus was well aware that there is always the possibility of fraud and pretence. Teachers too need to be tested. There must be a public test of the worth and value of any prophet who sets out the way for people to behave – the fruit tells. There is a fundamental difference between good and bad trees. If we do not believe that, then all we need to do is to taste the fruit. People may be able to put on a good show and present a convincing case, but in the end, the fruit of their lives will reveal the truth or falsity of what has been done and why. This is no light matter. Jesus pictured them as ferocious wolves. The sheep are in genuine danger from ravaging wolves. Yet the wolf can dress up in sheep's clothing and come with all the correct religious jargon and appearances. 'Lord, Lord', sits easily on the lips of the hypocrite. The false prophet may even achieve certain things like driving out demons or doing miracles, but these actions will also come to a final test.

I once took part in a Radio One programme with Annie Nightingale. In the *Radio Times* I was billed as a 'professional Christian'. There are extreme and real dangers in the Christian becoming a professional and losing the genuine reality of faith. That genuine reality is shown in the fruit and will be exposed in the final judgement. Evil, as well as goodness, has its reward.

The wise and foolish builders (Matt. 7:24–7; Luke 6:47–9)

It is as if we are given the story of the builders because Jesus was asked what kind of test fruitfulness is. Yet it is also a kind of summary of the seriousness of all that has been said. The picture of hearing the word of God is a regular theme in the Old and New Testaments, but hearing itself is never enough. People are not to go away and please themselves after they have heard the word of God. Nor are they simply to pick out the bits they want from the manifesto. The ethics of Jesus are the ethics of obedience: hearing must be matched with doing.

That doing is also to be tested. There seem to be two elements in the parable: the one is of the importance of having right foundations; the other is that the testing will be real and catastrophic in its impact and effect. The members of the kingdom have a right foundation if they hear and obey what Jesus has taught them; otherwise, they are like foolish builders who build on shifting sand. There is no way that such shoddy workmanship will last or stand the test of time or weather.

Summary (Matt. 7:28–9; Luke 4:17ff.)

This chapter has followed Matthew's account of the manifesto of the kingdom. We have tried to set down Jesus' teaching in its totality as Matthew recorded it. The ethics of Jesus are clearly expressed in the whole of the Sermon on the Mount. It would involve a false separation to try to filter out the ethics from such teaching as a whole. As has been shown, ethics and religion are inevitably interconnected in the Christian faith: the viability of the manifesto will be discussed in looking at the ethics of Jesus as a whole. What is evident is that Jesus gave a clear picture of the kind of life the disciple ought to be living if he is truly a member of the kingdom of God.

The impact on the hearers was quite obvious. Jesus taught as one who had authority. In essence this is a startling claim, for Jesus in this manifesto had set himself up as God's interpreter of the law and the prophets, as well as one who had the right and ability to set forth new laws and interpretations. This authority as expressed in the manifesto still exercises its claims on hearers and readers alike.

Jesus brought people to a crisis of judgement and response to himself and his teaching. As we read and hear his teaching we will respond by accepting it and living in the light of its truth, or by rejecting it – either avowedly, or simply by ignoring it.

4

How to Understand the Ethics of Jesus

We have outlined the ethics of Jesus, but some people believe that this is, in fact, an impossible task. They argue that you need to be an expert to read the ethics of Jesus. They then complain that you just end up with another set of rules. Others complain that the Church doesn't give us a very good example of the ethics of Jesus, so there must be something wrong with the ethics themselves. While others argue that they are just an ideology and can be separated from religion. Some feel that the ethics of Jesus are all about the 'inner life' and nothing else, and that they are in the business of helping us fulfil ourselves and be happy. All of these lines of attack suggest that we cannot get to the ethics of Jesus. So far we have tried to show what these ethics are, but we need also to show how we got there by replying to the criticisms offered.

One of the first lessons every philosophy student learns is that it is vital to define one's terms. The classic response to any statement by the philosophy teacher is, 'What do you mean by . . . ?' It is not always easy to say exactly what we mean, especially if we have to produce different words and ideas to express that meaning. One way of coping with the problem is to try to arrive at a better understanding of something and what it means by describing what it is not. By ruling out wrong ways of describing something, we may narrow the focus of what we do mean. Thus negative definition is very important for our understanding of complex issues. We shall use just such a set of negative definitions in clarifying what our approach is to the ethics of Jesus. In describing what Jesus' ethics are *not*, and how we should *not* proceed, it will be clearer what they are and how we should seek to uncover them.

Jesus' ethics are not impossible to discover

All too often the ordinary Christian finds that when he or she picks up a technical theological book they are all too easily put off. The technical expert seems more interested in the problems than the certainties. Indeed, the technical expert seems to have a serious case of scepticism, which ends up suggesting that there is little that can be genuinely known about the ethics of Jesus. Such scepticism is unwarranted and depends on one way of looking at the problem of cultural relativity.

Why are New Testament scholars so hesitant about the possibility of describing the ethics of Jesus, and so doubtful of their relevance for modern people? The answer is cultural relativity. Cultural relativism is the idea that what is true, right, good, or bad, is relative to particular cultural contexts, people, times, and places. In other words, it is impossible to make universal or absolute judgements about moral matters, because our understanding of morality varies from time to time, place to place, and person to person.

This general view of relativism bites into biblical scholarship in two particular ways. First, it suggests that every biblical passage or text was written in a particular context and for a particular context. Thus, it is argued, it is impossible for twentieth-century men and women to understand properly what was being said there and then, for we do not share that cultural context. As modern people, our world-view and beliefs are radically different from those of the biblical writers, so we cannot really appreciate what they are trying to say.

The further aspect of relativism which all too often affects biblical work is the notion that, even if we can arrive at some kind of understanding of the text, it is not *relevant* to twentieth-century people and life. The argument is that even if we are crystal clear about what the Old and New Testament writers were saying, we must judge it in light of our twentieth-century outlook and beliefs. Usually that will mean that we must dismiss the biblical picture or account as outmoded, irrelevant, and nothing more than historically quaint and interesting.

Both these assumptions need to be questioned and set aside. If we were to adopt them, they would remove much of the point of any biblical work, and especially any genuine purpose in trying to clarify the ethics of Jesus. But it is not because of that consequence that we reject relativistic approaches. We must reject the scepticism of the cultural relativist because it is wrong.

It is wrong at the theoretical level. To suggest that 'everything is relative' is to commit the logical howler of trying to state the unstateable. If 'everything is relative', then we have one absolute truth – i.e., that everything is relative – so relativism is false. If, on the other hand, it is only relatively true that in some people's particular cultural context everything is relative, then there is no universal threat to absolute or universal judgements, and each must then be judged on its merits. None can be ruled out as false from the start, because that would be to make an absolute or universal judgement.

Relativism is equally false in the sense that we see not endless variation, but many universal traits and characteristics. People and human nature seem to be remarkably the same down through the whole of history and across the greatest of cultural and geographic gulfs. In the realm of morality, it is fascinating to see the way in which different religious and moral codes end up covering the same kinds of areas and themes. Telling the truth, preserving life, caring for parents, sexual ordering in society, and rules concerning ownership seem universal. Of course, the expression of such rules may vary tremendously. Some groups may allow the taking of life under certain conditions, which other groups reject. Yet all seem to have a drawing of a line over whom it is permissible to kill and whose life is to be preserved.

If we were to listen to a discussion between a radical feminist and a conservative Roman Catholic on the issue of abortion, we might feel that there was no common ground. However, that is to misunderstand the moral debate, for the recognition that the life of the mother or the life of the foetus has value, and that the rights of the mother may conflict with the rights of the foetus, shows disagreement, but it is a disagreement over mutually recognised *moral* areas concerning the value of life and human rights. The very fact of moral language, discussion and debate points inevitably to a common moral base in humanity, past and present.

Relativism is not merely mistaken at the level of theory. It is also faulty at the level of practice. The fact that every biblical passage was written from and to a particular context is not in itself a sufficient basis for a leap to the conclusion that therefore we cannot properly understand biblical passages. All this does is to stress the need for careful and proper biblical scholarship which is sensitive to the role and influence of cultural context. We all engage in some kind of translation, not only from one language to another, but from culture to culture. While we may often get things wrong, that very fact can only be known if we also understand what it is to get such a translation correct. Indeed, all our historical work requires awareness of the cultural context and its influence, but that does not cause us to jettison historical work or to doubt all its findings.

The real danger is that the relativist has gone far beyond what is proper, for he has added a premiss to his argument, namely that twentieth-century people cannot understand first-century people and their writings. It is no more (or less) difficult for us to understand the writings of the first-century Christians than it is to understand the great historical works of the Jews, Greeks, Romans, Chinese, Indians, and every other great historic civilisation. Difference of outlook does not necessarily mean impossibility of understanding. Rather, it emphasises the importance of making sure the textual and contextual work is done properly.

The second aspect of the challenge from cultural relativism is over the issues of relevance and authority. These go together, for in the attempted rejection of New Testament truths and insights as irrelevant, the standard being used to judge relevance and irrelevance is that of the authority of twentieth-century thought-forms. If there genuinely is variation between the views of the first century and those of the modern age, it is not necessarily the case that the modern view is correct. Such a view rests on the belief that human judgement and understanding are developing and are thus 'more correct' now than in any previous time. This need not be so, and requires proof for its assertion. Modern presuppositions require careful argument, showing clearly the authority base for decision-making. It is perfectly proper to hold a strong view of the inspiration and authority of Scripture and of the Old and New Testaments. The grounds for such a view may be very different from the so-called test of relevance, and such claims cannot be set aside by the cultural relativist without cheating on his or her part.

The cultural relativists are ultimately suggesting that it is impossible to discover the ethics of Jesus. This is false because it rests on the basis of relativism, and relativism is fatally flawed. The discovery of the ethics of Jesus is not an impossible task, but one that requires sensitive textual and contextual work. The most the cultural relativists can say to us is, 'Be careful.' In that, they are correct.

Jesus' ethics cannot be understood without textual sensitivity

In every approach to Scripture, the text itself is special. We must be attached to the text if we are properly to understand it. However, the work of biblical criticism seems to threaten the text rather than to safeguard it.

What is biblical criticism? Like all literary and historical criticism, it is discriminating and applies various techniques to written documents to discover the original text, and the literary categories and sources, the modes of composition, date, style, authorship and purpose of that text. Literally understood, it is a neutral, scientific way of discovering objective truth about the text. Sadly, the history of biblical criticism in the last three centuries has not exemplified that scientific objectivity. All too often biblical critics make a subtle, if unconscious, move from textual study to an interpretation of the evidence in the light of their own presuppositions. Thus it is no surprise that the picture of Jesus we gain from nineteenth-century biblical critics is of an ideal liberal humanist, while the Jesus of the twentieth-century biblical critic is either an existentialist or a social and political revolutionary.

Biblical criticism is vital and necessary when it works properly. Its job is to clarify the sources, forms, categories, styles, life-settings and theological concerns of the biblical writers. Such work can be extremely valuable and insightful in grappling with the meaning and significance of the text. However, biblical criticism is limited. The job of clarification throws little light on the historicity of any particular incident or utterance, even if we can be crystal clear about a particular situation in the early Church which may then offer an explanation why some gospel incidents and sayings were preserved and recorded. This is very far from giving a reliable account of the origin of the saying or casting doubt on the historicity of the incident. While we need to be increasingly aware of the influences of early Christian life, witness and needs in the shaping of the gospel tradition, this need not call in question the integrity of what is said.

Different kinds of biblical criticism can lead to direct conclusions concerning the historical genuineness of the material without relying (whether implicitly or explicitly) on presuppositions about historical scepticism, divine possibility, inspiration and authority. My plea is not to abandon any positive work of textual, literary, form, tradition, or redaction criticism, it is to ensure that we recognise the limits of and procedures involved in making objective, historical claims. All too often the biblical critic behaves rather like the mythological character Procrustes. He enjoyed visitors and insisted that they spent the night in his home. He had a special bed which he loved them to occupy. As a perfectionist, he loathed to see the bed was not properly filled. So, if someone was too short for the bed, a quick stretch on the rack solved the problem and ensured an exact fit. If the visitor was too long for the bed, an axe soon lopped off the offending excess, again ensuring an exact fit. Let us beware of Procrustean approaches to the text which come with a framework which is then forced upon the text so that it is either stretched to fit the framework or parts of it are ignored because they do not fit properly. The genuine biblical critic remains committed to the text, and seeks to allow the text to speak for itself in the light of all the historical, literary and textual evidence.

One other complaint often levelled against the biblical critic is that of taking analysis too far. Michael Polanyi, a chemist-turned-philosopher, describes someone who plays the piano by ear without being able to read music. If the person is asked to play each individual note, then the whole flow of music grinds to a halt, for the totality is lost. We all know that too close attention to the detail of something may leave us unable to appreciate the whole picture and situation before us. There must be a proper balance between the analytic textual work which divides in order to understand better and the holistic approach which grasps the full sweep of the gospel accounts section by section and in their totality.

After the detailed work of textual, literary, form, and redaction criticism has been done, we are still left with the need to respond to the Gospels and the New Testament as canonically accepted. Are we to sit under the authority of Scripture as a whole, or set up some other standards by which to judge the validity, acceptability and authority of Scripture? In drawing up and closing the canon, the Church was drawing a clear distinction between the writings which might be relied upon as valid and those which could not be so relied upon. Historically, the Church has accepted the gospel accounts together as a canonical picture of the life, ministry and teaching of Jesus. To set aside that traditional picture requires both an overwhelming reason for its rejection and an iron-clad guarantee that whatever takes its place will offer a more certain basis for the life, ministry and witness of the Christ.

The gospel accounts do not simply exist as independent units. Biblical criticism has clearly shown the interwoven and interdependent nature of the Gospels. Thus, there are some simple internal tests we may make in looking for the teaching or ethics of Jesus.

The first is to enquire whether a particular account or saying coheres with the rest of the teaching of Jesus and the nature of Jesus. This double reference is important, for it relates both to the teaching of the Gospels as a whole and to our theological and

Christological understanding of who and what Jesus is. Does this fit with what the Gospels teach? Does this fit with the Jesus we have discerned?

Then we may look for multiple alternatives. The presence of a number of witnesses gives good grounds for accepting a particular account, especially if that account is an unlikely or a difficult one. If different gospel writers offer mutual support, we are as reassured as when witnesses in court corroborate each other's testimony. This is not at all to suggest that if there is only one witness, then the account or saying must be considered doubtful. At this point we come to the nub of the matter. We may approach any text, saying or story (especially if it is only recorded by one writer) in either a positive or a negative fashion. On the one hand we may argue that we must accept it as true until and unless falsity is shown (i.e., until the critic is able to disprove the reliability of the text, saying or account). Alternatively, we may argue that the text should be set aside until it is proved to be reliable. Not only common sense and legal practice, but also the normal standards and criteria of all historical and literary work clearly support the notion of accepting as true and valid what is given until it is proved otherwise. We must not be more sceptical about our biblical interpretation and understanding than we are about other areas of life, history and literature.

We cannot escape from doing the critical, textual work. It is vital if we are genuinely committed to the text and seeking to understand it fully and properly. However, we must also recognise that critical work has proper limits and be cautious about the role of the critics' presuppositions in making judgements as to the acceptability, historicity and validity of the text.

Jesus' ethics are not the domain of the expert alone

Jesus came to the ordinary people. His message is quite clearly expressed in ways which communicate directly with ordinary folk. While the Gospels make it perfectly clear that Jesus could more than hold his own with the teachers of the law, the teaching of Jesus is geared much more to the person in the fields and the street than to the groves of academia. This should give us all heart, for while the expert has much to teach us, it is not necessary to be an expert to appreciate the ethics of Jesus. By his stories, parables, illustrations, examples, as well as his own living and working, Jesus reveals to us all the heart of his message and its ethical significance. It is the childlike who can grasp the message.

Jesus' ethics are not in the form of a rule book

The traditional way of doing Jewish ethics laid great stress on the application of principles, rules and laws to situations. Soon this led to rules about rules and became the domain of the expert. As with the study and practice of law today, precedent and exception became the bread and butter of the expert. Any system of rules requires informed guidance as to application and interpretation. We have seen how this led to a legalism which judged others and justified one's self. The ethics of Jesus were no attempt to create a new or even a revised rule book. He did not design a complete moral code for each and every situation. He was not offering some detailed blueprint for all human activity. Jesus was concerned about a loss of focus concerning God's dealings with humankind. The rules and their interpretation were in danger of concealing the heart of morality, which God revealed to and required of men and women. Jesus' concern was to give a new direction and a new power to the moral life of people. He came to bring people to God and to give them the power to do and to be good. He constantly reminded his hearers of the absolute claims made on them by the presence of God's kingdom or reign. He did not try to present universal norms of conduct which were obligatory for all Christians in all circumstances. We must neither look for nor make the ethics of Jesus into a set of rules and regulations.

Jesus' ethics are not to be judged solely by reference to the Church

I once lectured to an Open University Summer School on the proofs of God's existence. I presented twenty-six such proofs and was rather pleased at the weight of such a cumulative argument. One questioner commented that there was only one thing that prevented him from becoming a Christian. It was that he saw no difference between the lives of Christians and non-Christian people. Sadly, he is all too often proved correct. There is a massive credibility gap between the pious mouthings of Christians and of the Church, and the quality of life and activity which most believers lead.

It is perfectly proper for us to wonder if the Church really takes seriously the ethics of Jesus. But that does not mean that the ethics of Jesus stand or fall by the success or failure of the Church, though the two are and must be closely related. If the ethics of Jesus make no difference in the lives of believers, then that suggests a basic flaw either in the believers or in the ethics of Jesus. However, the validity and moral worth of the ethics of Jesus are to be judged on their own merits rather than by reference to human success or failure in applying them. This is partly why non-believers remain fascinated by Jesus and his ethics, for they recognise the true value of Jesus and his teaching, independent from the impact of such teaching on the lives of his followers. Likewise, even if the Church perfectly obeyed the ethics of Jesus, that would not necessarily convince humanity of their genuine validity. The ethics of Jesus must be judged on their own merit. A proper judgement can only be passed in union with Jesus himself.

Jesus' ethics are not an ideology, but a matter of incarnation

Part of our difficulty with the credibility gap between the statements of the Church and its practice is that it is a gap between theory and practice. Such a gap encourages us to separate theory from practice. We shall fail to understand the ethics of Jesus if we divorce the ideas of Jesus and the life of Jesus. He *was* his ethics. He wasn't so much a teacher making clear ideas. He lived out his ethics, revealing the nature of the good life and how to lead it. We cannot and dare not separate the person and activity of Jesus from his message. Jesus incarnated his ethical standards.

His character and teachings were in perfect harmony. This is why his authority was so clearly recognised. There was no gap between his living and his proclamation.

This theme became crucial for the New Testament writers, for they saw that true Christian living is meant to reflect that incarnation of the ethics of Jesus. The imitation of Christ is not so much a matter of following his teaching or doctrine as incarnating his ethical standards. Thus in any reflection on the ethics of Jesus we cannot escape from the hard question of who Jesus is. If Jesus is Lord – and for the early Church he was the risen and present Lord – then his ethics make a fundamental claim upon us which is different in kind from cool reflection on an ideological system of ethics.

Jesus' ethics cannot be understood apart from religion

Philosophers debate whether we can separate religion from morality. But the ethics of Jesus cannot be separated from religion. There is an indissoluble link between the moral demands of Jesus and their religious basis. His ethical demands are religious in nature, for his ethical teaching is rooted in the nature of God. The ethics of Jesus were based on faith in God, arose out of a new relationship with God, and were sustained and expressed in living communion with God.

The ethics of Jesus entail living in and under the rule of God. Much of Jesus' dispute with the scribes and Pharisees was over the nature of religion and its ethical fruits. True religion should lead to true and high ethical living. False religion gives rise to the false moral values of self-confidence, hypocrisy, oppression and moral blindness which seem characteristic of the Pharisaic way of life. For Jesus, religion was inconceivable without the ethical expression of its reality, and ethics were unintelligible and impracticable without true religion as their motivating and empowering basis. The reality of God and his loving involvement with humankind meant that the ethics of Jesus were nothing less than the expression of God's nature and his will for men and women. Jesus called his followers to live as God wanted them to and so reveal themselves to be God's children. They are to live to please God.

Jesus' ethics do not emphasise the inner at the expense of the outer life

There is a popular misunderstanding that Jesus was primarily interested in the inner life of the person and not so much in the outward expression. As we have seen, it is certainly true that Jesus stressed the importance of the heart, the inner life, and our motivation in action. He was also extremely critical of the hypocrisy of mere outward show and appearance. However, the ethics of Jesus hold together a deeper insight: the importance of the inner attitude and instincts, along with the absolute necessity of expressing that attitude and motivation in real and practical ways.

The ethics of Jesus deal with the totality of human being, where there is no gap between the inner and outer aspects of human living. Our wills and our actions are to be in perfect unity. This is no merely mental activity, but a putting into practice of a fundamental orientation towards God. This may be seen more clearly by reflecting on the many things that Jesus taught his followers to do and refrain from doing.

As Jesus incarnated and acted out consistently the moral values of God, so we are to act. True morality cannot separate the inner from the outer, for such a dualism destroys human personality in its unity. The way in which the followers of Jesus live is an expression of what they believe, will and feel. The truly moral inner life finds its proper expression in the truly moral 'outer' life, as in the example of Jesus.

Jesus' ethics are not a matter of self-fulfilment, nor of hedonistic calculation

Among the wide variety of moral approaches and beliefs available today, there are two which stand out particularly in the

Western world. One is the pursuit of self-fulfilment. The other is seeking not only one's own happiness, but the greatest happiness of the greatest number. The ethics of Jesus stand in sharp contrast to both, for his teaching rests on the validity of God's revealed standards and principles as good and right in themselves, as opposed to any moral views which stress the consequences of actions as the *sole* ground for moral judgement.

The cult of self-fulfilment has made morality a selfish affair. My aim in life is to do what I want, and to do the very best for myself. My motivation is to find fulfilment. Jesus' teaching clearly showed that the path to God is one of self-denial and service to others. Of course, the critic will respond that what Jesus was offering was true self-fulfilment, so self-fulfilment cannot be such a bad thing. This reminds us of the importance of clear definitions and saying what we mean. Today's widely held notion of self-fulfilment is a million miles away from denying oneself daily, taking up one's cross, and following Jesus in a life of self-sacrifice for the sake of others. It is certainly the case that such a following of Jesus inevitably expresses a proper relationship with God in which we are truly ourselves. But that is not our motivation. It is a consequence of being obedient. If we were to follow Jesus in order to ensure that we found our true self, then our motivation and its successful expression would be doubtful.

Social morality is largely based on the greatest happiness of the greatest number. Christianity is in no way against human happiness, nor is it opposed to the greatest number enjoy-ing genuine happiness. However, the teaching of Jesus stresses that motives are as important as consequences, and that the proper motive for the Christian is *agape* (self-giving love). Christians are to do what is good for others because it is right and good so to do. We need to recognise that we can neither predict nor control the consequences of our own or other people's actions, and that an ethic based on consequences alone is fundamentally insecure. The ethics of Jesus rest on principles and standards which are derived from the nature and will of God for humanity. We are to live out these stand-ards, activated by love which is as concerned about the motive for and the means used in action as it is about their consequences.

Summary

It is not impossible for us to discover the ethics of Jesus. The theoretical problems of cultural relativity are not so much a bar to discovering the content and the relevance of the ethics of Jesus as an opportunity to do our biblical work properly. All the tools of a scientific biblical criticism which is genuinely an aid to understanding the text itself, its meaning and significance, and is not a Trojan horse for historical scepticism, may be put to work to uncover the ethics of Jesus, both in detail and in the broad sweep of the gospel accounts.

We need not be experts in every biblical language to discover the ethics of Jesus. We must not look for some guidebook to morality based on rules, nor be put off by the gap between the theory and the practice of those who claim to follow the ethics of Jesus. Rather, we must understand that the ethics of Jesus cannot be separated from the worship of God and a relationship with him, and that there is no division between the inner and outer expressions of morality, for both matter fundamentally in the ethical teaching of Jesus and in the reflection of his incarnation in his followers. The ethics of Jesus stand in contrast to the ethical standards of the world in which we live, not only calling those standards into question, but offering an alternative way of life for humankind.

5

The Ethics of Jesus –
Some Fundamental Questions

In the previous chapters we have tried to understand what the ethics of Jesus are and what significance and application they have for us today. But there are some hard questions which must be asked and answered about these ethics.

One of the key tests of whether we have understood something properly is that we are able to ask sensible and proper questions about it. We need to know enough to be able to ask questions about what we do not know. One of the hard things when you are a teacher is that if you ask students whether or not they understand something, they usually say that they do. The fear is that they do not know enough to realise that they do not actually understand it at all. Similarly, in trying to understand the ethics of Jesus, it may not be enough just to outline Jesus' ethical teaching in the way that we have done. There are questions which will have occurred to the reader, and these are proper and important questions. If you take the trouble to read lots of books about the ethics of Jesus, then you will find that there are a cluster of fundamental questions which come up time and again. In this chapter we shall try to ask and respond to some of them.

Are these the ethics of Jesus at all?

As they study the New Testament, and the Gospels in particular, some people may feel that they are not really confronted with the ethics of Jesus. What they find are rather the ethics of Matthew,

Mark, Luke, John, and the early Church. What lies behind this fear is the idea that the New Testament writers used Jesus as a starting-point for their own ethical teaching, but went far beyond what he taught, in order to make their own presentation of ethics. This might have been a deliberate ploy to give their own particular hobby horses the apparent authority and backing of Jesus and thus enable their views to play a crucial role in the early Church.

John's Gospel makes it clear that not everything in the life of Jesus is recorded in the gospel accounts (John 21:25). In deciding what was to be included and what left out, the writers must have been conscious of the problems, issues, and questions facing those early Christians, and it would be quite natural and make good sense to record any particular things that would help deal with these areas. This is very far from any deliberate intention to deceive; rather it is the inevitable result of selection and of being people of their times. We expect witnesses to tell their story from their own perspective: after all, what other perspective could there be? But that does not make the story unreliable. It makes the presence of other witnesses all the more important. The fact that we have four gospel witnesses to the life and teaching of Jesus makes the reliability of what we learn from the different sources beyond reasonable doubt.

But that may not satisfy the person who is determined to believe that all that we have in the New Testament are the ethics of the early Church and nothing else. What makes this a difficult point of view to argue against is that behind it may lie a thoroughgoing scepticism which refuses to accept any kind of answer at all.

One way of spotting and dealing with the sceptic is to ask what evidence *would* satisfy them. What would it take to show that these are indeed the ethics of Jesus, rather than just those of the New Testament writers? The common thrust of the various accounts seems to suggest four witnesses giving an accurate and reliable picture of what the teaching of Jesus was in reality. The variations of emphasis and detail reinforce the authenticity of the whole, for each witness sees the same event from their own particular angle and records it as such. That Jesus remains the same kind of person teaching the same kind of things and that the variations ring true seems to reinforce the view that we have the actual ethics of Jesus. If you were trying to 'doctor' the accounts to fit in with the needs of the early Church, then you would omit anything and everything which did not help fulfil that aim, or which was obscure or difficult or a direct challenge to the behaviour and outlook of the early Church. The presence of the occasional difficult and hard saying and the lack of any one-to-one relationship between the needs of the Church and Jesus' ethical teaching suggest that we have a genuine and not a concocted record.

In fact, the New Testament writers complement each other. Individually and together they present a coherent picture of the ethical teaching of Jesus. These writers were often eye-witnesses or gained their information from those who were. They wrote their accounts not only for those who did not know Jesus, but also for those who did. This means that there were many people who had heard Jesus preach and teach and who had had his teaching passed on in detail. These same people would have read these accounts and heard them read aloud. Yet we find no outcry that the gospel records were mistaken and misleading.

To this must be added the fact that the oriental and Jewish education process was based on rote learning. Endless repetition was the way people remembered exactly what they were taught. Those of us who learned our multiplication tables in this way are living witnesses to the effectiveness of learning by rote. The Jewish child and teacher were, and had to be, word perfect. In the light of this training, the writers would be word perfect about the teaching of Jesus. They would have committed his lessons to memory as part of their natural process of learning.

Coupled with this was their realisation that this same teacher was the Messiah and the Lord. All that Jesus taught therefore had amazing significance for his followers. This would provide the motivation to remember exactly what he had said. In the same way, we pore over exactly what our beloved has said to us, whether in a love letter or in the heat of an argument. Our minds go over and over the exact words used and look for every whiff of implication and every nuance. How much more would this happen with the words of the Lord of salvation?

The question whether or not we have the actual ethics of Jesus applies to every doctrine and teaching in the New Testament. Once you have asked the question, it must be asked of everything in the New Testament. We are then faced with a fundamental choice of believing and accepting the record as accurate, or of looking for some ulterior motive or need to adapt the record for another purpose.

Have we good reasons for calling the New Testament writers liars? Most of us would feel that it is up to the critic to show that these are *not* the ethics of Jesus and that there are good grounds for doubting the reliability of these records rather than the other way round. Not only does the Bible present them as accurate and reliable records, but from the earliest days the Church has pronounced these accounts as canonical, trustworthy and reliable. This should give us confidence in the reliability and authority of the New Testament accounts of the ethics of Jesus.

Are the ethics of Jesus only relevant for his day and not for ours?

We might have expressed this question as, 'Are the ethics of Jesus relevant today?', but what is being queried in this case is whether or not the ethics of Jesus are *always* relevant, or whether they were written only for that particular time and context. As we approach that query, we must be clear why someone might believe that the ethics of Jesus are only for his day.

There are two different reasons why someone might think that the ethics of Jesus have only relative and temporary significance. The first is a general literary reason, which argues that everything which is written is written in a particular context, for particular people in a particular place, at a particular time, and for particular reasons. Thus, what is written only has relevance for the there and then, but not for anything or anyone else.

The other reason is based on an attack on the relevance of the ethics of Jesus on the grounds that they are, it is claimed, tied to a view of eschatology (the end things) which was totally wrong. This view, typified by Albert Schweitzer, suggests that Jesus thought that the end of the world was about to happen. In the light of this, his ethical teaching was only for those who lived in the last days. Thus, his ethical teaching was and is irrelevant to ordinary life in normal conditions. Jesus was wrong about the end of the world, hence his ethics are not applicable to any other situation except the end days. The ethics of extremity are very different from the ethics of normality. So the only interest in the ethics of Jesus is a historical interest, to help us understand the views and attitudes of people who thought they were living on the brink of the end of the world.

The two different grounds of this view require different answers. The first attack has behind it a particular presupposition: cultural relativity. As we noted earlier, in relation to truth and morality, this view argues that what is right or wrong varies from time to time, place to place, and person to person. This means that there are no absolute or universal truths or standards. Thus, because everything is written in a specific context, its validity is only for that context, and nowhere else. The obvious retort is, 'Why?' There seems no prima facie reason why what is written should only be for the here and now rather than for a much wider audience over a much longer period of time. Surely to accept this sceptical relativist view requires more evidence and a more sustained critique of the alternative view.

In fact, cultural relativity as a view has serious problems: it is flawed, because it is self-contradictory. If I say, 'All views are relative,' then I am making an absolute statement. If this statement is only a culturally relative statement, and is therefore only relatively true, then it is only true for some people in some places at some times. We may therefore choose not to accept it. If, on the other hand, it is an absolute, universally valid statement, then it shows that in fact there *are* absolutes and universally true statements. But, if that is the case, it shows that cultural relativism itself is wrong. Thus, either I make a statement which destroys the view it tries to put forward, or I end up making a statement which is only relatively true and can therefore be easily dismissed as only true for particular contexts.

There is another sense in which cultural relativism is faulty. It is that the evidence of what we do know to be the case, what is true, and what is right and wrong, does not vary endlessly. In fact, the variations are variations on a set of themes. These themes are general and universal. In the whole area of morality it only *appears* that moral views vary from time to time and setting to setting. Examination of different societies' morality seems to reinforce a relativist viewpoint. But, the apparent endless variation of what is right and wrong in different societies is often really a matter of expression.

There is a common core of morality which lies behind the apparent differences. That core seems to include universal standards centring around proper parent-children relationships, sexual order in society, truth-telling, the sanctity of life, and rules about what belongs to me and us and what does not so belong. Cultural relativism obscures the common core of agreement by stressing the different emphases rather than the heart of the matter.

Cultural relativism is either saying something very obvious and harmless, or it is false. There is an obvious sense in which everything we say, write or do is done from and in a particular context. We all know that, but we do not therefore dismiss it simply on these grounds; rather, we seek to understand the background and the context, and in the light of that understanding try to see whether there is something of timeless, general and universal interest, significance and concern. We manage perfectly well to read the Greek plays of long ago and see in them human situations which are still relevant today. We read the great classics of the past and experience the same emotions as those portrayed in the texts, and the same as those felt and experienced by those who wrote and read the classics down through the years. The question we face in approaching these texts, as well as when we come to the New Testament, is whether there is some insight, truth and understanding which is universally true and generally relevant and so applicable in every period of history including the present age.

Before we examine whether there are such universal and general insights in the teaching and ethics of Jesus, we must respond to the second attack on the relevance of those ethics for today. This rests on theological approaches like those of Albert Schweitzer, who regarded Jesus' view of eschatology as entirely wrong, and so the ethics of Jesus as irrelevant. This assumes that Jesus was totally mistaken as to the future course of events, thereby depriving the ethical teaching of the Gospels of any and all relevance or authority for subsequent generations. It assumes that Jesus' ethics were designed only for a short interim period before the end times rather than for any longer period of time. Thus it is claimed that the ethics of Jesus cannot be lived or sustained over a long stretch of time, and indeed were never intended to be so. The problem seems to lie not so much in Jesus' view of eschatology, but rather in our failure to understand what the New Testament in general and the Gospels in particular teach as regards the *eschaton* or end time.

Eschatology is about the kingdom of God. Jesus did not suggest that the kingdom was about to arrive in some far off time, or even some near time, but rather that the kingdom had come. Jesus was the king who ushered in the kingdom. The eschatological reign of God is not something we await, it is already present. It has already happened, and in that kingdom we are moving inevitably forward to the final consummation of the world at the second coming of Christ.

Eternal life is not for the there and then; eternal life begins in the here and now. The same quality of life in the kingdom must begin now and is continuous into and through the consummation of everything. As we shall live in the heavenly realm, so we are to live now. The ethics of eternity are the ethics of the earthly life in the kingdom; there is no gap between the two. Schweitzer seeks to drive discontinuity between the two sets of ethical standards. The standards are the same, the only difference is in the setting in which the ethics are to be lived out.

Are the ethics of Jesus eternally relevant?

There is no discontinuity between the standards and the life of the kingdom in the present and in the future. The emphasis on the end of all things in the teaching of Jesus is not irrelevant to us in the twentieth century, nor will it be in the twenty-first. We live on the edge of ecological and nuclear holocausts. Global politics seem constantly to bring us to the verge of the end of everything. Our materialistic selfishness is in danger of destroying our world, ourselves, and our future. Set against this background of the end of all things, the teaching of Jesus has considerable relevance for us today. It calls for a perpetual expectation on our part, to be ready for the end and to watch for the signs of the times. There is a continual need to be vigilant, steadfast, and prepared for the end. The expectation that God himself is in charge and that he will move to consummate history gives a sense of urgency to our living and to our morality. If we live our lives in the light of the fact that Christ may return on this very day, then our morality will be very different from those who live only for the moment and who believe that nothing is going to happen to them or to the world.

Rather than belittling or undermining the importance of the ethical standards of Jesus, the stress on the imminent coming again of Christ gives motive and impetus to obey God's will and his laws. If we accept that in Christ God will act decisively to consummate history and end the world on his terms rather than on ours, and if we recognise that we do not know the hour or the day when that will happen, then in a real way we are in the same position as the members of the early Church, for they did not know when or where the end would come. Like us, they knew what were the ethical standards required of all Christian followers of the kingdom, and they tried to live as they ought in the light of those standards. We are to do the same.

The ethics of Jesus provide a constant reminder of the absolute claims made by the kingdom of God on the followers of Jesus. The content of the ethics of Jesus dealt directly with situations of conflict and troubling issues and debates which were going on all around. These were issues of marriage and divorce, paying taxes, obedience to the authorities, and the like. These hardly seem like a description of questions about some future state of affairs; rather, they are practical responses to the realities of daily living in the here and now. The ethics of Jesus are immensely practical for anyone facing such questions.

Both these attacks, and our responses to them, lead us to be clear about our basic approach to the ethics of Jesus and to the gospel records. We may, on the one hand, come in a sceptical, doubting way, based on a view like cultural relativism, where we refuse to accept the authority and relevance of Jesus' moral teaching for us today; or, alternatively, we may come in an attitude of faith, trust and expectation. Such faith believes that the ethics of Jesus are never out of date, because they present us with a set of transcendent claims on us which can never be rendered obsolete by the passage of time.

In Scripture, and through the ethics of Jesus, God in Christ has spoken to us and has revealed his will for humanity. It is because of who Jesus is, the basis and source of his teaching, the content of that teaching and the difference it makes and has made in transforming people and situations, that we recognise the authority of Jesus and of his moral teaching. It is also because we find in the content of the ethics of Jesus the general universal moral principles of love and justice, which are universally valid and are recognised as such by everyone. Loving one another and loving one's enemies are not in any way just the fashion of the moment. In fact, they are never very fashionable or acceptable; but they are deeply significant moral revelations of how God requires human beings to relate properly to one another.

Moreover, these principles speak to the reality of human nature, which remains the same down through the ages and across the cultures. Relativism will always fail as long as it refuses to recognise that human nature is universally the same: we are a mixture of good and evil. We are made in the image of God, destined for glory; yet we are fallen and sinful. By the grace of God we are still able to be transformed into complete and whole human beings. The capacity for good and evil remains the same in us all. By God's action in Christ, we can be saved from evil and enabled to do and be good. The universality of these principles and of our human nature mean that the teaching of Jesus is always relevant as long as there are people.

We have argued that the ethical teaching of Jesus is universally relevant. There remain questions about whether or not this way of life can be sustained over a long period of time. Even more fundamentally, we may be asked whether the ethics of Jesus are possible to live at all.

Are the ethics of Jesus impossible standards?

C. E. M. Joad expresses our dilemma thus: 'We may know, in fact, that we ought to live very much as Christ enjoined. We may say that Christ's prescription for good living is wholly impracticable or is much too difficult; but that does not alter our conviction that it is the right prescription.' Jesus himself seems to have put the matter in a nutshell for us: 'For I tell you that unless your righteousness surpasses that of the Pharisees and the teachers of the law, you will certainly not enter the kingdom of heaven' (Matt. 5:20); and again, 'Be perfect, therefore, as your heavenly Father is perfect' (Matt. 5:48).

The followers of Jesus are expected to do more than the scribes and the Pharisees and to exceed even their rigorous standards. Such a requirement in itself seems to be unattainable in this world. It suggests an absolute ethical norm and goal which makes our poor efforts seem totally inadequate. How then are we to respond to this dilemma? If we actually accept this analysis, we are in fact suggesting that the ethics of Jesus are irrelevant for human living and meaningless as far as the ordinary person living a normal daily human existence is concerned. Various attempts to 'save' the ethics of Jesus have been made.

We might suggest, for example, that the language that Jesus used was full of oriental imagery and exaggeration: it was never meant to be taken literally, and to try to do so makes a mockery of the sublimity of the ethical teaching in itself. This escape route is a difficult one. It assumes that we can know what is meant literally and what is simply imagery and pictorial. It assumes an intimate knowledge of oriental thinking and language such that we can confidently set aside what is peculiar to that culture as irrelevant to everywhere and everyone else. It is in constant danger of being reductionist, and so throwing away the baby with the bath water. It also fails to realise that humanity has much in common down, through and across the ages. People are people, and they share a common humanity, nature and basic creation so that we can have confidence that there is little which is exceptional or unique either to individuals or to groups.

Another escape route might be to suggest that the ethics of Jesus really take the law of Moses to the nth degree. The function of the law, as the apostle Paul so clearly expressed it in the book of Galatians, is to bring humanity to acknowledge its weakness and sinfulness. The law shows us how far short of the ideal we fall. If that is true for the Mosaic law, how much more will it be true for the law of Christ as expressed in the gospel pages and in the manifesto of the kingdom in Matthew in particular?

This does at first sound like a worthy argument which leads to a stress on the necessity of salvation through Christ alone. Obviously there is a great deal of truth in such an emphasis on grace. However, we must be aware that this argument carries a sting in the tail. In the end it fails to take seriously the actual content and nub of the ethics of Jesus: it makes them simply a means to another end – the end of salvation – rather than an end in themselves and worthwhile in themselves. The teaching of Jesus then has no validity or worth in itself. Such worth and validity would only be found in its success or otherwise in bringing people to a sense of need and inadequacy. While this may be part of the role of the ethics of Jesus, it is not a total or sufficient explanation of them.

A third strategy is found in the extreme form of fundamentalism which stresses literalness to the exclusion of common and obvious sense, thereby ruling out all literary and linguistic appreciation and insight. This may find expression in a proclamation of the ethics of Jesus such that they seem to be totally at odds with and irrelevant to everyday human existence and our ordinary experience of common sense. The fundamentalist retort is, 'So much for our experience and common sense then!' However, the danger is that we ourselves make the ethics of Jesus seem impossible by *our* presentation of them. This makes the ethics of Jesus not impossible in themselves, but merely because of our expression of them.

Another argument is that what we have in the ethics of Jesus are counsels of perfection. As such, they were never meant for everyone, but only for a few special people – the saints. This strategy has two main thrusts. The ethics of Jesus were meant for the few in the sense that they were only for Christians, and for no one else. But, there is a second level of exclusivism, that the ethics of Jesus are only for the special and chosen few who are able to sacrifice themselves utterly and bear this hard way. The generality of Christian men and women are not and cannot be expected to live by such impossible standards. This attitude may be seen in religious orders, especially within the Catholic tradition, but it is well matched in the Protestant tradition, where the majority of people inside and outside the Church expect higher standards of ministers and Christian leaders than of other so-called 'ordinary' Christian folk. Ministers, priests and clergy are expected to be perfect.

One main difficulty with such an approach to the ethics of Jesus is that it strikes at the root of the universality of the lordship of Christ. That lordship, and the teaching of the Lord, will be severely limited if we follow this suggestion.

None of these responses to the alleged impossibility of the ethics of Jesus seems to be adequate. A more adequate response must take account of the nature of ideals, of humanity, and of the doctrine of the Trinity. We shall examine each in turn.

The nature of ideals

I watched spellbound as Torvill and Dean, in their various Olympic and World championship ice-dance competitions, beat the rest of the world and were awarded the perfect score of six by every single judge. It was the same with the Romanian gymnasts and their scores of six. But as each and every gymnast seemed to be awarded that perfect score of six, it raised the question whether or not we were truly witnessing perfection. Could they all be perfectly perfect? If they had managed to achieve perfection, then what was left to aim for? How could you improve on perfection? Perhaps the scoring was at fault and the dancers and gymnasts were not totally perfect after all.

There is a genuine tension between having an ideal and being able to attain it. Some might argue that if it is actually attainable then it is not an ideal. The very nature of ideals is to be unattainable. In fact, the role of ideals is to serve as proper goals. As Paul could say, 'Not that I have already obtained all this, or have already been made perfect, but I press on to take hold of that for which Christ Jesus took hold of me' (Phil. 3:12). In this way the ethics of Jesus are never out of date, because they present a transcendent claim which cannot be made redundant or obsolete by the passage of the years. Ideals are thus universal and absolute, and must be so if they are genuinely ideal. They will always be hard to put into practice, otherwise they would stop being ideals.

It may also be the case that, though ideal, they may not necessarily be unrealistic. In the incarnation of Jesus we see the ethics of Jesus incarnated and made flesh. We see in the life of Jesus life at its very best and life lived as God intended it to be lived. Perhaps if people were to take the ethics of Jesus more seriously, then human relationships would improve and we would find that the ethics of Jesus were far more possible than we imagine. The more seriously the standards and their practice are taken, the better the results. As C. H. Dodd comments: 'The nearer we get to love for our enemies, to uncalculating self-sacrifice, to a serene freedom from all self-regarding cares, and to a broad charity that never judges our neighbour, the finer, truer, holier and happier would human life become.'

All too often when we talk about the impossibility of the ethics of Jesus and their impracticality, we really mean that when we do try to follow and put Christian ethics into practice they do not produce good results – by which we usually mean the results that we expect or desire. But then, in a sense, what we are really saying is that the ethics of Jesus cannot be lived or introduced easily or smoothly. They require effort and may create hardship. This is especially the case in a secular environment where the claims of God are ignored. This is quite a different thing all together from saying that they cannot be made to work at all. Many hold that pacifism has never really or consistently been tried, and until and unless that happens it is unfair to dismiss pacifism as impossible in our world. We don't know it is impossible, because it has never really been tried.

Some might draw attention to the *tu quoque* ('You are in the same boat as I am') type of argument which too few Christian apologists use. When confronted by the impossibility of the ethical standards of Jesus, we ought to look very carefully at the success rate of alternative moral and ethical views. Do any non-Christian ethics work any better or any more than Christian ethics? Are we here again returning to the nature of ideals and their inherent impossibility and unattainability? Christians must be more responsive and positive than we have been thus far.

The apparent impossibility of the ethics of Jesus may have a positive role. It is clear that Jesus indicated the goal and direction that should characterise the life and actions of the followers of the kingdom. I can no longer claim everything I have as my own and dispose of it as I wish; all my talents, treasures and abilities are to be put to the service of God and used in the service of the neighbour in need. This is the thrust of the radical teaching of Jesus. In living between the two comings of Christ and between the cross and the *eschaton*, we are confronted with a situation of continuous growth and development. So much of the teaching of Jesus, especially in Matthew's Gospel, was trying to prepare the Church for a period of life before the return of Christ. It was important that the Church knew precisely how to regulate its life until then. Such regulation will always be improving and seeking to be ever nearer the ideal. The ethics of Jesus call for continual effort in order to overcome the obstacles and shortcomings of the present moment.

There is a long tradition in Christian ethics which tries to cope with the impossibility of the standards and the ethics of Jesus. It tries to show how to cope when we fall short of the ideals set out in the manifesto of the kingdom. We shall return to this theme, but it is important to notice that the Christian must never be content when he or she fails and falls short of the ideal. We ought always to have an uneasy conscience when we notice the discrepancy between what Jesus demands and what we actually do. The art of compromise and adaptation to our present needs and desires can all too easily destroy the desire to fulfil the perfect standards of Jesus. To be light and salt means that we are to mourn over our shortcomings and strive to do better. Without ideals we would have no means or basis for such a struggle. The Christian life would then become a settling for what can be achieved rather than what must or ought to be achieved. The tension between the ideals and the accommodation of those ideals to the world around us is part of the tension between the present and the future. The history of the Church and of Christian ethics may be seen as some people forgetting the future and living only in and for the present, while others have forgotten the present and tried to live only for the future. Both lead to a mistaken and false sense of security. Instead, there ought to be a divine unease as we try to live out the demands of the kingdom life, true to both the present reality and the future fulfilment.

Humanity and the Trinity

One constant complaint heard about Christian ethics in Christian circles today is that they are not sufficiently theological. This charge cannot be levelled against the ethics of Jesus. The very problem of the alleged impossibility of the ethics of Jesus raises some key theological themes and doctrines.

Someone might say that to give an ideal is pointless if people cannot possibly attain it; indeed, it may end up bringing nothing but despair. What on earth is the point of striving for perfection if, in the end, it is totally elusive? As we have seen, the ideal may be a difficult goal, but it is still a goal and an opportunity and stimulus for growth and development. But it does more than provide a goal. It reminds us that we are fallen men and women who live in a fallen and distorted world. Our failure to keep and fulfil the ideals of Jesus may tell us far more about us than it tells us about the ethics of Jesus. Yet we may go further, for our human inability to live up to and according to the strenuous moral teaching of Jesus is a constant reminder of our need of God's mercy, grace and forgiveness. We must always see our sin, and indeed the sins of others, in the light of God and his mercy. The apparent impossibility of the ethics of Jesus reveals again our sinful, fallen human nature and our constant need of God.

When we fall short of the ideals of the kingdom, that is no reason to hold up our hands in horror and disgust at the impossibility and difficulty of the task facing us. Instead, it is a constant reminder of our need for God's renewing grace and of our dependence upon him. There is no other way to achieve the ethics of Jesus except by relying on the grace of God. The very height of the standard is itself the death of all human achievement and the basis of the grace of God. In this way the ethics of Jesus are not simply a demand made upon us; they are also God's gift to us.

But here again there is a subtle trap for the Christian. If we seem to over-emphasise God's part, his grace and initiative, then it may appear to reduce the worth, value and importance of our moral effort. If our eternal destiny does not depend on our success in fulfilling the ethics of Jesus, then why should we make the effort at all? In the New Testament there is no hint that the moral life and struggle are trivial or insignificant; rather, such a struggle is the very mark of a genuine follower of Jesus. The proof that we shall obtain God's gift of salvation is that we obey God's will, as expressed in the ethics of Jesus. Such obedience is futile if we are persuaded that by obeying we may earn God's approval. Grace does not remove the moral seriousness of the moral effort. What a proper understanding of grace does is to remove our self-centredness in the moral struggle and leave us open for God and for our neighbour.

But all this talk of grace and sin need not make any practical difference, for the ordinary person still asks whether or not the ethics of Jesus are impossible to attain. The cure for sin and the extent of God's grace are shown in the incarnate life of Jesus Christ. Here is the fundamental difference between the ethics of Jesus and most other moral codes, the feature that makes Jesus' ethics unique. Jesus incarnated and lived out his own moral teaching. He did not stand on the sidelines and point in the direction of a golden life and future for everyone if they would only walk in that way. Rather, he left the glory of heaven, humbled himself, took on the reality of humanity, and lived the life of a full-blooded, genuine man. He was subject to all the temptations we are; yet he did not sin. He fulfilled and attained his own ethical teaching. Are Jesus' ethics then possible? The answer must be that they are, and the proof of that contention is the example and the life of Jesus.

Yet this is more than just an example to be emulated and

applauded. Jesus came in order to make us what he taught us we should be. The ability to fulfil and attain the ethics of Jesus comes to us through the third person of the Trinity. The Holy Spirit is the source of the power which enables men and women to live them out. To the natural person, the ethical norms of Jesus are impossible ideals, but in the power of the Spirit all may fulfil and attain God's standards. When we read the Sermon on the Mount and find there the very hard things that are required of a Christian, we must read it in the light of the Spirit and with the realisation that this is a picture of the sort of life we shall live when the Holy Spirit is having his perfect way in our lives. The falling short of the perfect standard is a commentary on human weakness and sin. It is not a failure on the part of the Godhead; it is our failure to allow God to have his way and to do his will. It is our disobedience which is at the root of the impossibility of the ethics of Jesus.

In his teaching Jesus drew no distinction between those commandments and ideas which are easy to keep and those which are difficult. We cannot properly distinguish between what is required and what is optional. It is not at all like Bertrand Russell's comment on the ten commandments, that ten questions were set, but only five could be attempted. All the ethics of Jesus are requirements. There are no optional areas or topics. But this is no cause for despair. In the gospel accounts Jesus constantly commanded people to do the impossible. To the lame, he said to walk; to the man with a withered hand, to stretch it out; to the dead, to wake up and come out of the tomb. The difference is that with the command Jesus also gave the power to obey and fulfil the command. We shall not understand the heart of the ethics of Jesus if we simply proclaim the standards and forget to proclaim the availability of the power to fulfil the commands and to keep the standards. The ethics of Jesus are *not* impossible standards.

Are the ethics of Jesus for everyone?

As we saw earlier, one way many Christians cope with the gap between the standards of Jesus and our failure to attain those standards is to suggest that the ethics of Jesus are only for members of the kingdom. No one who is not a member of the kingdom can ever hope to attain these kind of standards, so there is no point in even presenting the ethics of Jesus to unbelievers. There is an obvious sense in which the moral teaching of Jesus is part and parcel of what it means to be a Christian. We cannot separate the moral principles from their theological and religious basis or from the living reality of a relationship with Christ. In that sense, the principles are only possible for those who know the power of God's Holy Spirit at work in them through the indwelling Christ.

But that does not mean that the standards are not for all. If Jesus is Lord of all, then his standards are for all. They embody the way everyone ought to live. They express God's will for the whole of humanity. This is how we should do God's will on earth as it is done in heaven. Thus, the moral teaching of Jesus is universal in its scope. It also operates in a way that shows its universal validity. It reveals God's will and standards to all and so acts as a challenge to those who fail to keep God's standards and as a warning of the results of such failure. It is also a promise for all, for it offers the encouragement that if we do follow Christ, then we shall have the power to fulfil the standards of the kingdom.

The ethics of Jesus are for us all, both as individuals *and* as members of God's society. The problem with the English language is that our pronouns do not distinguish between what is addressed to 'you' in the singular and 'you' in the plural. With our Western individualistic bias, we tend to read the Gospels as if they were spoken to us only as individuals, forgetting that often Jesus addressed the believers as a group and as members of God's society.

The picture of humanity assumed and given in the New Testament is that of a corporate body of people. We are not islands entire of ourselves; we were created to live together. The ethics of Jesus are for the whole community, and for each and every one of us as members of that community. This means that we should strive to put the ethics of Jesus into practice both as individuals and also in the context of all our relationships. In fact, Jesus' ethical standards would make little sense if we did not live in relationships. Ethical principles guide our attitudes, dealings and responses to other people. We must not separate the individual from the corporate.

This is highlighted by Jesus' stress that our primary concern is to be for our neighbour in need. In the parable of the Good Samaritan Jesus made it clear that our neighbour is whoever is in need. Our pathetic attempts to limit the scope of neighbour love are doomed to failure and deserve condemnation. Jesus did not present a blueprint for every society; rather he presented the fundamental principle which should underlie every society. To love our neighbour in need is the challenge and vocation of every follower of Jesus, and the way that every person ought to live as a truly and fully human being.

Are the ethics of Jesus unique and distinctive?

There is a genuine distinctiveness in the ethics of Jesus. Such distinctiveness begins with the stress on self-denial. This is not some mere Stoic view of holding oneself in check; rather, when we acknowledge and accept the claims of God and of other people on us, we are summoned to subordinate our self-interest for the sake of loving God and our neighbours as ourselves. Such self-sacrifice for the sake of others is the central theme in Christian ethics.

Jesus condensed and concentrated his ethical teaching. It is not so much that there is novelty at every point, but that there is greater depth and intensity in Jesus' teaching. His concern was not so much to formulate a new moral code as to lead human beings into a relationship with God of such a kind that they received the power to do the good and right they knew they ought. Jesus did not only present lofty ideals, his distinctiveness lies in the power he gives us to realise those ideals. The distinctiveness of the ethics of Jesus lies also in his stress on incarnation, inspiration and imitation. We are to incarnate the ethical teaching of Jesus and make it live in our human flesh and bodies. We are given the inspiration to do so by the power and presence of the Holy Spirit. We are to imitate Christ in our living, and thus fully incarnate God's will for humanity. This blend of a recognition of the image of God in humanity and the grace to fulfil and restore that image is part of the unique emphasis in the ethics of Jesus.

Are there contradictions in the ethics of Jesus?

Many of these apparent contradictions have been explored in the previous chapters; nevertheless, it is worth bringing the points together. These so-called contradictions are between a morality of rewards and punishments over and against grace, the rejection of this world, and Jesus' attitude towards the Pharisees.

When considering the apparent tension between Jesus' emphasis on the grace of God and his talk of rewards and punishment, it is important to understand the motives at work in morality. The person who does what is good and right because he or she wants a reward is not acting morally. Likewise, the person who avoids doing evil simply because he or she is afraid of hell or punishment is not acting morally. They are acting either from selfish desire or from fear. We are called to do what is right because we love God and wish to please him. We are to do what is right because it is right and good. We are to avoid what is evil, because it is evil. God gives us the grace to know what is good and evil and to seek the one and avoid the other.

Immediately the critic replies that this removes our free will. If God does all this in us, then we do not do it. The Bible is quite clear at this point; it talks quite happily about each and every person's responsibility and answerability before God. We are responsible for what we do or fail to do, and why we do or don't do things. We are also answerable to God for all we say, think and do. We have the freedom to obey or to disobey, to act or to refuse to act. The Bible also talks from a different perspective. It talks of God revealing his will and way to us; it talks of the Holy Spirit at work in us enabling us to obey the commands of Jesus. There is no embarrassment or difficulty about either or both ways of talking; each is from a different perspective. One is from the human point of view; the other from the divine perspective. Both perspectives are necessary and appropriate from their own point of view: there is no contradiction.

The critic may feel that Jesus' talk of rewards and punishments contradicts the moral nature of his teaching. As we have seen, this is to misunderstand the nature of rewards and punishments. These are not presented by Jesus as the motivation for action or the refusal to act; rather, they are the logical and necessary outcome of certain ways of living.

In C. S. Lewis' *The Last Battle*, death is pictured as a door into a new and glorious life. When the children in the story pass through that door they find some dwarfs there. The dwarfs had let down the children and the cause of good in their life before death. They were only out for their own concerns. Now they seem blind and fail to see the beautiful table and good things set out to eat that are spread before them. They cannot see the glory of the new world. One of the girls asks Aslan, the Christ-figure portrayed as a lion, to help.

'Dearest,' said Aslan, 'I will show you both what I can, and what I cannot, do.' He came close to the Dwarfs and gave a low growl: low, but it set all the air shaking. But the Dwarfs said to one another, 'Hear that? That's the gang at the other end of the table. Trying to frighten us. They do it with a machine of some kind. Don't take any notice. They won't take *us* in again!'

Aslan raised his head and shook his mane. Instantly a glorious feast appeared on the Dwarfs' knees: pies and tongues and pigeons and trifles and ices, and each Dwarf had a goblet of good wine in his right hand. But it wasn't much use. They began eating and drinking greedily enough, but it was clear that they couldn't taste it properly. They thought they were eating and drinking only the sort of things you might find in a stable. One said he was trying to eat hay and another said he had a bit of an old turnip and a third said he'd found a raw cabbage leaf. And they raised golden goblets of rich red wine to their lips and said 'Ugh! Fancy drinking dirty water out of a trough that a donkey's been at! Never thought we'd come to this.' But very soon every Dwarf began suspecting that every other Dwarf had found something nicer than he had, and they started grabbing and snatching, and went on to quarrelling, till in a few minutes there was a free fight and all the good food was smeared on their faces and clothes or trodden under foot. But when at last they sat down to nurse their black eyes and their bleeding noses, they all said:

'Well, at any rate there's no Humbug here. We haven't let anyone take us in. The Dwarfs are for the Dwarfs.'

'You see,' said Aslan. 'They will not let us help them. They have chosen cunning instead of belief. Their prison is only in their own minds, yet they are in that prison; and so afraid of being taken in that they cannot be taken out.' (*The Last Battle*, Collins Lions, 1980, pp. 139–40)

If we live in good and wholesome ways, then rewards will follow as night follows day. If we live in evil ways, then punishment comes. Both rewards and punishments are the corollaries of particular ways of life; they are not the motives for behaviour. Jesus was simply telling it 'like it is' when he described the positive and negative results and fruits of certain ways of living.

Some argue that Jesus denied the worth and value of the world. This is an odd suggestion, for the teaching of Jesus is full of pictures from nature, of the birds, the trees, and of the weather. He delighted in using the natural world as an illustration for spiritual truths. He gloried in the world of nature. Of course, he resisted the view of life which believes that the here and now is all that there is to human being and living; but in no way did he seek for his followers to withdraw from living life to the full. He was to be found among those whom polite society rejected and avoided. Jesus got involved in the rough-and-tumble of human being, and his morality teaches love as the practical norm in the here and now for all human beings in need. As a part of God's created world, humanity is to be loved and cared for by every Christian.

One other apparent contradiction is between the emphasis on love in the teaching of Jesus and his treatment of the Pharisees. We have already looked at this issue, but it brings us back to the necessity for truth and love. In Jesus' attack on the injustice and hypocrisy of the Pharisees, there is no sign of personal hostility or resentment, though they had given Jesus every reason to feel both; rather, Jesus is deeply and properly concerned about the debasement of religion and the harm this has done to others. His attitude is typified in the driving out of the money-changers from the temple. Here was injustice and the defilement of religion; God's house had become a den of thieves: the worship of greed and profit had taken the place of the worship of God. Love is not afraid to speak the truth and to act on it. Jesus revealed his love for all by acting so that all might realise the seriousness of what had been done. Hypocrisy and injustice had to be condemned. Love condemns evil, for it describes evil as it is. Love is concerned to change and to transform that evil into goodness; that is why it speaks and acts forcefully. The problem is not a contradiction of love, but our failure to grasp the strength and purity of love. We substitute weak and meek acceptance of anything and everything for a violent love that seeks the best for others.

The incident of the cursing of the fig tree (Matt. 21:18–22) may make some feel that Jesus did violence to nature. As always, the whole context of a story is important, and in Matthew's account there is a very clear lesson for the disciples. They are amazed that the fig tree withers so quickly at the command of Jesus. He shows not only that he has power over nature, but that faith is able to do remarkable things. The incident is a clear challenge to the faith of the disciples. How big is their faith?

But what about the poor fig tree which was cursed because it did not produce fruit? It may seem like a selfish, petty response to not getting something to eat. Gardeners will be conscious of the real point at stake. Trees and bushes are meant to produce fruit. If they don't, they are good for nothing and have to be removed and destroyed. Christmas holidays can be a great time for a project for the whole family. One family I know usually makes up a monster jigsaw puzzle. They love to add a few pieces and see the whole thing grow over a week or so. Imagine the tragedy if they put it all together and found that just one piece was missing. It seems very harsh to throw away the whole puzzle just because one bit isn't there. But the one piece makes the difference between a jigsaw puzzle and what is no real good as a puzzle.

By this example, Jesus showed that fruit is the point of the fig tree. If there is no fruit, then there should be no fig tree. Jesus used a perfectly common gardening experience to teach a lesson about faith.

Does the Church take the ethics of Jesus seriously?

This seems to be a crucial question at two levels. In its teaching and in its practice, has the Church taken the ethics of Jesus seriously? The history of Christian ethics has been that of a failure to insist on the radical teaching of Jesus. There has been a distinct lack of dynamism and a lack of expectation of continual growth and conversion. Part of the reason for this has been the accommodation of the gospel to the present situation and context of the world and society. The Church seems to have given up on the possibility of fulfilling the ethics of Jesus, and even in its proclamation has failed to make the case out for that possibility.

At a conference of ethics teachers the complaint was voiced that Christian ethics had failed to make any difference to the world and to the Church. This seems to me a fair charge and complaint. At times the Church has used the negative forms of the ethics of Jesus as sticks to beat people with. The scholar has been more interested in linguistic analysis, literary styles, and in theological solidity than in making a genuine difference to the lives of Christian men and women. Our Christian ethics have been, and still are, too often incomprehensible and irrelevant, and have no practical application.

The great preachers of the past were great precisely because their messages and expositions were always readily applicable. They helped people live out the gospel and put the teaching of Jesus into practice. The need and responsibility of those who teach the ethics of Jesus is to expound and expose the ethics of Jesus in all their fullness; yet to do it in such a way that they speak into ordinary situations and also carry the power to transform the lives and contexts of societies and individuals. We are to make living stones and genuine incarnations of Jesus who not only know the ethics of Jesus, but *do* the ethics of Jesus.

The fault also lies in the lives of Christians. All too often there is no difference at all between the lives of Christians and non-Christians. If we are honest, we have to admit that our own lives are little different from those around us. This does not invalidate the ethics of Jesus. It is no excuse for giving up trying to live as Jesus taught and lived; rather, it is a summons and a challenge to every Christian to live by the teaching of Jesus. His grace and power are available to fulfil the commandments he gave. That we strive to be more and more like him shows the world that we do take seriously the ethics of Jesus.

Genuine questions have answers. We have tried to ask and answer some real questions which people have, but there comes a time when even the questions have to stop. Jesus himself was a master of cutting through questions to the heart of the matter.

One issue which still remains is how original the teaching of Jesus is, and for that we need to look at the roots of his teaching.

6

The Ethics of Jesus – Their Roots

In looking at the ethics of Jesus, and trying to understand them properly, we need to be clear where their roots lie – in Judaism.

Religious art is a useful means of expressing our worship and praise, but it also expresses our view of the objects depicted. Jesus figures largely in painting and sculpture and seems to take on the appearance and form of the culture in which the art finds its expression. All too often we picture Jesus as we see ourselves, in some idealised form, forgetting that this may be an expression of our cultural values stated in artistic form. Jesus was neither a white Anglo-Saxon nor a black revolutionary. Jesus was a Jew. He was not born into some state of general human limbo, but rather in a particular human, historical, cultural context. This was no accident. The history of God's dealings with the world flows through the history of his dealings with the Jewish people. We shall never understand the ethics of Jesus unless we are crystal clear concerning his Jewish context and the interaction between that context and his ethical teaching.

Not only was Jesus a Jew, he was born at a very particular time in the history of the Jewish people. It was to an occupied country that Jesus came. It was a setting where political questions overshadowed religious issues and the religious divisions were drawn along political lines. It seemed that the time was ripe for some new prophet to manifest God's revelation in dealing with the Jews. As the Son of God, the ethical teaching of Jesus goes far beyond a mere reiteration of traditional Jewish ethics.

Nevertheless, we cannot properly understand the ethics of Jesus without understanding his Jewish roots.

'In the beginning God . . .'

The starting-point for Jewish and Christian ethics is the same place. It is God himself. Judaeo-Christian ethics are fundamentally the ethics of revelation. We do not create our own moral standards, they are given to us by God. They are not expressions of our highest ideals, but revelations of the nature and will of God. God is the source and ground of Judaeo-Christian ethical principles. These reveal not only what we, as human beings, should do, but also what God is like.

For the Jews, and therefore for Jesus, the revelation of God's standards was to be found in the history of God's dealings with his chosen people in creation, covenant, law, and through the prophets. These were not separate features stuck together to build a moral system, but rather part of a patchwork quilt which God provided to cover the needs of his people. Each links to and complements the other. They are part of God's salvation-history for humankind.

Because Judaeo-Christian ethics are rooted in God's initiative, they come to us with the full force and demand of the omnipotent Lord. They are not a matter of taking or leaving it, as if this were some light matter. They are crucial for the very life of humanity and the living in obedient relationship with God, who created and continues to sustain the world and all of us. While humankind is free to accept or reject God's standards, this decision is not without the most serious consequences. To reject God's way of life is to choose death and separation from God.

That the Judaeo-Christian ethic finds its root and ground in the nature and will of God means that it is no humanistic ethic. God's standards confront and call in question all human attempts to design moral ways of living. We cannot get behind the ethics of God to have other criteria by which to judge those ethics. The ethics revealed by God are the ultimate criteria and means by which to judge all moral systems and principles. They are the point by which to level the world.

Covenant

Revelation is a three-term relationship. There is the revealer, the revealed, and those to whom the revelation comes. For the Jew, God was the revealer. His moral standards were revealed, and we shall need to examine the content of that revelation as far as the Jew was concerned.

The Jewish nation was the community to whom God revealed his moral will. It is vital for us to understand that this relationship of revealer and those to whom the revelation was given was no mere formal relation. It was a mutual covenant. Israel and God were two factors in the same equation. The covenant was a two-way mutual relationship. The history of the Jewish people in the book of Genesis is of God entering into covenant relationship with individuals and thus with the whole Jewish nation. It was in the light of a covenant relationship like that of God and Abraham in Genesis 17 that the Jewish people interpreted the revelation of God to them. There we see God taking the initiative in revealing himself to Abraham and making a covenant not only with Abraham but with Abraham's descendants (Gen. 17:1–8). But Abraham and his descendants had a part to play in the covenant. It takes two to make a covenant. Both parties have roles and responsibilities to fulfil, for this is what it means to be in a covenant relationship. For Abraham and his descendants, the mark of being in covenant relationship with God was circumcision (Gen. 17:9–14).

While Abraham's covenant was seen as the root of God's choice of the Jewish nation, the basic covenant relationship found expression in passages like Exodus 19. In the wilderness of Sinai, God re-established his covenant with the Jewish people: 'Now if you obey me fully and keep my covenant, then out of all nations you will be my treasured possession. Although the whole earth is mine, you will be for me a kingdom of priests and a holy nation' (Exod. 19:5–6). Israel was appointed by God and chosen to be a priest-people among the nations. This obliged them to be the people of God and to live out what it meant to be chosen. They were to illustrate and carry out the implications of humanity's Godlikeness in all individual and social relations of human life. They were to reflect fully and accurately the character of God. They were to show what God was like by being like him. The path to such Godlikeness was explicitly stated in the Mosaic tradition.

It was to fear God and to keep all his statutes and commandments (Deut. 6:2). It was to love God: 'Hear, O Israel: The Lord our God, the Lord is one. Love the Lord your God with all your heart and with all your soul and with all your strength' (Deut. 6:4–5). It was to be holy as individuals and as a community, for God was holy (Exod. 19:6; Lev. 19:2; Deut. 14:2, 21; 26:19; 28:9). It was also to educate the next generation in the ways of God and their responsibility to fulfil their covenantal obligations:

> 'And these words which I command you this day shall be upon your heart; and you shall teach them diligently to your children, and shall talk to them when you sit in your house, and when you walk by the way, and when you lie down, and when you rise. And you shall bind them as a sign upon your hand, and they shall be as frontlets between your eyes. And you shall write them on the doorposts of your house and on your gates.' (Deut. 6:6–8, RSV)

It is no accident that the Jewish people have a tremendous stress on the importance of education. The need to alert consciousness of God and to reinforce the Jewish purpose in living begins and is sustained in the home. Parents have a key responsibility so to educate their children. In the celebration of the Passover feast the Seder-children have a special place because they are to ask what the feast and its symbols mean. The enactment of the Passover is not simply a memorial to the Exodus dealings of God with his chosen people. It is also a moral and religious lesson for all who are present. In reminding people of what God is like and has done, those present are called to live like that God and to be holy, to fear him and keep his commandments, and to love him. It is to be reminded of what it means to be a covenant people.

Ethics and religion

Some are confused as to whether such Passover celebrations are cultural, religious or moral events. Such categories are in danger of misleading us. For the Jew, and so for Jesus, there was no notion of any separation between ethics or morality and religion. All ethics were theological in the sense of being based on and reflecting God. Jewish ethics are based on the fundamental concepts and teachings of Judaism. Jewish moral principles regulate the conduct of those who follow Judaism in the context of the ritual and ceremonial observances of the Jewish religion. At the same time, Jewish moral principles are the expressions of God's ultimate aims, as apprehended by Jews, and are the ideals and part of the destiny they must set before humanity.

However, it is more than the mere form which binds ethics and religion together, for the demands ethics make are the focus of faith. There is to be no withdrawal from life and the world. When God's will is revealed, the task of the Jewish people is to embody and incarnate that will in their living. Morality is the embodied will of God. This is why those of us who try to set aside the ritual and ceremonial aspects of the Old Testament teaching are in danger of doing violence to the very heart of Jewish life. All of life is to be lived in the light of God and in God's way. All of life, in that sense, is spiritualised or endowed with moral and religious significance. In personal terms, life is to be preserved, honoured and enjoyed. In social terms, justice, truth, perseverance and peace are to mark our relationships. In terms of motivation, every good act is to be done for the sake of God. Thus when the Jew lives chastely, humbly, truthfully and compassionately, this is part of a separation from the world and a consecration to God. Morality and religion are inseparable and interdependent.

What is revealed?

In trying to understand the Jewish background to the ethics of Jesus, we have concentrated on the God who reveals himself and his will in a covenant relationship in which morality and religion are united; but the form of that revelation for the Jewish people was in their sacred writings. The Jews were 'people of the book' long before Christians claimed that title. The Torah was the cornerstone of God's revelation to the Jewish people, but to that was added not only the rest of what we know as the Old Testament, but also commentaries, interpretations and applications of the Torah. It is not our task to investigate how Jews interpret or apply their scriptures in all their detail. Rather, we must try to see the general background and teaching which Jesus and his audience took for granted as we do with the air we breathe. The context and approach of the Jewish scriptures were part of the way every Jew lived and thought. These scriptures were taught and were entirely natural to Jewish life and practice. In Jewish ethical teaching there are key themes which would be central to the understanding of Jesus and his contemporaries.

Jewish writings in general

What we have in the Old Testament is a series of writings which reflect a wide variety of conditions and settings. Some are written from the context of nomadic shepherd tribes; others show the refinement of life and law of an urban population. For the Jew, the Torah was the main focus of God's revelation of what was required by him from his people. However, the Jew knew that all too often the life of the Torah was not lived by God's people. Thus the historical, wisdom and prophetic books expressed God's continual call to the Jews to be his consecrated people. With these also grew various traditions of interpretation which seem to have had almost as much authority as the Torah, for they offered the means of understanding and putting into practice whatever the Torah required of the Jews. The starting-point of the Torah and of the Jewish approach to ethics was the God who revealed himself and his will. That revelation began and was reflected in the creation.

Creation

The Jews did not look to the world as a means to argue in favour of the existence of God. They could not conceive of a world unless God existed. There was no need to prove God's existence. It was simply taken for granted, as a fish regards water. There was no doubt God created and sustained the universe. The goodness to be found in creation was a direct result of God's hand in it. God created something of himself and his nature in the world and the people he made. There are a number of different ways we may approach and understand how creation offers the Jew, and us all, an account of God's will and values.

Natural Law

God made the world out of nothing, and sustains it by his power (Gen. 1–2; Ps. 24:1–2; 96:5; Isa. 40:12–26; Jer. 10:6–16). The natural order reflects God's nature, including his moral nature. God may be seen as having built morality into both the nature of the world and human nature. God has so made the world, and us in it, that some things are good and right for us and other things are harmful and wrong. What is bad tends to harm us, while what is good helps us to flourish. This natural order in things and in people may be witnessed to by the remarkable unanimity over what constitutes morality in different societies and cultures. While the expression and form of morality may vary greatly, the content of morality seems to have a common core and content. That content may be known by reasoning, for it is an *objective* feature of reality. The way the world and human beings are reflects objective moral standards. We are thus able to describe what is good and what is bad for people.

For example, we know that it is not good for people to be alone. We are by nature gregarious and flourish best in loving and supportive company. There is something wrong, we feel, with the totally isolated 'loner' life. The Genesis account of creation notes that it is not good for man to be alone, so God is pictured as creating a community of male and female, who together complement and fulfil each other. Living in community is natural and is good for us.

Thus, Jew and Gentile alike may refer to the natural order of things, seeking to discover objective moral standards and principles by which to live. For the Jew, such morality is the direct result of God's creation and endowing of the world and humanity with morality.

Made in God's Image

Despite being united with nature, humanity is distinguished from the rest of creation in the Genesis story by the account of man and woman's creation in God's image (Gen. 1:26–7). As daughters and sons bear the marks of resemblance to their parents, so humankind bears a resemblance to the God who created us.

Inevitably there are different understandings of what 'image' means, but it is clear that in moral terms God created human beings as moral creatures. The Jew understands this to mean that people are responsible human beings and are answerable to God. Not just any kind of living is appropriate for human beings. There are some things which fit in with what people are and their purposes in life; and there are other things which are inappropriate for men and women who bear the divine image. This fact created a tension for the Jews, for such teaching implied that all who were created, Jew and Gentile alike, were in some senses made in God's image. This in itself could not be *the* distinctive moral feature of life. But that did not mean that it had no moral significance. The purpose of human life was to reflect the unity and holiness of God, in whose image humanity is made. The moral law is not a contingent feature of life. It is a necessary feature, in which human beings have an obligation to fulfil the divine intentions for living. That moral law rests on the nature of humanity as a reflection of God's likeness.

Conscience

Some have suggested that conscience is the essential moral faculty of human beings. It is the 'voice of God' within us. It is seen as the ability to reflect morally on any and every situation and to know directly and intuitively what is right or wrong. For others, conscience is interpreted more as the mind of humans making moral judgements. This refers more to the moral reflection itself, rather than the ability to engage in such reflection. In both instances conscience may be helped or hindered by education and support. It is possible to interpret the moral and religious education of the Jewish child as part of the development of conscience.

Creation Ordinances

For the Jew, God is the Creator Lord, who appoints humanity to rule over all the earth. As the Creator, God may be understood as ordaining or ordering creation, and humanity's place in that creation, in particular ways. In a sense, this is to suggest not only that God created the world and people, but also that he gave some 'maker's instructions'. God's instructions for living deal with our relationships, and they are to be found in the Genesis account:

God and humanity

The Genesis picture is of God making man and woman in his image. No one forced God to make them. He just did it. In his sovereignty, he is the Creator and humanity is the creature. Thus, we are created by God for God. We are created to be his creatures and to live in harmony with him. God gave humankind all they required, but he also set a limit. God told the man and woman not to do something. They were forbidden to eat of the tree of the knowledge of good and evil. The appropriate human response was meant to be one of obedience. The proper relationship between humankind and God is one of obedience and trust. That is the way to live in relation to God.

The human community

As we have seen, people are created to live in community, and part of that communal life is sexual differentiation. Without woman, man is incomplete and inadequate. For the Jew, God ordained the relationship between man and woman. It is the basis of the human community, and it created the context of family life. They were to be fruitful and multiply (Gen. 1:28). The Jew sees the basis of marriage in these pages from Genesis. This is God's way of ordering society and the human community.

Humanity and nature

Humanity and the world are both created by God, but that does not mean that he gave equal value to both. Humanity is differentiated from nature, not only in being made in God's image, but also in the specific role to be performed by men and women. Work is God's purpose for men and women. They are given a command to 'fill the earth and subdue it' and to have dominion over the created order (Gen 1:28).

God's creative ordinance is for humanity to be a steward over nature and to exercise responsible dominion over it. This is not the same as irresponsible domination. Responsible dominion is typified in the naming of the animals (Gen. 2:20). This is the same kind of loving action as we perform when we give pet nicknames to those we love. Humanity is to care for and maintain the world and is to develop the resources of the world in responsible stewardship before God (Gen. 2:15). From this analysis of the Genesis creation account it is possible to see that both marriage and work are creation ordinances. They were given by God as ways of ordering human life according to his purpose and will for humankind.

The Fall

The Jew is neither optimistic nor pessimistic about human beings, rather he is realistic. The Genesis narrative expresses this realism in terms of the fall. The perfect harmony of the creation paradise was lost because of the entry of sin into the world. Disruption, disorder, chaos, toil, death, are all the results of sin. Humanity disobeyed God and broke his commandment. The results of disobedience are disastrous (Gen. 3:22–4). Humanity and nature are no longer in a proper relationship. It is now a struggle against the elements to produce enough to live. Man and woman's harmonious relationship is broken down. The fall account pictures blaming others, complaints, and the refusal to accept responsibility. Shame and concealment follow. God is blamed and the open relationship between humanity and God is transformed into one of hiddenness, fear and punishment.

The creation narratives provide an account of the purpose of humanity and of how life is meant to be lived. They also reveal that humanity fails and falls short. The impact of the fall is even more serious for the Jew, because it removes the natural relationship between the Creator and the created. No longer may men and women read off from nature what God's intentions and purposes are. We cannot rely simply on the fact of being made in God's image to please him. That image is now twisted. Our consciences, like our reason, are subject to the fall and may be twisted in ways which elude us. We cannot build on the creation ordinances properly, for both the world in which we live, and we ourselves, are less than God created us to be.

As the rest of the book of Genesis proceeds, we are presented with the same struggle between good and evil. The likes of Enoch, Noah and Abraham lead virtuous, moral lives, well pleasing to God. But we read also of Cain's murder of Abel, the sins of Noah's day, and the corruption and vice of Sodom and Gomorrah, and much more of human depravity and wickedness. God is required to remedy the situation, for there is no other solution to the problems of the world.

The law

With the loss of any immediate and reliable awareness of good and evil, and the ability to obey God's commands, the Old Testament scriptures portray a covenant God, who enters into binding relationships with his chosen people. The very word 'testament' really means 'covenant'. God takes the initiative in making a covenant (Deut. 7:7–8). He promises reward and blessing to those who keep his covenant. He promises to keep his side of the agreement if we keep ours. He also promises to punish those who fail to keep their promises (Deut. 30:1–10). Covenant finds expression in law. God is pictured as revealing his standards to and for humankind by means of laws. The best-known set of laws is the Decalogue, or the ten commandments, but this is simply part of a much more complex series of civil, ceremonial and moral laws, contained, for the most part, in the Pentateuch. This law is an expression of the nature of God, his will, his character, and his pattern for human life in its totality.

These laws are basic and essential to any moral and communal life (Lev. 19). God is not only the law-giver, he is the only ruler of Israel, as well as its judge and helper (Isa. 33:22). God's law is Israel's highest standard for living. This revealed law consists of statutes and judgements. God mediates his moral demands to his people through the proclamation of his commandments. There are two overlapping ways in which God's demand and standards are expressed for the Jewish people:

'And now, O Israel, what does the Lord your God ask of you but to fear the Lord your God, to walk in all his ways, to love him, to serve the Lord your God with all your heart and with all your soul, and to observe the Lord's commands and decrees that I am giving you today for your good?' (Deut. 10:12–13)

and

'Love the Lord your God with all your heart and with all your soul and with all your strength . . . and love your neighbour as yourself.' (Deut. 6:5 and Lev. 19:18; cf. Luke 10:27)

In practice, this meant that all of public and private life was consecrated to God. The marks of such life were justice, truthfulness and solicitude for the weak, obedience to and reverence for those in authority, regard for the rights of others, a forgiving and candid spirit, love for one's fellow humanity, and mercy towards the animal kingdom. The context in which such a life was to be lived was that of a relationship to God.

It is no accident that the Decalogue begins with duties to God (commandments 1–4) and then moves to our responsibilities to each other (commandments 5–10). The Jews were required to have allegiance to the one and only true God, and to worship God alone on his terms. They were to be completely loyal to God and to observe his Sabbath day. Then the commandments for the people of God deal with relationships with parents, the sanctity of life, sexual relations, stealing, truth-telling and possessiveness (Exod. 20; Deut. 5).

The scope and detail of Jewish ethics is far greater than these sets of rules. Idolatry is forbidden, for it is seen as leading to vice, oppression, contamination, and corruption (Exod. 20:3;

23:24; Lev. 19:4; Deut. 4:15–31). Parents are to be revered (Exod. 20:12; Lev. 19:3). Sexual perversion is abhorred (Lev. 18:22–3; 20:13, 15, 16). Adultery is seen as a sin against God (Exod. 20:14; Lev. 20:10). Fornication is condemned, and the importance of chastity stressed (Exod. 20:14; Lev. 18:18–20; 20:10; 21:9; Deut. 22:13–21). There are limits to permitted marriage relationships – e.g., consanguinity is forbidden (Lev. 18:6). Slavery is also limited (Exod. 21:2–3, 20, 26). Concern is to be shown for the stranger (Exod. 12:49; 22:21; Lev. 19:33–4). The poor, the widow and the orphan are to be cared for (Exod. 22:26; 23:6; Lev. 19:9; Deut. 15:7–11). Justice is to be shown to all, regardless of wealth or poverty (Exod. 23:1–3; Lev. 19:15, 18, 35–6; Deut. 16:18–20). Bribery, robbery, and oppression are to be avoided (Exod. 23:8; Deut. 24:14).

The observance and keeping of these laws is not some light matter. The book of Deuteronomy makes it crystal clear that the penalty for breaking the commandments is as serious as the blessing which follows from obedience:

> 'And if you obey the voice of the Lord your God, being careful to do all his commandments . . . the Lord your God will set you high above all the nations of the earth. And all these blessings shall come upon you and overtake you, if you obey the voice of the Lord your God.' (Deut. 28:1–2, RSV)

Then follows a detailed picture of the blessing in terms of prosperity and success. That is in sharp contrast to the disasters of every conceivable kind which are the result of disobedience:

> 'But if you will not obey the voice of the Lord your God or be careful to do all his commandments and his statutes which I command you this day, then all these curses will come upon you and overtake you.' (Deut. 28:15, RSV)

(This picture of blessing and cursing is found in Deut. 27–8.)

The law of Moses was the starting-point for the Jews of all that God demanded of his people. It set before them their duty as the chosen people of God. However, in the keeping of the law abuse was possible, and we have seen how Jesus in his struggle with the Pharisees challenged some patterns of life based on the law. But there could be no mistaking the fact that the law was revealed by God to be obeyed, and that the consequences of the Jews' response affected their well-being.

The wisdom literature

The books of Psalms, Proverbs, Job and Ecclesiastes provide a different slant for Jewish ethics. They include highly specific moral teaching which is presented as relevant for all men and women. The good person is a person and not simply a Jew. There is a universal character to the Jewish ethic at this point. In response to the question of who is worthy to live in the presence of God, the psalmist responded:

> He who walks blamelessly, and does what is right,
>   and speaks truth from his heart;
> who does not slander with his tongue,
>   and does no evil to his friend,
>   nor takes up a reproach against his neighbour;
> in whose eyes a reprobate is despised,
>   but who honours those who fear the Lord;
> who swears to his own hurt and does not change;
> who does not put out his money at interest,
>   and does not take a bribe against the innocent.
>
>   (Ps. 15:2–5, RSV)

The general emphasis of the ethics of the wisdom literature is on the holiness of the truly human. This is no ascetic morality. In some ways, the content is of 'laws from heaven for life on earth'. Such wisdom stresses the differences between good men and women and evil people (Job 31; Ps. 1; 24:4; 34:13–15; Prov. 5:1–14, 20–3; 6:12–15; 13). The teaching is often by way of positive and negative contrasts – e.g., telling the truth and spreading gossip (Prov. 26:28; 28:23; 24:5; 10:19; 11:13; 12:18; 16:27–8; 25:9–10). The general thrust of such specific teaching seems to assume that it pays you to be good. The book of Job tries to put the other point of view, that worldly wisdom does not always work. However, this is not to call in question the fact that the worldly wisdom of a book such as Proverbs is correct most of the time. It is for the Jew to do what God asks willingly and in freedom, for the world is good and good things will generally result from following God's ways.

The prophetic writings

The tone of the prophetic writings is one of rebuke. The Jewish people are chastised for ethical transgressions. The demand is for ethical perfection with no compromise. The writings reflect the standards and ideals of a good person (Isa. 33:15; Ezek. 18:5–9). The essence of Jewish ethics is to do what is right and just. The people of Israel were chosen by God. This choice meant that their conduct was under scrutiny (Amos 3:1–2). They were bound by a love covenant (Jer. 31:33–4; Hos. 2:19–20). All this was sealed by righteousness and loyalty (Hos. 12:6).

The prophets did not claim to be introducing a new morality. Their aim was to restore the morality taught by the law. They wished to recall God's people to God and to transform their beliefs into action. The prophets sought to restore the original covenant relationship between God and his people. Breaking God's moral law meant separation, defeat and exile. Keeping God's moral law meant the opposite.

There were various facets of teaching which highlighted particular issues. The people of Israel did not practise what they preached. Religion was a travesty. Even the sacrificial system was abused (Isa. 1:11–17; Jer. 6:19–20; Hos. 6:6; Amos 5:21–4; Mic. 6:6–8). Religion meant true morality. The immorality of the people of Israel was seen as stemming from false religion and idolatry. The adulterous abandoning of God led to vice, oppression and untruthfulness (Isa. 5:22; 59:3–6; Jer. 9:2–8; 23:14; Amos 6:4–7).

The social life of the children of Israel was marred by dishonesty and social injustice. The demand and standard of God was crystal clear:

He has showed you, O man, what is good;
   and what does the Lord require of you
but to do justice, and to love kindness,
   and to walk humbly with your God?
(Mic. 6:8, RSV

Those who had power and wealth in Israel and Judah were guilty of abusing their power. They were condemned in the strongest possible terms by the prophets. God was summoning his people back to his ways by means of the prophets (Isa. 5:7–23; Jer. 7:5–7; Mic. 2:8–9; 6:10–11; Zeph. 3:3).

Is not this the fast that I choose:
   to loose the bonds of wickedness,
   to undo the thongs of the yoke,
to let the oppressed go free,
   and to break every yoke?
Is it not to share your bread with the hungry,
   and bring the homeless poor into your house;
when you see the naked, to cover him,
   and not to hide yourself from your own flesh?
(Isa. 58:6–7)

Along with the condemnation of social injustice went a powerful attack on immorality (Ezek. 22:6–12; Hos. 4, 6).

However, it is a mistake to read the ethical teaching of the prophets as purely condemnatory. The aim of condemnation is always restoration. The prophets proclaim God's response to the people of Israel and their behaviour. Sin is a serious matter. God must respond, for sin is a reflection on his good name and an offence against his nature. This response is twofold. Firstly, the prophets must pronounce judgement on those who sin (Hos. 5:1–10; 7:12, 16; 8:1, 7; 13:7–8; Amos 2:6; 3:2; 8:7–14). God's judgement is expressed in very real terms in Hosea. It covers famine (4:10), captivity (8:13; 9:3–7); war (8:14), death (9:12–16) and the removal of God's presence (5:6, 15). The other theme is that of God's mercy. Punishment was designed to bring repentance, forgiveness and restoration. The very punishment itself was a sign of God's forgiveness and restoration. The very punishment itself was a sign of God's forgiving steadfast love (Isa. 9:1–7; Hos. 14; Amos 9:11–15; Zeph. 3:11–20). Such prophetic material provides a rich source of ethical teaching.

The apocryphal and rabbinic writings

The apocryphal material (such as Ben Sira, Tobit, and the Testament of the Twelve Patriarchs) and the rabbinical writings were an attempt to build a fence around the law and to apply it to life. Obedience to the commands of God meant that the whole word of God was to be obeyed. There was no genuine distinction between major and minor commandments. True religion's seal and earnestness meant total watchfulness and care over every detail. On the negative side, the rabbinic concern was with three cardinal sins. These were idolatry, adultery and murder. These were matched by a concentration on ceremonial sins of omission.

At the same time there was a stress on the positive virtues of love for one's fellows, industry, simplicity, sobriety, compassion, and benevolence to the poor. Rabbi Hillel summed up the heart of the moral attitude to others in a negative version of the golden rule: 'What is hateful to you, do not do unto another' (b *Shabbath* 31a). This is often spelled out in terms of 'wherefore do not hurt him, do not speak ill of him, do not reveal his secrets to others – let his honour and his property be as dear to thee as thine own' (Ab. RN Text B 24, 29, 30, 33). It was in the context of such rabbinic teaching that Jesus began his ministry and propounded his own distinctive ethical message. Yet it is clear that Jesus drew on and used the whole of his Jewish tradition. His teaching shows both continuity and discontinuity with what we call the Old Testament.

Summary

Jesus was brought up and lived as a Jew. His background and context were the roots of his ethical teaching. He saw all of life in relation to God and his covenant with the Jewish nation. The practice of the Jewish faith did not separate ethics from religious observance. They were one and the same thing for Jesus. He was steeped in the Jewish writings, from the understanding of creation and its ethical implications through the law, the wisdom teaching and the prophets, to the apocryphal and rabbinical writings and teaching of his own day. We must now examine in some detail how Jesus used this teaching, and in what ways he challenged the tradition from which he came.

7

The Ethics of Jesus –
Continuity and Discontinuity

If we are to understand properly what is new in the teaching of Jesus, and what builds and relies on Jewish roots, we need to see what degrees of continuity and discontinuity exist in Jesus' ethics.

The gospel writers were quite clear that Jesus was a regular attender at the synagogue, and that he taught there. Luke records how Jesus began his public ministry after his temptation in the wilderness. His first reading and brief comment sum up both the continuity with the past and yet the discontinuity of a new era:

> [Jesus] went to Nazareth, where he had been brought up, and on the Sabbath day he went into the synagogue, as was his custom. And he stood up to read. The scroll of the prophet Isaiah was handed to him. Unrolling it, he found the place where it is written:
>
> > 'The Spirit of the Lord is on me
> >   because he has anointed me
> >   to preach good news to the poor.
> > He has sent me to proclaim freedom for the prisoners
> >   and recovery of sight for the blind,
> > to release the oppressed,
> >   to proclaim the year of the Lord's favour.'
>
> Then he rolled up the scroll, gave it back to the attendant and sat down. The eyes of everyone in the synagogue were fastened on him, and he began by saying to them, 'Today this scripture is fulfilled in your hearing.' (Luke 4:16–21)

Jesus was seen by the ordinary people in the light of the Old Testament. He was thought to be Elijah, one of the prophets, or even John the Baptist resurrected. He is pictured by the gospel writers as fulfilling Old Testament prophecies, from the stories of his birth to the post-resurrection appearances. In the Transfiguration accounts, Jesus was legitimated by Elijah and Moses, the symbolic representatives of the prophets and the law. In general terms, this underlines the unity between what we call the Old and New Testaments. Jesus is the servant – the embodiment of Israel. His messianic fulfilment of the Old Testament prophecies created a new community of the true people of God, who worship God in spirit and in truth by lives of service and obedience.

Jesus and the law

The nub of the question of continuity or discontinuity with the Jewish roots of Jesus' teaching comes in relation to the law of Moses. As we saw in the last chapter, it was one of the key starting-points for Jewish ethics, for it embodies God's demands on his people. The law was an expression of God's taking the initiative and his setting up of moral standards. The law is God's revealed will and offers a definition of humanity's duties and responsibilities. Within the covenant relationship as expressed in the ten commandments, we saw that the first four emphasise our relationship with God, while the other six stress our relationship with our fellow men and women. There is no break in the continuity of these commandments with the teaching of Jesus. It is in putting right a breakdown in how the law was understood that Jesus' teaching becomes crucial.

Jesus and the dangers of formalism and legalism

You cannot read the gospel stories and avoid the conclusion that Jesus constantly came into conflict with the scribes and the Pharisees. Some of his strongest language and condemnation is used by Jesus as he warns about the dangers of following the scribes and the Pharisees. We must be clear that it is not each and every scribe and Pharisee who is condemned. Jesus was quite clear as to the nature of his criticism. It was not aimed at the genuine seeker of the truth who was struggling to apply the law of God in an honest, obedient fashion. It was against the dangers of formalism and legalism that Jesus warned. Why?

The wrong kind of Pharisaism makes no distinction between different parts of the law. In trying to make each and every part of the law equally significant, the danger is that nothing is really important. If everyone I meet is addressed as 'my love', the term is quickly devalued. There are parts of God's law which are crucial in significance. The heart of God's law is summed up in our relationships with God and with one another. These are to have priority over ceremony, things, and our own selfish interests and concerns.

The wrong kind of Pharisaism substitutes a routine, mechanical obedience for a thoughtful, sensitive obedience. The letter of the law becomes more important than the spirit of the law. Rules become ends in themselves, rather than the means of serving God and each other. It is not just a mistaken application of rules which is at stake. We may also change the very meaning of the heart of the rule. When Peter is recorded in Matthew 18:21–35 as asking how many times we are to forgive, it looks like a request for rules for forgiveness. Jesus rejected this demand; for even to try to frame such a rule would be to miss the true nature of forgiveness. It is not about sitting with a calculator, adding up failures until the magic number is reached and we can get our own back with a vengeance. The heart of forgiveness is that there is no recording of wrong done and no hoarding up of a tally.

The wrong kind of Pharisaism is also in danger of putting such a stress on outward appearances that the inner reality may be ignored. Such a concentration on appearances may lead to hypocrisy and a serious gap between what we think and feel and what we do. Legalism may encourage us to make such a gap. Jesus came to bridge the gap and to create a unity of the inner and outer; the appearance and the reality.

There are at least two other dangers implicit in the formalism of the Pharisees. They are of so stressing the ceremonial law that failure and omission become the key factors in moral behaviour, rather than any positive moral behaviour. People may all too easily be forced so to concentrate on avoiding mistakes that they do little or nothing. This is one way of avoiding error and failure, but it is very far from the positive keeping of the law which seeks to do and bring about good, rather than failing to keep some detail of the law. Behind such a danger lurks a further misunderstanding about the nature of righteousness. The Pharisee might do what was right only for the sake of being able to stand uncondemned before God on judgement day. Not only is this a failure to do what is right because it is right in itself and is God's will, it also makes fear of punishment and seeking of reward the key motives in ethical behaviour.

We have seen how Jesus used the conflict with the Pharisees to clarify the proper understanding of the law and to restore people's view of God's will for humanity. Jesus came to reinstate the true nature of the Mosaic law. He tried to disentangle the heart of the matter from the later accretions of the commentators. In their zeal to give detailed applications of the law, they had buried the essence in a mass of minutiae which required an expert to untangle. Goodness was meant to be for all, from the simple to the wise. It was not the sole domain of the legal genius. Jesus laid bare the essential teaching of the law in terms of the original spirit, not the letter. He also kept the heart of the law, as may be seen from his requiring of those healed from leprosy to show themselves to the priest (Mark 1:40–5; Luke 5:12–16; 17:11–19; cf. Lev. 13:49; 14:2–32). He clarified doubtful points, stated the heart of the law afresh, and gave simple examples and definitions. He restored the law to its original expression as the will of God. It is in this way we are to understand the claims of Jesus:

'Do not think that I have come to abolish the Law or the Prophets; I have not come to abolish them but to fulfil them. I tell you the truth, until heaven and earth disappear, not the smallest letter, not the least stroke of a pen, will by any means disappear from the Law until everything is accomplished. Anyone who breaks one of the least of these commandments and teaches others to do the same will be called least in the kingdom of heaven, but whoever practises and teaches these commands will be called great in the kingdom of heaven.' (Matt. 5:17–19)

Jesus taught the complete fullness of the law. He fulfilled the law. He brought it to its full validity by completely keeping it. He did all that the law required. He fulfilled it *perfectly*. In this way, he made the law fully valid, for he gave men and women the power to put it into effect. It was no longer merely an impossible standard. With Jesus, it became a possible reality. This ability to fulfil the demands of the law in himself, and by others through him, rested on his authority.

The challenge to the formalism and legalism of the Pharisees is focused on the authority of Jesus. So often he began his teaching with, 'You have heard that it was said ... But I tell you ...' Jesus spoke not simply as another rabbinic scholar and teacher. He taught as the Son of Man and the Son of God. Here we return to the theme of the impossibility of separating the teaching of Jesus from the person of Jesus. Who he is makes all the difference to the value and validity of his ethical teaching. He did not teach in a deductive way from the Torah, but taught in his own authority. To put it more correctly and biblically, he taught in the authority of God, his Father (see John 5:31–47; 8:12–58).

Jesus taught the corrective to legalism. He returned women's and men's attention to genuine morality and purity of motive. He showed how it was possible to justify one's life before the holy God. This was not by threat of punishment or promise of reward, but by the service of God and humankind, in love and obedience to the will of God.

The actual content may be seen in two ways from the gospel accounts. The conflict with the Pharisees provided an opportunity for a clear account of God's will and the meaning of the law. Jesus also revealed that law and its meaning in his own teaching, especially through his parables, in his dealings with

people, and in his own use of Scripture in his personal life. The
standards Jesus taught are not some kind of lowering of the high
standards set by the scribes and the Pharisees. Matthew is quite
clear how Jesus regarded the 'new' morality: 'For I tell you that
unless your righteousness surpasses that of the Pharisees and the
teachers of the law, you will certainly not enter the kingdom of
heaven' (Matt. 5:20).

Jesus' conflict with the Pharisees

The gospel writers record the dispute with the Pharisees in
terms of who Jesus was, the claims he made about himself
and what he did and was able to do, and the authority under
which he acted and spoke. While all of the teaching of Jesus is
liberally sprinkled with allusions to passages, texts and figures
from the Old Testament writings, this is particularly evident in
his debates with the Pharisees. The very fact of conflict, and
the essential issues at stake in that conflict, may lead us to
overlook the content of the message of Jesus. He was offering
a reinterpretation of the law which was a direct challenge to
the currently accepted rabbinical interpretations. The detailed
reinterpretation presented specific moral teaching, but that was
set in the overall context of a biting critique of the Pharisees'
way of life.

Jesus' attack on hypocrisy

The most swingeing attack on the Pharisees is to be found in the
pages of Matthew's Gospel. Jesus drew attention to the fatal gap
between what they preached and how they lived:

'The teachers of the law and the Pharisees sit in Moses'
seat. So you must obey them and do everything they tell
you. But do not do what they do, for they do not practise
what they preach. They tie up heavy loads and put them on
men's shoulders, but they themselves are not willing to lift a
finger to move them.

'Everything they do is done for men to see: They make
their phylacteries wide and the tassels on their garments
long; they love the place of honour at banquets and the most

important seats in the synagogues; they love to be greeted in the market-places and to have men call them "Rabbi" . . .

'Woe to you, teachers of the law and Pharisees, you hypocrites! You shut the kingdom of heaven in men's faces. You yourselves do not enter, nor will you let those enter who are trying to.

'Woe to you, teachers of the law and Pharisees, you hypocrites! You travel over land and sea to win a single convert, and when he becomes one, you make him twice as much a son of hell as you are.

'Woe to you, blind guides! You say, "If anyone swears by the temple, it means nothing; but if anyone swears by the gold of the temple, he is bound by his oath." You blind fools! Which is greater: the gold, or the temple that makes the gold sacred? . . .

'Woe to you, teachers of the law and Pharisees, you hypocrites! You give a tenth of your spices — mint, dill and cummin. But you have neglected the more important matters of the law — justice, mercy and faithfulness. You should have practised the latter, without neglecting the former. You blind guides! You strain out a gnat but swallow a camel.

'Woe to you, teachers of the law and Pharisees, you hypocrites! You clean the outside of the cup and dish, but inside they are full of greed and self-indulgence . . .

'Woe to you, teachers of the law and Pharisees, you hypocrites! You are like whitewashed tombs, which look beautiful on the outside but on the inside are full of dead men's bones and everything unclean. In the same way, on the outside you appear to people as righteous but on the inside you are full of hypocrisy and wickedness.

'Woe to you, teachers of the law and Pharisees, you hypocrites! You build tombs for the prophets and decorate the graves of the righteous. And you say, "If we had lived in the days of our forefathers, we would not have taken part with them in shedding the blood of the prophets." So you testify against yourselves that you are the descendants of those who murdered the prophets. Fill up, then, the measure of the sin of your forefathers!

'You snakes, you brood of vipers! How will you escape being condemned to hell? . . .' (Matt. 23:2–7, 13–17, 23–5, 27–33)

Jesus drove home the content of these charges in a number of other contexts. Luke comments on the Pharisees' love of money, after Jesus relates the parable of the shrewd manager (Luke 16:1–15). Matthew records Jesus' attack on the Pharisees' understanding of clean and unclean and its importance for living. There Jesus is pictured as setting tradition as interpreted by the Pharisees against the word of God in its true intention (Matt. 15:1–20). In John's account of the woman taken in adultery, Jesus challenges the scribes and Pharisees to carry out the sentence of the law if they are themselves pure and spotless in the light of its standards (John 8:1–11).

These are not simply examples of how Jesus attacked hypocrisy. He was not introducing some new moral standards. The heart of the Mosaic law was what was at stake. The issue was one of consistency between words and actions. The Pharisees claimed to follow Moses, but Jesus charged them with failing to meet their own avowed standards: 'But do not think I will accuse you before the Father. Your accuser is Moses, on whom your hopes are set' (John 5:45).

Jesus and the Sabbath

One widely reported dispute between Jesus and the Pharisees was over the issue of Sabbath observance. The examples range over healing on the Sabbath to the disciples pulling grain for a snack (see Matt. 12:1–13; Mark 2:1–12; Luke 6:1–10; John 7:14–24). Jesus used the Old Testament scriptures to defend his and his disciples' behaviour, to attack the Pharisaic interpretation of the Sabbath law, and to stress God's intention in the framing of the law. Jesus drew on Exodus (20:8–11; 23:12), Leviticus (24:9), Numbers (28:9–10), Deuteronomy (5:12–15), and the books of Samuel (1 Sam. 21:1–15; 2 Sam. 8:17) to show that God's law was for the benefit and good of men and women. If and when the interpretation and application of the law refused to allow such good to be done, it was a harmful interpretation and a wrong application. The true purpose of the law needed to be reiterated

Jesus and purity

Jesus was concerned at the way the distinction between what was clean and unclean was being drawn. In the dispute with the Pharisees over 'clean' and 'unclean' (Matt. 15:1–20) and in the record in Mark (7:1–23), Jesus drew heavily on Old Testament teaching and was concerned about the Pharisaic focus on things rather than people, and on empty forms which ran the risk of ignoring human needs and distress. Outward show might conceal inner evil and uncleanness. This was the enemy to be attacked, and proper teaching about good and evil would focus on the right issues.

> 'What comes out of a man is what makes him "unclean". For from within, out of men's hearts, come evil thoughts, sexual immorality, theft, murder, adultery, greed, malice, deceit, lewdness, envy, slander, arrogance and folly. All these evils come from inside and make a man "unclean".' (Mark 7:20–3)

Jesus was all too aware of how wrong attitudes corrupt. In his response to the money-changers in the temple, we see not some hasty reaction, but, by putting the various accounts together, a pattern of visits which culminated in the driving out of evil in order to restore what was right and good. The reaction of the Pharisees was typical of those who are not truly concerned for what is clean and good (Matt. 21:12–17; Mark 11:11–19; Luke 19:45–8).

Jesus' own behaviour also called in question the way the Pharisees drew distinctions about what was morally significant. In Luke 5 Jesus is challenged over his eating and drinking rather than following in the footsteps of the disciples of John and of the Pharisees. In his response, Jesus highlighted the new order of his reign in terms of the new garment and the new wine. The celebrations for the Bridegroom are part of the new kingdom, and they overrule patterns of behaviour which may be nothing more than show (Luke 5:33–9; Mark 2:18–22).

Jesus, the righteous and the sinners

A constant source of complaint for the scribes and the Pharisees was the company Jesus kept. The calling of Matthew to be a disciple led to such a dispute:

> While Jesus was having dinner at Matthew's house, many tax collectors and 'sinners' came and ate with him and his disciples. When the Pharisees saw this, they asked his disciples, 'Why does your teacher eat with tax collectors and "sinners"?'
>
> On hearing this, Jesus said, 'It is not the healthy who need a doctor, but the sick. But go and learn what this means: "I desire mercy, not sacrifice." For I have not come to call the righteous, but sinners!' (Matt. 9:10–13)

Jesus came to the rejected, the sick, the outcast. He fraternised with groups and individuals who were on the fringe of respectable society. He was to be found with tax-collectors, publicly known 'sinners', women, and Samaritans. He identified with the segregated, the cut off, the despised. He quoted Hosea 6:6 in his own defence and challenged the existing view of righteousness and respectability. To be righteous was to enter into God's kingdom, and only those who recognised their need and responded appropriately were given the righteousness which stemmed from God, rather than mere human effort. The conversion of Zacchaeus is a typical example of Jesus bringing radical change in unexpected areas (Luke 19:1–10).

Jesus and divorce

Another area of controversy with the scribes and Pharisees and their interpretation of the Mosaic law may be seen in Jesus' teaching on divorce (Matt. 5:31–2; 19:1–12; Mark 10:1–12; Luke 16:18). Jesus was not simply concerned to overcome the trap questions set by the Pharisees, but also to deal with the laxity in divorce and remarriage and to restore a proper understanding of marriage for both women and men. He used God's original intention in creation to make his case, and drew on both Genesis (1:27; 2:24) and Deuteronomy (24:1–4) to return people's attention to God's standards for the marriage relationship.

Jesus and the beatitudes

We have already given this teaching of Jesus extended treatment, but it is important in the context of Jesus' response to the scribes and the Pharisees to see how he questioned the authority invested in traditional interpretations and applications by stressing his own authority. On the issues of miracles, adultery, divorce, oath-taking, punishment and revenge, and genuine love for one's neighbours and one's enemies, Jesus used a whole range of Old Testament references and gave his own authoritative interpretation of how God expects men and women to live. As we saw, the distinctive teaching of Jesus is novel in comparison with the traditional interpretations of the law, but is in continuity with the original statement, aim and purpose of the law (Matt. 5:17–18).

Jesus' positive teaching – continuity and discontinuity

Much of Jesus' own positive teaching is expressed not in contrast with that of the Pharisees and scribes, but in the light of and by reference to the traditional Jewish scriptures.

In his teaching on the limitless nature of forgiveness (Matt. 18:15–35) and his account of the proper understanding of who is a neighbour in the parable of the Good Samaritan (Luke 10:25–37), Jesus drew on Leviticus and Deuteronomy (Lev. 19:17–18; Deut. 6:5; 19:15). In his teaching on humility in the parable of the wedding feast (Luke 14:7–14) and the parable of the two sons (Luke 15:11–32), Jesus drew on Deuteronomy and Proverbs (Deut. 21:15–17; Prov. 25), Genesis and Zechariah (Gen. 41:42; Zech. 3:4). In his parable about Dives and Lazarus (Luke 16:19–31), Abraham, Moses and the prophets are used to drive home his point about loving God rather than money.

There can be no doubt that Jesus stood firmly in the direct line of God's moral will as expressed in the law and the prophets. At the same time, Jesus was concerned to distil the essence of the law and the prophets in terms that were easily understandable to all. He expressed the heart of this, not in the negative form of the golden rule, but in its positive affirmation, requiring action: 'In everything, do to others what you would have them do to you, for this sums up the Law and the Prophets' (Matt. 7:12). While this turned round the emphasis of the traditional understanding of the rule, Jesus was at pains to reinforce the original sense of the greatest commandment:

> One of them, an expert in the law, tested him with this question: 'Teacher, which is the greatest commandment in the Law?'
>
> Jesus replied: '"Love the Lord your God with all your heart and with all your soul and with all your mind." This is the first and greatest commandment. And the second is like it: "Love your neighbour as yourself." All the Law and the Prophets hang on these two commandments.' (Matt. 22:35–40; cf. Mark 12:28–34; Deut. 6:5; Lev. 19:18)

Jesus was unafraid to apply the law in a way that was relevant to the needs of individuals. The story of the rich young ruler (Matt. 19:16–22; Mark 10:17–31; Luke 18:18–27) shows Jesus going beyond the mere fulfilment of the law to the specific needs of one person. This was the mark not only of his perceptive evangelism, but also of his ability to confront people with the key moral issues for them (see also John 4:1–42).

Jesus also made use of the Jewish scriptures in his own personal life. Luke records the temptations of Jesus, and how Jesus responded to the moral dilemmas he was confronted with. The devil challenged Jesus to give up the pattern of the suffering servanthood of the Messiah who came to die, and to replace it with that of Jesus the Provider of bread for all, the All-powerful, who is simply given earthly authority and power, and Jesus the Performer, whose tricks from temple tops would create a popular Messiah. Using passages from the Psalms and Deuteronomy, Jesus resisted the temptations to live a life other than God's intended one (Luke 4:1–13; cf. Deut. 6:13–16; 8:3; Ps. 91:11–12).

Summary

We have seen that Jesus lived and taught in the context of the Judaism of his day, and how he used and fulfilled much of the content of what we call the Old Testament scriptures. He was the perfect fulfilment of God's will for humankind. He taught the dangers that stem from a formalistic and legalistic approach to morality and law, and in his conflict with the scribes and Pharisees he was able to restore the original force and simplicity of God's moral standards. He drew freely on the Jewish writings in expressing his own teaching, in his dealings with people, and in coping with the moral pressures and demands of his own life. There is much more continuity than discontinuity with the themes and aims and purposes of the law and the prophets. That continuity again shows how far Jesus is truly the Son of God and at one with the Father.

8

The Ethics of Jesus – So What, Then?

Inevitably we must ask whether the ethics of Jesus are relevant to us today. We need to remember that this is not a new question, and we are not the first to ask it. The question was as important to the early Church as it is to us today. To answer the question properly, two levels need to be explored. These are the relevance of the ethics of Jesus *then*, and the relevance of the ethics of Jesus *now*. In this chapter we will deal with the first level.

So what for the early Church?

So, what did the ethics of Jesus mean to Christians after the death of Jesus? We have looked at the way in which the gospel writers have tried to set out the ethical teaching of Jesus in their clear and concise fashion. But even before they had done their job of recording the teaching of Jesus, the growing early Church was faced with the problem of applying the ethics of Jesus and trying to live the new life of the kingdom in a world which was seeking to mould men and women into its own fashion.

As we live in a world where the alternative philosophies and ideologies to Christianity pose genuine threats to living the Christian life, so in the time of the early Church alternative philosophies, religions and ideologies threatened to submerge the new faith of Christianity and to infiltrate its very heart, so that it became an amalgam of all the views it was supposed to challenge.

The world around us easily squeezes us into its mould. The social conventions, accepted norms and cultural outlooks of the day are strong pressure points on any emerging view. The purity of any morality or religion is soon tainted by contact and infiltration by the surrounding culture and environment. This made the task of the writers in the New Testament all the more important. Their task was to help people understand what the moral teaching of Jesus actually was and how to apply and live that teaching in the real world in which they lived, moved and had their being. They were trying to show the difference Jesus made and to help Christians develop the moral attitudes and aspirations of members of the kingdom of God and thus enable them to make decisions on issues of conduct. Their job was to show how the ethics of Jesus worked in practice.

The picture we have of the early Church is one of growth. The reality of faith and the coming of men and women into that faith is all too obvious in the pages of the Acts of the Apostles. Such growth meant an increasing need for teaching, and that teaching happened in the context of the fellowship of Christian believers. Growth brought problems. The early Church was confronted with a wide range of problems ranging from how to ensure fair shares for all the widows and fatherless, to whether it was all right to eat meat offered to idols, to issues of immoral behaviour among Christians, to uneasy relationships between Jews and Gentiles. The letters to the churches in the New Testament are not only filled with teaching about the new faith, they also deal in very direct terms with the problems facing the churches. They are attempts to apply the ethics and teaching of Jesus to the issues that faced Christians then. The New Testament writers showed what Christians were supposed to do with the teaching of Jesus.

There is a sense in which all the moral teaching of the New Testament depends on the ethics of Jesus. Who Jesus was and what he did form the foundation of all that is said in the New Testament. However, that says too much and too little. It is too little, in that we can never exhaust all that it means, no matter how long we try to do so. But it is also saying too much, in that it may blind us to the very specific ways in which Jesus and his moral teaching were used by the New Testament writers. It is important for us to understand what the writers were saying. They were quite clear that if we understand the ethics of Jesus, then certain things will follow. If you have received the gospel and know Jesus, then you will live like this. If you have received the Holy Spirit – the Spirit of Jesus – then you will live like this. Our attention will not focus on all that these two statements imply, but will concentrate on the explicit way the writers use and refer to the moral teaching of Jesus and to Jesus himself.

The motives of the writers

Paul summed up his motive and aim as a Christian in Philippians: 'For me, to live is Christ and to die is gain' (Phil. 1:21). There seem to have been three kinds of motives which influenced the epistle writers. The first was that they understood that those who had been called by God were meant to live in a particular way. They were to be conformed to the purposes of God, and that meant to be like Christ (Eph. 1:11–12; 1 Pet. 1:1–2).

The second motive was that the writer felt a compulsion to ensure that Christians behaved as they ought to. In a sense, it is like a teacher preparing his pupils for an examination. The good teacher tries to make sure that all his pupils will pass: he wants them to be as perfect as possible.

I am jealous for you with a godly jealousy. I promised you to one husband, to Christ, so that I might present you as a pure virgin to him. (2 Cor. 11:2)

We proclaim him, admonishing and teaching everyone with all wisdom, so that we may present everyone perfect in Christ. (Col. 1:28)

The third motive seems to arise from the writer's own situation, where he felt that he was in a position to call on the Christians in other places to live as they ought to live: 'As a prisoner for the Lord, then, I urge you to live a life worthy of the calling you have received' (Eph. 4:1).

The writers obviously felt a responsibility to help fellow Christians be consistent to their calling and to help them fulfil the role and duties which are part and parcel of being a member of Christ's kingdom. They carried out this responsibility in various ways, but we shall examine their understanding of the theological basis, the nature and the content of the ethics of Jesus, and the context in which we apply them today.

The theological basis

Some people suggest that to be a Christian is to have a new set of perspectives, patterns and priorities. This is to under-estimate the change that happens when someone becomes a Christian. To be a Christian is to be a new creation. Conversion is a total and radical change, not just in attitude, but in being. It is to be a different kind of person with a different status and goal. In theological terms, this is seen as being a new creation, having salvation, being justified, rejecting sinfulness and seeking righteousness and being obedient to Christ. We shall examine each of these aspects of the New Testament writers' attempt to unpack and apply the ethics of Jesus.

New creation

'Therefore, if anyone is in Christ, he is a new creation; the old has gone, the new has come!' (2 Cor. 5:17). Paul encapsulated in this statement the truth of the radical change that occurs when someone becomes a Christian. It recaptured the kind of thinking that is so clear in Romans 6. There Paul argued that in baptism we die and are buried with Christ. As we arise from the water, we arise to a new life. The old self has been crucified. We have died to the life of sin which we used to live. Now in Christ, we are to count ourselves 'dead to sin and alive to God' (Rom. 6:3–14). Elsewhere, Paul argued that we are to get rid of the old yeast and be a new batch. We are to be the bread of sincerity and truth

(1 Cor. 5:7–8). There is a mutual death involved here, for it is argued that we are dead to the world and the world is dead to us (Gal. 6:14–15). This new way of life is to be marked by clear ethical behaviour which rejects certain ways of life and embraces others:

> You were taught, with regard to your former way of life, to put off your old self, which is being corrupted by its deceitful desires; to be made new in the attitude of your minds; and to put on the new self, created to be like God in true righteousness and holiness . . . (Eph. 3:22–4)

Such a new life means that we are saved and enjoy the salvation of God.

Salvation

> For the grace of God that brings salvation has appeared to all men. It teaches us to say 'No' to ungodliness and worldly passions, and to live self-controlled, upright and godly lives in this present age, while we wait for the blessed hope – the glorious appearing of our great God and Saviour, Jesus Christ, who gave himself for us to redeem us from all wickedness and to purify for himself a people that are his very own, eager to do what is good. (Tit. 2:11–14)

This passage from Titus makes clear what the impact of salvation is meant to be. We are saved from a particular way of living in order to follow an alternative way of life. There is much that could be developed here, but the New Testament writers were concerned that salvation should show itself in a moral way of living. Jesus died in order to save men and women. That salvation means that they now follow a different form of behaviour. They are no longer subject to the world's way of doing things (Col. 1:22; 2:20; Heb. 13:12). This salvation is not yet complete and looks forward to the return of Christ as the final fulfilment of that salvation. Nevertheless, in the mean time, Christians are to behave in upright and godly ways, eager to do what is good, and in this way they show that they are those who belong to the kingdom of God. They are those who have been saved by Christ.

Justification

For those who came from a Jewish background, the way to please God was by keeping the law. Those who kept the law were justified before God. They were regarded as just, as if they had never sinned. Paul argues that this is not a successful way of being freed from the penalty of sin and finding favour in the eyes of God:

> We who are Jews by birth and not 'Gentile sinners' know that a man is not justified by observing the law, but by faith in Jesus Christ. So we, too, have put our faith in Christ Jesus that we may be justified by faith in Christ and not by observing the law, because by observing the law no-one will be justified. (Gal. 2:15–16)

It was this understanding of justification by faith which transformed the life and understanding of Martin Luther.

The law still has a vital role in leading us to faith: 'So the law was put in charge to lead us to Christ that we might be justified by faith. Now that faith has come, we are no longer under the supervision of the law' (Gal. 3:24–5).

Paul also writes in Romans about how Jesus was delivered over to death for our sins and was raised to life for our justification: 'Therefore, since we have been justified through faith, we have peace with God through our Lord Jesus Christ, through whom we have gained access by faith into this grace in which we now stand' (Rom. 5:1).

The picture is one of a rescue mission by Jesus to save people from the evil age in which they live. Christians are justified by the blood of Jesus and thus are saved from the wrath of God. This means that there is and ought to be a fundamental difference between the way of life of those who are not justified by Jesus and those who are justified. Paul reminded the Corinthians:

> Do you not know that the wicked will not inherit the kingdom of God? Do not be deceived: Neither the sexually immoral nor idolaters nor adulterers nor male prostitutes nor homosexual offenders nor thieves nor the greedy nor drunkards nor slanderers nor swindlers will inherit the kingdom of God.

And that is what some of you were. But you were washed,
you were sanctified, you were justified in the name of the
Lord Jesus Christ and by the Spirit of our God. (1 Cor.
6:9–11)

Those who are new creations and saved are also justified by faith
in Christ and accordingly live a new life in Christ.

Sinfulness

While there is some disagreement about whether in Romans 7
Paul was talking about life before becoming a Christian or
afterwards, it is quite clear that he was talking about the
experience of a struggle between good and evil that we all
know only too well. He said, 'I do not understand what I do.
For what I want to do I do not do, but what I hate I do.' And
so he came to this conclusion:

When I want to do good, evil is right there with me. For in
my inner being I delight in God's law; but I see another law
at work in the members of my body, waging war against the
law of my mind and making me a prisoner of the law of sin at
work within my members. What a wretched man I am! Who
will rescue me from this body of death? Thanks be to God –
through Jesus Christ our Lord! (Rom. 7:15, 21–5)

What it means to be a Christian is to put an end to sinfulness
and to live a life worthy of being a member of the kingdom
of God. Those who are sinful will not and cannot inherit
the kingdom of God (Gal. 5:19–21; Eph. 5:5). Paul entreated
Christians to be very careful in their dealings with those who
are still in sin and unbelief:

Do not be yoked together with unbelievers. For what do
righteousness and wickedness have in common? Or what
fellowship can light have with darkness? What harmony is
there between Christ and Belial? What does a believer have
in common with an unbeliever? (2 Cor. 6:14–15)

The avoidance of sin and sinfulness is crucial for the Christian.
But there is still some comfort for the Christian who finds that he

or she is not totally successful in the struggle against evil in their own lives: 'My dear children, I write this to you so that you will not sin. But if anybody does sin, we have one who speaks to the Father in our defence – Jesus Christ, the Righteous One' (1 John 2:1). The very same Jesus who freed men and women from the power and force of sin and evil is the one who intercedes for the Christian who falls short of the standard expected of those who live the life of the kingdom. But it is not simply an escape from and an avoidance of sin which is to mark the Christian life: we are to seek after righteousness.

Righteousness

Paul expressed the contrast between sinfulness and righteousness in Romans 6:

> But thanks be to God that, though you used to be slaves to sin, you wholeheartedly obeyed the form of teaching to which you were entrusted. You have been set free from sin and have become slaves to righteousness. (Rom. 6:17–18)

This process of being slaves of righteousness has its beginning in what Jesus Christ has done for us. While using Abraham as an example for justification by faith, Paul focused attention on the idea of crediting righteousness to Abraham and to Christians:

> The words 'it was credited to him' were written not for him alone, but also for us, to whom God will credit righteousness – for us who believe in him who raised Jesus our Lord from the dead. He was delivered over to death for our sins and was raised to life for our justification. (Rom. 4:23–5)

Paul was arguing that those who are in Christ are changed from lives of sin to lives of righteousness. This is achieved by the work of God in and through Christ. We are the beneficiaries of what Jesus Christ has done for us. However, this is not a matter of choice or an optional extra. It is fundamental to being a follower of Jesus: 'For the kingdom of God is not a matter of eating and drinking, but of righteousness, peace and joy in the Holy Spirit, because anyone who serves Christ in this way is pleasing to God and approved by men' (Rom. 14:17–18).

One of the motives and desires of the New Testament writers is that the members of the kingdom of God will show the righteousness of God in their lives. This in itself will bring praise and glory to God and show the reality of God's power and new life to the world:

> This is my prayer: that your love may abound more and more in knowledge and depth of insight, so that you may be able to discern what is best and may be pure and blameless until the day of Christ, filled with the fruit of righteousness that comes through Jesus Christ – to the glory and praise of God. (Phil. 1:9–11)

Obedience

The only path to righteousness comes from obedience. As we have seen, the movement is from being a slave to sin to becoming a slave to righteousness. Slaves obey their masters. Thus, the picture is a change from obeying the master of sin to obeying the Master of righteousness. This is the very purpose for which God called Paul into his ministry: 'Through [Jesus] and for his name's sake, we received grace and apostleship to call people from among all the Gentiles to the obedience that comes from faith' (Rom. 1:5).

John argues that this obedience is the distinguishing mark of being alive in Christ and one of his followers (1 John 3:24). It is not necessarily an easy thing to achieve or fulfil. Paul pictured the struggle to obey as part of his total ministry and work: 'We demolish arguments and every pretension that sets itself up against the knowledge of God, and we take captive every thought to make it obedient to Christ' (2 Cor. 10:5). The struggle has its point and purpose, which is to bring honour and glory to God:

> Because of the service by which you have proved yourselves, men will praise God for the obedience that accompanies your confession of the gospel of Christ, and for your generosity in sharing with them and with everyone else. (2 Cor. 9:13)

We have tried to show how the New Testament writers began

to apply the moral teaching of Jesus to the early Church and its issues and problems. In order to apply the teaching properly, they made certain theological assumptions which they expressed quite explicitly. It was on the basis of being a new creation and enjoying salvation and justification that the writers could appeal for an end to sinfulness and advocate a seeking after righteousness by obedience to the teaching and commands of Jesus.

However, all this is merely to describe the framework in which the teaching of Jesus was applied. We must now explore the ways in which that teaching was actually applied to the Church and Christians, and what was enjoined upon them in terms of the lifestyle they should follow.

The lordship of Christ – in him, like him, with him

While a living relationship with Jesus Christ is the underlying assumption of the New Testament as a whole, and of all the moral teaching for the early Church, there are very specific ways in which the relationship between Jesus and his followers is used to encourage certain ways of living. The Christians' relationship with Jesus is presented as an ethical example and motive for living the good life. This stems from the notion of obedience, which itself rests on the clear understanding that Jesus is Lord and that Christians are his servants or slaves. The following of and obedience to Jesus the Lord blossoms so that Christians are one with Christ or are in him, are to be like him and are to be with him.

Jesus the Lord

For the early Church, Jesus was not simply some figure from the past to be remembered and revered. He was also the present and living Lord. He was the ruler of the Church and the one who inspired and motivated Christians to live his life in the world. He was the Lord who lived and reigned and who would return in glory to bring in the fullness of his kingdom. This lordship of Christ united all Christians, as Paul reminded the Corinthians:

'To the church of God in Corinth, to those sanctified in Christ Jesus and called to be holy, together with all those everywhere who call on the name of our Lord Jesus Christ – their Lord and ours' (1 Cor. 1:2).

Paul pictured this relationship in terms of the movement from being a slave of sin to becoming a slave of Christ (1 Cor. 7:22; 9:21). In the epistle to the Colossians it is quite clear what the implications of this relationship are: 'So then, just as you received Christ Jesus as Lord, continue to live in him, rooted and built up in him, strengthened in the faith as you were taught, and overflowing with thankfulness' (Col. 2:6).

The Christian who calls Jesus 'Lord' is to preach Jesus Christ as Lord (2 Cor. 4:5), to rejoice in the Lord (Phil. 4:4–7), and to set apart Christ as Lord in his or her heart (1 Pet. 3:15–16). The lordship of Christ is to be obvious to unbelievers and those who are watching the Christian: 'So then, men ought to regard us as servants of Christ and as those entrusted with the secret things of God' (1 Cor. 4:1). It is also to make a significant difference to the way Christians live. Relationships are to be conducted and framed in the light of the lordship of Christ. Thus, in Ephesians and Colossians, the relationships between husbands and wives, parents and children, and masters and slaves are to be conducted in light of Christ's lordship (Eph. 5:22–6:9; Col. 3:18–4:1).

The fact that Jesus is Lord is to affect everything that is done by the Christian: 'Whatever you do, work at it with all your heart, as working for the Lord, not for men, since you know that you will receive an inheritance from the Lord as a reward. It is the Lord Christ you are serving' (Col. 3:23–4; cf. Rom. 14:5–12). The morality of Christians is to be guided and directed by the fact that Jesus is their Lord and they are his servants. This means that their body is for the Lord (1 Cor. 6:13–15), that their role and place in life comes from the Lord (1 Cor. 7:17), and that the only proper boasting is to be in the Lord (2 Cor. 10:15–17).

It is clear that some of the problems which affected the early Church were caused because of a failure to live in the light of the lordship of Christ:

I urge you, brothers, to watch out for those who cause divisions and put obstacles in your way that are contrary to the teaching you have learned. Keep away from them. For such people are not serving our Lord Christ, but their own appetites. (Rom. 16:17–18)

Jesus is Lord, and that means a transformation of the status, behaviour and relationships of Christians. The application of the ethics of Jesus takes place in the light of the relationship of Lord and servant.

Union with Christ

We have already seen that John argued that those who obey the commands of Jesus live in him and he lives in them (1 John 3:23–4). There are a whole series of pictures which together form a cluster that expresses what it means to be in Christ and in union with him. Union with Christ begins with an honest self-appraisal: 'Examine yourselves to see whether you are in the faith; test yourselves. Do you not realise that Christ Jesus is in you – unless, of course, you fail the test?' (2 Cor. 13:5).

The relationship of being in Christ begins with Christ in the believer. The New Testament offers a series of pictures to sum up what this means. It is to be in Christ (1 Cor. 1:30; 2 Cor. 5:17). It is to belong to and be of Christ (1 Cor. 3:21–3). It is to be a member of Christ (1 Cor. 6:15). It is to be a citizen of heaven (Phil. 3:20). It is to have clothed oneself with Christ (Gal. 3:26–8).

The New Testament writers go a stage further in their account of union with Christ. They argue that because of this relationship we are called on to behave in certain ways and to exhibit certain qualities. The union with Christ is used as a moral call and challenge to the Christian. In Romans, the Christian is called to clothe himself with the Lord Jesus Christ and not even think how to gratify the desires of the sinful nature (Rom. 13:12–14). There is also the call to follow Christ (Rom 15:5–6). In 1 Corinthians, because the Christian is a member of Christ he is therefore to behave in particular ways (1 Cor. 6:13–15). In Galatians, the apostle writes often harsh things in order that Christ might

be formed in his readers (Gal. 4:19). In Ephesians, where the
discussion is of the roles that God gives to his people in order
to fulfil his will and purposes, union with Christ is pictured as
a corporate activity and state. God gave the roles 'to prepare
God's people for works of service, so that the body of Christ
may be built up until we all reach unity in the faith and in the
knowledge of the Son of God and become mature, attaining
to the whole measure of the fulness of Christ' (Eph. 4:12–13).
This is clearly linked with the prayer that Christians might be
strengthened through the Spirit

> so that Christ may dwell in your hearts through faith. And I
> pray that you, being rooted and established in love, may have
> power, together with all the saints, to grasp how wide and
> long and high and deep is the love of Christ, and to know
> this love that surpasses knowledge – that you may be filled
> to the measure of all the fulness of God. (Eph. 3:17–19)

It is obvious that the Christian is to be filled with the full
measure of Christ, to know him and to have Christ dwell in
him as fully as possible.

In the letter to the Philippians, Paul argues that if there
is any genuine encouragement and benefit from being united
with Christ, then we are to show the moral qualities of being
like-minded, having the same love and being one in the Spirit
and in purpose (Phil. 2:1–4). Part of the onward aim of the
Christian is to fulfil the purpose for which Jesus took hold of
each believer (Phil. 3:12–14). John sums up unity with Christ
in very direct terms: 'Whoever claims to live in him must walk
as Jesus did' (1 John 2:6).

There are benefits which come to the Christian who is united
to Christ. Religious and traditional distinctions are broken down
(Gal. 6:15). In situations of suffering we are comforted (2 Cor.
1:5–6). There is nothing that can separate the believer from the
love of God which is experienced in Christ (Rom. 8:35–9).

There is a job to be done which stems from being in union
with Christ. Saints and believers have been 'chosen to make
known among the Gentiles the glorious riches of this mystery,
which is Christ in you, the hope of glory' (Col. 1:27). It is not

only evangelism which is the task of those who are united with Christ: 'For we are God's workmanship, created in Christ Jesus to do good works, which God prepared in advance for us to do' (Eph. 2:10). Building on the Old Testament picture of a sweet-smelling sacrifice, Paul pictures the Christian now as an aroma of Christ rising up to God in the midst of those who believe and those who do not (2 Cor. 2:15).

Union with Christ brings a new status, a call to grow into even and ever closer union with Christ, positive benefits and a task for the Christian in the world. That task may also be expressed as being like Christ.

Christlikeness

For many Christians down through the ages the heart of the ethics of Jesus has been the imitation of Christ. We are to be like him. In Philippians and in 2 Corinthians we are told that the Christian is to be like Christ in his death and in his life (Phil. 3:10–11; 2 Cor. 4:10). Paul expressed the content of this in two ways – as *conformation* and *transformation*. From the beginning of God's purposes for those who follow Jesus, God's will was that they were to be conformed to the likeness of his Son (Rom 8:28–30). All the pictures of union with Christ seem to point in the direction of a process of being conformed. But this is not a do-it-yourself matter: 'And we, who with unveiled faces all reflect the Lord's glory, are being transformed into his likeness with ever-increasing glory, which comes from the Lord, who is the Spirit' (2 Cor. 3:18).

Unity with and in Christ

Too often when we read the New Testament, we imagine that the writers are addressing us as individuals and forget that their letters were to groups and communities. To be in and with Christ is not simply a one-to-one personal relationship. It is to be part of belonging together with each other and with Christ. This is captured most of all in Paul's metaphor of the body: 'Now you are the body of Christ, and each one of you is a part of it' (1 Cor. 12:27).

There is no more intimate union with Christ and with each

other than to become flesh. Each and every Christian is part of that body and is to fulfil a specific role in its functioning (1 Cor. 12:12–26). In that body, we all belong to each other as we belong to Christ (Rom. 12:4–5).

Here the ethics of Jesus are applied in the context of the community of faith. We are the body of Christ and he is the Head of the body. We are to act together in the light of those facts. There is no alternative:

> Instead, speaking the truth in love, we will in all things grow up into him who is the Head, that is, Christ. From him the whole body, joined and held together by every supporting ligament, grows and builds itself up in love, as each part does its work. (Eph. 4:15–16)

Applying the ethics of Jesus

We have seen how the theological basis underlying the ethics of Jesus was crucial for their application in the world. How that application happens is equally crucial. It is in the context of the relationship with Jesus as Lord, the union in and with him, and the gradual growth into Christlikeness that the ethics of Jesus may be applied. However, this still leaves unanswered the questions regarding the qualities and results of applying the ethics of Jesus, and it is to these that we now turn.

The qualities required

The writer to the Hebrews says:

> Since the children have flesh and blood, he too shared in their humanity so that by his death he might destroy him who holds the power of death – that is, the devil – and free those who all their lives were held in slavery by their fear of death. (Heb. 2:14–15)

This same theme is picked up by Paul in his letter to the Galatians: 'It is for freedom that Christ has set us free. Stand firm, then, and do not let yourselves be burdened again by a yoke of slavery' (Gal. 5:1).

As we have seen, to be a Christian is to be released from sin and its power and hold. This is pictured as freedom (2 Cor. 3:17–18). This freedom is a precious commodity and needs to be preserved. The early Church faced threats from within the fellowship from those who tried to force a return to a legalistic and slavish following of the law and religious customs (Gal. 2:4). There was, however, a more subtle threat to the Church arising from a fundamental misunderstanding of the freedom which came in Christ. Some Christians seemed to think that if they were now free in Christ that meant they were free to do absolutely anything and everything. Freedom was seen as licence. It was crucial to counteract this heresy and to ensure that Christians understood that freedom in Christ meant freedom to be like him. It was a freedom to serve others in love. Therefore Paul wrote: 'You, my brothers, were called to be free. But do not use your freedom to indulge the sinful nature; rather, serve one another in love' (Gal. 5:13), adding that the entire law may be summed up in the loving of one's neighbour as oneself (Gal. 5:14).

The example of Jesus was held up as the basis and the reason for our love of others:

> This is how we know what love is: Jesus Christ laid down his life for us. And we ought to lay down our lives for our brothers. If anyone has material possessions and sees his brother in need but has no pity on him, how can the love of God be in him? Dear children, let us not love with words or tongue but with actions and in truth. (1 John 3:16–18)

It is hard to imagine that the great hymn of love in 1 Corinthians 13 is not based on the example of Jesus and his life. All the qualities of loving expressed so eloquently in that passage are exactly those that Jesus lived and embodied. The Christian will only be able to love in that way when Paul's prayer is answered:

> that you, being rooted and established in love, may have power, together with all the saints, to grasp how wide and long and high and deep is the love of Christ, and to know

this love that surpasses knowledge – that you may be filled to the measure of all the fulness of God. (Eph. 3:17–19)

The appeal to the example of Jesus is matched by appeals to the experience we have in Christ and to his explicit moral teaching. For example, we are to forgive each other. We are also to forgive whatever grievances we have against each other: 'Forgive as the Lord forgave you' (Col. 3:13); and Paul exhorted Christians to give by referring to the words of Jesus: 'It is more blessed to give than to receive' (Acts 20:35).

In summary, then, we can see how, by urging Christians to show the qualities of freedom, love, forgiveness and giving, the New Testament writers used the ethics of Jesus and the example of his life as the basis for a call to morality.

The call to morality

An analysis of the New Testament shows how the ethics of Jesus were applied directly to the early Church and its problems by a variety of calls to morality. There are many summons to live as Jesus requires. We shall try to uncover something of that variety and to see both the strategy underlying them and the implications of these calls for morality.

There is a general strategy which is used in the epistles to make a moral point. It is to present the theological facts and arguments and then to state that the ethical result must follow. We have this kind of link at the beginnings of the fifth and twelfth chapters of Romans. There is, however, a more specific motive which is used as the ground of a call for morality. When confronted by those who were not behaving as they ought, Paul argued: 'Such people we command and urge in the Lord Jesus Christ . . .' (2 Thess. 3:12). Jesus himself was used as the basis of a moral appeal.

There are many instances where the New Testament writers use the example of Jesus as the basis for the Christian to behave in certain ways and to adopt certain attitudes. Christians are to follow the example of Jesus Christ and not to please themselves (Rom. 15:1–3), to accept each other (Rom. 15:7ff.), to give to the needy (2 Cor. 8:7–9), to be kind, compassionate and forgiving

(Eph. 4:32), to love (1 John 3:16), to have the same attitude as Jesus (Phil. 2:5–11), to endure and not grow weary or lose heart (Heb. 12:2–3). They are called on to suffer as Jesus suffered (1 Pet. 2:20–1). They are to be imitators of Paul, Jesus and of God (1 Cor. 11:1; Eph. 5:1–2; 1 Thess. 1:6).

It is not only to the example of Jesus that the writers appeal. They also use the name of Jesus as a ground for the call for morality: 'And whatever you do, whether in word or deed, do it all in the name of the Lord Jesus, giving thanks to God the Father through him' (Col. 3:17; cf. 1 Cor. 1:10; 5:4–5).

The appeal to Jesus also takes other forms. It may be a plea on behalf of Christ (2 Cor. 5:18–21), or an appeal to have the qualities of Christ (2 Cor. 10:1), or a plea to have the same attitude as Christ (1 Pet. 2:13), or to act out of reverence for Christ (Eph. 5:21).

Paul himself was quite clear as to his motive for evangelism and the ministry of reconciliation: 'For Christ's love compels us . . .' (2 Cor. 5:14–15). But he was also clear that the death and sacrifice of Jesus ought to make a great difference to the way in which we live: 'You are not your own; you were bought at a price. Therefore honour God with your body' (1 Cor. 6:19–20).

Paul often made reference to the return of Christ and the day of judgement which Christ's second coming brings. This was clearly a reason for behaviour which is worthy of the Lord Jesus (1 Cor. 1:7–9; 4:4–5; Phil. 3:14). He also argued that Christians were to walk and live in ways which were worthy of the gospel and of their Lord (Phil. 1:27; Col. 1:10), and to be servants of the Lord (2 Tim. 2:24), as well as to fulfil the law of Christ (Gal. 6:2).

Paul wrote to the early Church in the belief that the Christians were letters of Christ and living epistles to be read by the world (2 Cor. 3:3). In seeking to present these believers as pure and spotless, he often made appeal to his authority and asked to have his teaching followed. In matters of morality he did, however, make it clear when he was expressing his own opinion and when he believed that his teaching came from Jesus Christ (Rom. 14:14–19; 1 Cor. 2:15; 7:10, 12, 25; 1 Thess. 4:2).

The appeal to the authority of Jesus stressed the importance of the moral teaching and the awful risk entailed in neglecting to obey such teaching.

Throughout this section we have seen the ways in which the New Testament writers in general and Paul in particular called the early Church to a particular kind of moral life. Jesus has been used in terms both of his example and his name. There are a cluster of ways of expressing what Jesus has done for the Christian and how his example and teaching ought to be emulated and copied in the lives of believers. If we are clear what the ethics of Jesus are, then it is quite clear what we are supposed to do with them: they are to be lived as Jesus lived them. About that there can be no mistake or special pleading. The Christian is inevitably to imitate Christ in all he or she does.

Judgement, reward and punishment

We have seen how the New Testament writers used the example of Jesus as the basis of their call to morality. They also appealed to the fact of judgement and to the notions of reward and punishment. We argued earlier that this was no crude attempt to frighten or blackmail people into the kingdom, but that reward or punishment is the necessary corollary of the particular way of life we choose. Such appeals need to be seen in their context as motives and encouragements to behave in appropriate ways:

> So we make it our goal to please him, whether we are at home in the body or away from it. For we must all appear before the judgment seat of Christ, that each one may receive what is due to him for all the things done while in the body, whether good or bad. (2 Cor. 5:9–10)

The importance of appearing before the judgement seat of Christ is clearly implied in stressing the need to follow certain ways of life (Rom. 14:10–12; 1 Cor. 4:4–5; Phil. 2:14–16; 4:4–7).

While it is clear that those who are in Christ have been given the gift of eternal life (Rom. 6:22–3), there still remains the fact of judgement before God (Rom. 14:5–12). This will be a time of testing what has been done, to see whether it is good and lasting (1 Cor. 3:1–15). Those who remain faithful to Christ will indeed receive their reward (Rom. 8:17, 31; 1 Cor. 3:21–2; Eph. 6:5–8). The obverse is also true. Those who continue to sin will likewise receive their reward, which is punishment (Rom. 14:12; 1 Thess. 4:3–7).

The Spirit of Jesus

Inevitably, by using the ethics of Jesus as the focus for our approach to the rest of the New Testament, we run the risk of putting a false emphasis where the text itself tends in a slightly different direction. While it is true that Jesus and his moral teaching are clearly at the heart of the New Testament, the emphasis in the Bible seems more concerned with how it can be possible for ordinary men and women who have passed from death into life to live the life of Christ in an alien and antagonistic world. The solution to the charge that the ethics of Jesus are impossible for people is quite simply the person and work of the Holy Spirit. He is the source of the power and capacity to be like Jesus.

In John's Gospel, Jesus quite clearly pointed forward to the Holy Spirit as his Spirit who would enable men and women to know the truth and to do it. The pages of the New Testament are not so much full of the way to know the teaching of Jesus as of how to put it into practice. The Spirit is the one who brings the teaching of Jesus within the grasp of the Christian. He is the supernatural, ever-present guide and enabler who gives us the power to obey the commands of Christ. This work of the Spirit is most clearly seen at work in the context of the fellowship of Christian believers – the body of Christ. The ethics of Jesus are only possible in the context of the fellowship of believers. It is the Spirit-filled body which is the bride of Christ (Eph. 4:4; Rev. 22:17). The link between Jesus and the Spirit is made clear in Galatians 4: 'But when the time had fully come, God sent his Son, born of a woman, born under law, that we might receive the full rights of sons. Because you are sons, God sent the Spirit of his Son into our hearts . . .' (Gal. 4:4–6). Paul had already made the point, in the previous chapter, that '[Christ] redeemed us in order that the blessing given to Abraham might come to the Gentiles through Christ Jesus, so that by faith we might receive the promise of the Spirit' (Gal. 3:14). In practice, this means a different way of life and a different controlling focus:

> You, however, are controlled not by the sinful nature but by the Spirit, if the Spirit of God lives in you. And if anyone does not have the Spirit of Christ, he does not belong to Christ. But if Christ is in you, your body is dead because of sin, yet your spirit is alive because of righteousness. And if the Spirit of him who raised Jesus from the dead is living in you, he who raised Christ from the dead will also give life to your mortal bodies through his Spirit, who lives in you. (Rom. 8:9–11)

This gift of the Spirit is a seal of God's ownership and a deposit guaranteeing what is to come (2 Cor. 1:21–2).

The presence of the Spirit in the lives of the New Testament believers had certain distinctive marks. At the Council of Jerusalem, the early Church was able to make a moral decision about what should be required of Gentile believers. In setting out the basic requirements as abstinence from food sacrificed to idols, from blood, from the meat of strangled animals and from sexual immorality, the apostles, elders and brothers expressed the reason for their decision as follows: 'It seemed good to the Holy Spirit and to us . . .' (Acts 15:28–9).

The early Christians were to realise that what they did was of supreme importance: 'Do you not know that your body is a temple of the Holy Spirit, who is in you, whom you have received from God? You are not your own; you were bought at a price. Therefore honour God with your body' (1 Cor. 6:19–20).

Living in accord with the guidance of the Spirit is a liberating experience which brings us nearer to being like Christ:

> Now the Lord is the Spirit, and where the Spirit of the Lord is, there is freedom. And we, who with unveiled faces all reflect the Lord's glory, are being transformed into his likeness with ever-increasing glory, which comes from the Lord, who is the Spirit. (2 Cor. 3:17–18)

This growing more like Jesus ought to be marked by the fruit of the Spirit: 'love, joy, peace, patience, kindness, goodness, faithfulness, gentleness and self-control' (Gal. 5:22–3).

Paul summed up what it is to live in the Spirit: 'Since we live by the Spirit, let us keep in step with the Spirit' (Gal. 5:25).

The Spirit is the one who interprets to the believers the mind of Christ. He takes the teaching and will of Jesus and reveals them to humanity. The life of the kingdom is realised and is made possible only by the coming of the Spirit.

Summary

This chapter began by asking, in the light of knowing the ethics of Jesus, 'So what?' The answer the early Church gave was in terms of new creation, salvation, justification, righteousness, obedience, and escape from sinfulness. As the New Testament writers tried to apply the ethics of Jesus, they talked of union with Christ, being like Christ, and the imitation of Christ. These things were only possible in the relationship of service to the risen Lord. Such a relationship meant freedom, love, forgiveness and genuine giving. Readers of the New Testament were summoned to show these qualities by being reminded of Jesus' teaching about the reality of judgement, reward and punishment. We must never forget that the moral teaching of Jesus was not presented as some impossible standard which Christians were to try ever harder to achieve. The power and presence of the Spirit meant that it was possible to live the life of the kingdom and to be like Jesus as men and women kept in step with the Spirit. What was true for them then is still true for us here and now.

9

The Ethics of Jesus – So What, Now?

It is always possible to read a book, watch a television programme, hear a talk or listen to a radio show, and when it ends to say, 'Thank you very much' and that is that. It is even possible that you have endured to the end of this book and have understood more about the ethics of Jesus and what they mean for us today and are thinking that is all there is to it. If that is how you feel, you are in danger of missing the heart of the ethics of Jesus. They are not simply a set of lessons to be learned: they are a way of life.

All of us have to have a basic starting position, a set of presuppositions, a point by which to lever the world. For the Christian, the basic given is the living reality of Jesus. Jesus is the living Lord. His teaching, then, is the Lord's teaching. His ethics are the standards we are meant to live by. To know Jesus is to want to obey him.

When people heard Jesus as he taught his moral framework for living, they were brought to a moment of crisis. He provoked extremely strong reactions. He confronted people with the choice of following him or rejecting him. Neutrality and fence-sitting were hard in the presence of Jesus Christ; you were either for or against him, with little room for being in-between. The ethics of Jesus demand a response from us. They make certain claims on us. They are a clear statement about how we are to live. They offer the basis of a life which pleases God. They challenge us to genuine human being.

A current diagnosis

When Jesus confronted people with the need for repentance, that implied there was something wrong that needed to be put right. The fact that people did change dramatically reveals the accuracy of his diagnosis and the success of his cure.

The bottom line was that people were sinners. I almost wrote that the bottom line *is* that people *are* sinners. Until and unless we admit that there is a problem with the world, society and ourselves, the ethics of Jesus will seem irrelevant and just an interesting set of ideals. For those who met Jesus, the values and new life of the kingdom came like a helping hand to a drowning person.

Living in the kingdom means an end to sin. It sounds so easy, but the hardest part is admitting that you and I are sinners. We have something wrong with us. There are lots of ways of describing that disease and its manifestations. But the challenge Jesus brought by his life and teaching was to selfishness and self-centredness.

It's almost a truism to say that the West is a materialistic greedy society. Certainly so many of us seem more and more focused on ourselves and looking after number one, that other people not only can go to hang, but, if they get in our way, then we'll trample over them to get where we want to be.

The rise of personal debt is just one small indication of how we seem to want all the so-called 'good things of life' immediately. We take the waiting out of wanting and have instant satisfaction. Only it doesn't satisfy. The growing number of drug addicts, alcohol-dependent people and mentally disturbed folk needing tranquillisers of every kind is very far from a picture of humanity enjoying itself.

The problem is not the goal of happiness and pleasure. God made us to enjoy good things. The problem is the pursuit of good things. It is ourselves and the way we destroy even the good and the wholesome. God loves to give human beings good things to enjoy, but we soon get caught up in the wrong kind of reliance on material things. We become so concerned with them, and they can dominate us and our lives so much, that they begin to control us. It isn't wealth itself which is a problem, but that we come to rely on it. We can so easily overstate and over-estimate its importance. Then it has become our master and we are slaves to it. This is the worldliness which takes away our attention from what is really important. Jesus taught that if anyone is to live in the kingdom, then it means denying oneself, taking up the cross and then following in the footsteps of Christ.

The hard bit is the first step of self-denial. It means that other people are more important than me. It means that other interests are to come before mine. It means *agape* love. It means loving the unlovely, the undeserving. It also means forgiving those who do us harm and evil.

We've seen that to forgive is not to write a blank cheque, but is a genuine openness to being restored and to living in fresh harmony with others. For those of us who have been victims of racial, sexual, political and religious abuse that is a tall order. But if the values of the kingdom are to mean anything, they must offer a starting-point in places like the Middle East, Northern Ireland, South Africa and Cambodia. It is where people recognise that all of us have failed and fallen short of the standards we hold and God gives, and that none of us is blameless, that we may be able to take the first step of asking for forgiveness. We may then find that such a bold initiative provokes exactly the same response from those who were called 'enemies'. We won't know if this will work until we try. But we do know that it is the way of those who follow Jesus and live in his kingdom. So we are to do it not because it will work, but because it is right and good.

The challenge of Jesus for today

Every aspect of our life today can and should come under the scrutiny of the ethics of the kingdom. These standards provide us with a way of testing how we should live. There are lots of books to be written on how to apply the kingdom values, but four main areas seem of immediate relevance.

Cosmic issues

As the threat of nuclear holocaust has seemed to recede, the fear of ecological disaster has replaced it. In reality, both are and will remain perhaps the ultimate challenges for the twenty-first century. Both are strikingly similar in the scenarios they offer as warnings to us all. A world devastated and human beings destroyed is the common core. Whether the cause is a nuclear accident, a nuclear war, or the increasing pace of ecological disturbance and dis-ease, the end result will be the same.

We don't seem to lack strategies or strategists who produce peace plans and control agreements for nuclear waste and pollution problems. But the root problem of human being seems strangely intractable. It is both what human beings do and what drives and motivates them which is the problem. We are selfish and we pursue our own interests.

In the kingdom, there is a double command. The King is the one through whom the world was called into being. He is the one who sustains the world as well as the one who died to restore it with humanity to its proper place and relationship with God. Thus Christians have a double motivation to act responsibly in ecological and nuclear matters. Our salvation is bound up with the well-being of the world itself.

But there is also in the ethics of Jesus a challenge and a cure for the gap between our actions and our motives. Jesus showed the clear relationship between what we are and what we do, and between the inner motive and its outward expression in action. The values of the kingdom give us the right moral motivation of concern for others, for creation itself, and for the animal kingdom. These matter to God, so they must matter to us.

However, the correct attitude must lead to the correct action. The fruit must tell and be shown. Our good motives must be translated into action as peacemakers, where nuclear war threatens. In ecological terms we are to be good stewards of all that God has given. The world belongs to God and to those who come after us, and we must return it to its rightful owner in good shape.

Sexuality and marriage

In an age when the West is obsessed with sexuality, we have reduced sexual being to genital activity. Jesus challenges our self-centred approach to sexuality. Sexual expression is not just about pleasure-seeking. It is about relationship. Jesus pointed back to God's creation plans for humanity. Sexual differentiation was part of God's gift in overcoming the loneliness and isolation of a human being. But proper sexual expression needs that context of mutual love and reciprocal care. It takes two who have broken the old sets of ties and left parental homes. It means being committed to each other in an exclusive way. These then allow the expression of sexual unity which is called becoming one flesh.

That is God's pattern for kingdom living, and so it calls us all in question. Heterosexual and homosexual alike are challenged by the standard of male and female marriage as the only proper setting for that ultimate expression of human love. None of us can pretend that it is easy, and we long to make exceptions. The standard remains the standard for us all, both within and without marriage. If we want to live as Christ showed and God commanded, then we need not be married or have sexual intercourse to be fulfilled.

There is no evidence whatsoever that Jesus ever had any sexual relationship with anyone in the clear sense of genital activity; yet he was fully a man. Indeed he offers us a perfect picture not just of human being, but of manhood. That picture should challenge the mixed-up ideas of masculinity which are around in our society today. Yet Jesus clearly held up the pattern of marriage as the setting where human love can grow and flourish and human beings can find unity from their isolation.

Jesus also stressed the importance of children, and marriage is the God-given context for the creation and sustaining of family life. That there are other patterns, and that these are not total disasters, is a triumph of God's goodness. But their existence does not call in question the ideal set out for those in the kingdom. Furthermore, the care of children is not just for parents. Jesus warned everyone of the importance of treating children properly and of the serious risks to all those who harm the innocent child. Some of his sternest warnings are reserved for those who do damage to children.

If we bring every aspect of our sexuality — from who we are, to the ways we express sexual love — to the example of Jesus and his explicit teaching, we will find a standard to bring *shalom* and wholeness to us all.

Citizens of earth and heaven

Living in the kingdom means that we are citizens of two different yet related realms. On the one hand, we are citizens of heaven and our hope and future lies in living in accord with the values and perspectives of eternity. God's realm is the heart of our existence. At the same time that rule begins in the here and now and extends into the future. That implies that the here and now is of the utmost significance. We dare not separate how we live now from what we shall be in the new life after death. The continuity between this life and the next means that what we do and how we live in this world matters.

This is part of why the incarnation of Jesus is so important. He came and entered into our human setting as well as our very humanity. He lived as a citizen of a land which was occupied and under foreign rule. It is no wonder that this has been a comfort and challenge to many people in similar settings who have seen Christ's coming into that situation as providing a model for liberation. While the excesses of liberation theology may show the danger of building too much on too small a biblical base, there can be no doubt that the reality of liberation was the result of the ministry of Jesus and the coming of the kingdom.

In the same way, Christians are to be bringers of liberation at every level. We can so easily focus that liberation on freedom from the shackles of sin and on the ministry of healing. While these are crucial, they are only part of that liberation ministry. Jesus brought a freedom from the slavery of oppression, but not as others expected. He did not seek to overthrow the civil powers and authorities by force or violence. That had been tried often enough in Jewish history without success. Instead, he brought the freedom of men and women set right with God and seeing the true values which matter.

Jesus was not afraid to be critical of those who abused their power over others. His tongue-lashings of the Pharisees show a concern for the terrible impact they were having on people who knew no better and were thus being given a false view of religion and, indeed, of God. But Jesus recognised that civil authority found its basis in God. There is no civil power which is not ultimately a shadow of God's power. That is not to say that all civil powers behave as God wishes. That is only too obvious. But even twisted, abused power is still power over others. The question, then, is how is that power exercised, and what is the aim of the use of such power? The aim must be for the benefit of the citizens. It should be to do good to others and to restrain evil. Jesus taught that even Caesar was to have his proper dues, for without civil authority we are all vulnerable and anarchy is the result. Bad government is still better than no government at all.

That is no excuse for letting governments do anything and everything to others. Jesus was crystal clear that God's rights and dues were to have priority over those of civil authorities. If it comes to any kind of crunch, and the civil authorities are breaking God's laws and standards and putting people at risk, then it is perfectly proper for them to be challenged. This clearly follows the role of the prophets in the Old Testament who acted as God's judgement-bringers, proclaiming God's unhappiness with the ways in which rulers abused the people.

Thus we have a simple test for all those in civil authority. Do they do as God wants or not? Do they restrain evil and reward and encourage goodness? If they fail these tests, then Christians must speak out, not in the name of politics, but in the name of Jesus. They must state clearly and unequivocally what standards God requires of those who have power over us. This provides an acid-test for voting in a democracy. We must look carefully at which parties offer a programme and a track record of policies which do restrain evil and seek to foster good in society. They deserve support as well as loyalty.

But what if the government is unjust and we suffer as Christians for our faith? The example of Jesus is that we must suffer and turn the other cheek when we ourselves are the object of attack. Jesus was roused to anger and action when he saw others being abused and suffering wrongdoing. He did not express that anger when wrong was done to him. So we are to follow him in being zealous to protect others and slow to defend ourselves. This is genuine love which puts others before ourselves.

Life and death

Many wish that Jesus had been explicit concerning what we should do about abortion and euthanasia and the host of moral and medical issues that face us today. But that would have been to deny the genuineness of the incarnation at a very particular time in history and in a specific setting. It would also have led us further into the trap of using the teaching and example of Jesus as a rule book where we look up what to do in every situation. That destroys responsibility and stunts our growth as adult men and women making our own moral choices and taking responsibility for them.

Yet we find that Jesus' response to death was often grief and a desire to put right the wrong of death. Whether it was at the tomb of Lazarus or beside the bed of Jairus' daughter or with the widow of Nain, Jesus acted decisively to raise the dead. This was not just a miracle of life over death. It was a foretaste of what it means to be in the kingdom of God. Eternal life is here and now as well as in the life to come. Death is not the last enemy who will win. It is the last enemy which has been defeated in the resurrection of Jesus.

This leaves us with the clear understanding that medicine, properly following in the steps of the Great Physician, is meant to preserve life and resist death. But that preservation and resistance must never be at all costs and by all means. Death is not the worst thing that can happen to people, and Jesus was quite adamant that we should not fear those who can destroy the body, but those who destroy the soul and very essence of what it is to be human.

When medicine refuses to accept that death has come, and strives officiously to keep alive what is now the remains of a person who has gone to be with Christ, it does far too much. But that does not mean that we should not be in the business of pushing back the frontiers of medical skill and knowledge in order to resist the evils of disease and of death which can be properly avoided.

At the other end of life, with all that is happening on the genetic engineering, infertility and abortion fronts, there is obviously no direct teaching. Jesus was at pains always to treat people as people. In technical language, he treated people as ends in themselves, not as means to another end. This means that from the earliest stages of life people must have their own integrity and not be used by us for some other sake than their own. Some may feel that to use the word 'people' from the very earliest stage of life is to beg the question in favour of a particular view of human being.

There is a fascinating incident in Luke's Gospel which many see as significant in matters concerning the status of foetal life (Luke 1:39–45). The pregnant Mary goes to visit the pregnant Elizabeth. Mary has just been told that she is to bear the Son of God. She has also been told that her cousin Elizabeth is pregnant, even though she is well past the age of child-bearing. When Mary enters the house of her cousin, the baby in Elizabeth's womb stirs and leaps for joy. The six-month foetus, who was John the Baptist, seems to be acknowledging the arrival of the Lord. It is interesting that it is the Lord as far as Dr Luke is concerned, even though the pregnancy has just been announced. For many, the unmarried mother and the elderly first-time pregnant mother would have been classic cases for abortion. The descriptions of Jesus and John the Baptist show that even at such stages foetal life has awareness, and that in terms of our salvation these foetal lives were fundamental.

Of course, we know that these foetuses were Jesus and John the Baptist because we have the advantage of hindsight. We look back from the full-grown men to the babes in the wombs and recognise the continuity between then and now. While it is less clear that we can reverse the argument and project from every foetus forwards to the person they will be when adult, it is clear that they would be that person, all other things being equal. If there is no natural calamity, or human intervention, then foetuses will grow up into adults. Any such intervention is interrupting a natural, normal process and requires the most serious of justifications, if any are actually possible.

The importance of children and of not harming them have already been emphasised, so in all matters which affect children the well-being and safety of the child should have precedence over other things. The innocent child is to be protected and nurtured, not abused and destroyed.

The compassion of Jesus and its expression in a non-judgemental way has attracted all kinds of people. That compassion should characterise all those who live in the kingdom as they confront the hard ethical dilemmas of modern medicine, particularly in matters of life and death. That compassion is always geared towards the hurting and the helpless. Love's priority was for the needy, the vulnerable and those who cannot speak for or protect themselves. In conflicts between different compassions, then, the vulnerable must be foremost. Living in the kingdom will not remove us from the effects of the fallen world, and hard choices will still need to be made. In making those choices, the recognition that we are answerable to God and have good grounds for what we choose is vital. God's good grace is far greater than the conditions of sinfulness in which we have to decide.

Character development in the kingdom

There is a move in modern thought away from seeing ethical and moral reflection as a kind of problem-solving game towards a greater stress on character development. This fits extremely well with, and has much of its root in, Christian ethics. Jesus did not want to produce expert decision-makers. He wanted to produce men and women of Christian character who showed the virtues and qualities of kingdom people.

The development of character is in the end shown by the kinds of lives people live. These reveal the qualities which mark people as members of the kingdom. It is a sad reflection on most of our Sunday schools that they seem to have produced so little not only in terms of people in Church, but — more importantly — in terms of Christian lifestyle. As Jesus taught, it is the fruit that counts and inevitably shows what kind of people we are.

Good teaching, whether in Sunday school or in Church, must be aimed at producing men and women of God. The same is true in theological colleges. Too often we seem more interested in producing people who are experts in pastoral, counselling, liturgical and theological skills, without making them men and women of God. Christian education of every kind must be in the business of growing Christian character.

I believe that a radical shift is necessary if we are to regain moral force and integrity in our world. It is a shift away from simply telling people what Jesus taught; rather, it is a move to living out what he taught. This is what it means to be genuine members of the kingdom of God.

So where now?

Our world and societies face a whole selection of brand-new moral questions. How we ought to live as individuals and societies is crucial for the survival and well-being of ourselves and our world. Jesus offers the best hope for our world. He did not leave a blueprint with the answers to every single moral dilemma we shall face. But he did offer and embody the fundamental principles and attitudes which make human life complete, fulfilled, and as it ought to be.

Our task, then, is to apply these principles and show these attitudes in every walk of life and to all the myriad problems we face and will encounter. To properly understand the ethics of Jesus is to enter into a living relationship with Jesus. It is to live according to his needs. It is to live with his power at work in us. It is to put Jesus Christ first in everything.

This book has tried to show what Jesus said and what that means for us. The accuracy and authenticity of my account of the ethics of Jesus can only be checked by going back to the New Testament, and to the Gospels in particular. By reading the gospel accounts it will be possible to see whether or not I have been fair and accurate in telling the story of the moral teaching of Jesus.

If we do this, then we will again come face to face with the risen Christ. How we respond to him and his authority will decide what we will do with the ethics of Jesus. Jesus is God incarnate. His ethics can be summed up in terms of *incarnation* – making them live in human flesh; *imitation* – putting them into practice by copying and being like Christ; and *inspiration* – all of this is possible only in and through the power of the Holy Spirit of Jesus. The qualities and way of life of Christ are meant to be shown in the lives of Christians everywhere. Other people should be able to see the reality of Jesus from the living copies before them.

For the Christian, the ethics of Jesus offer both a comfort and a challenge. It is a comfort to know that these standards are possible, for we have seen them lived by Jesus. It is a comfort to realise that these are the ethics of grace and that we are not required to manage them on our own. God helps us keep his standards by the gift of his Spirit. But there is also a clear element of challenge which comes as we read the ethics of Jesus. Whenever we look at the very best in human beings we are forced to recognise how far short of perfection we fall. When we look at Jesus and his teaching we must admit that we are very poor ambassadors for him and his kingdom. All too often we have failed to live as we are meant to live. The ethics of Jesus summon us to be more like him. They challenge us to be what we are created and destined to be.

If all of us as individuals and communities took the ethics of Jesus seriously and put them into practice, then this would transform the world. So what are we waiting for?

For Further Reading

J. Gustafson, *Jesus and the Moral Life*. San Francisco: Harper & Row, 1968.

Anthony E. Harvey, *Strenuous Commands*. London: SCM Press, 1991.

Pinchas Lapide, *The Sermon on the Mount*. Maryknoll, NY: Orbis Books, 1986.

T. Ogletree, *The Use of the Bible in Christian Ethics*. Oxford: Basil Blackwell, 1984.

Jack T. Sanders, *Ethics in the New Testament*. Philadelphia: Fortress Press, 1975.

A. Verhey, *The Great Reversal*. Grand Rapids, MI: Wm B. Eerdmans, 1984.

Scripture Index

Subject Index